D1133257

THE CAVE OF ROUFFIGNAC

For Mimi
from Eevee
May 1963

THE CAVE OF ROUFFIGNAC

by

LOUIS-RENÉ NOUGIER

and

ROMAIN ROBERT

Translated by David Scott
from the French
ROUFFIGNAC, OU LA GUERRE
DES MAMMOUTHS

LONDON
GEORGE NEWNES LIMITED
TOWER HOUSE, SOUTHAMPTON STREET,
STRAND, W.C.2

Published 1958

PRINTED IN GREAT BRITAIN BY
WYMAN AND SONS, LTD., LONDON, FAKENHAM AND READING

AUTHOR'S NOTE

THIS book does not claim to be a scientific work on the paintings and incised drawings in the cave of Rouffignac-en-Périgord. We shall work for a long time yet to complete the exploration of our six miles of galleries, to record hundreds of painted or incised drawings, to decipher the thousands of "macaronis" and interlacings drawn on the ceilings, to make a plan of the hundreds of bears' "nests"[1], to classify and analyse the archaeological material in the many flint-cutting workshops in the deep galleries, to sift the innumerable hearths and reconstruct the late pottery, to collect remains of extinct fauna and draw up a list of their species, and to study a great many other subjects!

The examination of pollens, the chemical analysis of soils, the changes in the walls and their hygrometric content, the movements of the air, the nature of the vehicles used in colouring matter, the true origin of the "dust of centuries", as our Master, Abbé Breuil, rather poetically terms the dirt which is nothing but an impalpable manganese powder—these are so many more problems posed pell-mell but which will be solved with the efficient aid of scientific good will.

This work is intended to be simply the "record book" of the Rouffignac cave. It records the impressions conjured up by the cave of very ancient prehistoric origins, when bears, mammoths and men wandered on the face of the earth. It recalls adventurous expeditions as long ago as the 16th century, when men entered the cave "in large numbers and with brands, torches and lanterns". It tells of the amazement caused by the sensational discovery, in a cave more often described and more frequented than any other in History, of animal pictures in true proportion to the vast size of the cave itself.

PUBLISHER'S NOTE TO THE ENGLISH EDITION

IN the course of the narrative, the Rouffignac cave is sometimes referred to as Miremont and the Cro de Granville—names by which the cave was known before its re-discovery by MM. Nougier and Robert.

[1] See p. 7.

CONTENTS

I

THE PREHISTORIC ERA AT ROUFFIGNAC

II

THE HISTORY OF ROUFFIGNAC

III

THE DISCOVERY OF ROUFFIGNAC

IV

APPENDIX OF DOCUMENTS ON ROUFFIGNAC

LIST OF ILLUSTRATIONS

ILLUSTRATIONS

I
THE PREHISTORIC ERA AT ROUFFIGNAC

ROUFFIGNAC AT THE TIME OF THE GREAT CAVE BEAR

A mantle of Ice

About 40,000 years ago a thick sheet of ice lay over Europe and followed its northern fringes, overflowing the limits of the future Baltic Sea.

In the west, hills, plateaux and old Hercynian mountain masses lay under a rigorous climate, held as in a vice between the great glaciers of the North and those from the Alps abutting on the plain of Bavaria or dying out on the Fourvières ridge above Lyons. Icy winds blew fiercely from the heart of Europe, bringing Arctic conditions.

This was a powerful and active age, during which our soil was formed and moulded in the shapes which were to become familiar. The mountain heights sank, worn down by eroding torrents. Morainic deposits covered thousands of square miles along the fringes of glaciers, spreading over deeply frozen lands. The last hollows of the great valleys were scooped out, or their last terraces built up. Fine loess dust, carried by the continental winds, covered like a veil the lower levels of the countryside.

The west changed steadily to take on new and final shapes. And the living world changed in time with the mineral world, but in the opposite sense. The cold and mossy tundra, with its sparse vegetation and frozen swamps, took the place of an earlier Mediterranean flora such as fig-trees, Canary laurels, broad-leaved spindle-trees and Judas-trees. Gales, even more than cold, attacked trees, which could gain a footing only in sheltered areas or in the more clement lands near the Atlantic or southwards.

The great straight-tusked elephant, the hippopotamus and the terrible sabre-toothed tiger disappeared, yielding place to species better able to face the new rigours of the climate, such as the woolly rhinoceros, with its divided nostrils, the mammoth and the great carnivores: cave lions, hyenas and cave bears.

"*The most bear-like bear*"

The cave bear, which was the commonest carnivore of the last Ice Age, known to geologists as the Wümian era, was the most bear-like of bears. It was very large, about one-third larger than the present-day brown bear. When standing upright it reached a height of over 6 ft. 6 in. It was a heavy beast, with a well-rounded brow, a rather large head, massive, powerful arms and short, sturdy thighs. It had a very different "line" from that of the present-day bear, for the body was dominated by the forepaws and shoulders, and these were accentuated by the heavy head, lowered to sniff at the ground.

The creature was to be feared for its sharp claws, six to eight inches long, and for its long canine teeth, both upper and lower, which rubbed together as it chewed. None the less, it had the habits of a home-keeper. The "most bear-like bear" was above all a cave bear. It sought its vegetable food in the tundra or on the plain, but as winter drew near it liked the warm seclusion of the caves. There it found the protection of Mother Earth from damp winds and extreme cold. It sought a winter shelter in the deep caves and hibernated there until spring, with its life and loves, came round again.

During the winter the bear went to sleep, saving his energies and practically doing without food. Only his thirst had to be slaked, and the bear's retreat is always a damp cave, where water oozes from the walls or a stream flows underground.

North-east of what was to be called later the Eyzies-de-Tayac district, the cave bear frequented the Combarelles glade, a narrow cleft 230 yards long and averaging six feet in width. In the north-west he was particularly fond of the Cro du Cluzeau, which was to be Rouffignac.

The Cro du Cluzeau

The Cro is a great cave with a total depth of nearly six miles, three-quarters of which was big enough to accommodate the tribe of bears with ease. The original opening, in the Ice Age, was no doubt as high as it is today, but wider. It was the only entrance, and it quickly led to a network of great galleries with a complex plan. After a distance of several miles these galleries become diversified, fork and fork again, ending in a maze of underground passages which become steadily narrower and lower.

The main structure of the Cro consists of a large east-to-west gallery with an eastern and a western branch. The east-to-west gallery and the western branch form a sudden right-angled bend at the south-west end of the great underground system. This arm of galleries used to communicate with the open air through a chimney or vertical well, thirty to ninety feet deep, emerging on the limestone plateau beneath which the Cro lies.

Today this chimney is blocked, but it is possible to make one's way slowly along winding galleries marked at their angles by cones of gravel, pebbles and iron-stained sand. These various materials have slid gradually down from the surface of the plateau to the world underground. They are the traces of a powerful stream of water which used to sweep the surface, plunge into this chimney and spread throughout the depths in the shape of a delta, forming an underground Mississippi in miniature. There is a striking similarity between the course of the Cro and that of the greatest river in the world. But the former Cro watercourse was destructive, while the Mississippi is creative. The former is negative: a reversed reproduction of the latter.

From this peculiar chimney it is easy to follow the two great arms of the underground torrents; the right arm forms the eastern branch, while the more powerful arm forms the great western branch. In fact, the entrance to the Cro is merely the natural exit of one of the secondary torrents, forming a branch of the underground delta which returns to daylight after covering about one-third of a mile in the depths. The Cro network was already formed in the last Ice Age. It was to be filled up slowly by clay formed by decalcification and by matter which infiltrated from the surface. The busy water continued to delve, to dig and to dissolve, farther and farther towards the lower levels.

The main galleries are as much as 15 or 30 ft. wide, with roofs of varying height, rising to 30, 45 or 60 ft. or sinking as low as 6 ft. and sometimes less than 3 ft. And in the outer fringes of the underground delta the galleries become corridors, the corridors become flues, and the flues shrink to impassable fissures.

The Cro, a "Pyrenean cave" in Périgord

Extending as it does for about six miles, an exceptional distance in the Périgord district, the Cro du Cluzeau is more like the caves of the Pyrenees; it is also reminiscent of the great cave of Niaux, with its extensions to the caves of Sambart and Lombrive, a system which also covers several miles. Combarelles and Font-de-Gaume are typical "Pyrenean" labyrinths. The Cro du Cluzeau is a deep cave which has strayed into Périgord. Is not this fundamental natural anomaly one explanation of the fact that the Cro was not found by the people of Périgord, but was rediscovered by men from the Pyrenees? In Périgord, the archaeologist is an explorer of narrow corridors a few hundred yards long. The Pyrenean archaeologist is an explorer of wide galleries several miles long. Human traces, drawings and paintings are quite differently distributed in the two districts, and at different depths. The prehistoric drawings of La Mouthe begin 93 yards from the entrance; those of Font de Gaume at 65 yards and those in the Combarelles corridor at 120 yards. No doubt these drawings and paintings are far in by comparison with the 800 yards of bare walls that must be passed at Niaux in order to admire the frescoes in the Black Hall.

At the Cro du Cluzeau you must traverse at least 100 yards to reach the great mammoths on the "Red Ceiling"; 650 yards along the "Sacred Way" to see the Rhinoceros frieze; 800 yards to see the animal groups on the "Great Ceiling", and nearly 1,000 yards to view the "Mammoth with the Roguish Eye".

In the eastern branch of the Cro, again, you must follow nearly 500 yards of winding galleries to reach the Red Ceiling of the Snakes.

The two anthropomorphs facing each other in the continuation of the Breuil gallery and the last mammoths painted in a terminal chamber of the western delta are between 1,000 and 1,200 yards from the entrance. Even so, you must take care not to lose your way in the maze of galleries, but take the shortest path. One mistake may easily double the distance to be covered.

No doubt, it is easy to understand why the explorers of Périgord had neither the patience nor the courage to push on so far underground in their search for traces of man which are usually exposed to view in the open air. Périgord is essentially prehistoric; it is essentially accessible as well. This very accessibility provided an excuse for neglect in these easy conditions. Necessary as they proved, these excuses might have eased the local explorers' recognition of the true fact in the first place, and their confession afterwards. Instead, they roused all the more bad feeling as the goal had been missed so narrowly, and that to a point at which no excuse will serve to cover so blameworthy a failure. The Cro was a "Pyrenean" cave in Périgord. It kept its secret for the Pyreneans.

The first occupants

Hundreds or thousands of the great cave bears were the first occupants of the Cro du Cluzeau. As winter approached, long lines of bears went underground. Plump, with thick, shining coats and tense masses of flesh under the fat, they wandered through the long galleries in search of resting-places. The mother bears, heavy with the promise of offspring, scratched the yellow, slimy clay to make their nests and give birth to their young, in the first winter months, in the warmth of the cave. The holes are irregularly spaced in the galleries: they are true "bears' nests", 9 to 12 ft. across and 3 ft. deep, and there are hundreds and thousands of them.

The walls of the galleries, and sometimes their roofs, consist of regular strata of smoothly rounded flints, encrusted in the miry clay. These twisted "kidneys", often reddish brown in colour, form natural friezes which heighten the whiteness of the limestone. But the kidneys are sometimes cracked; then they break up and fall to pieces. They fall on the clay and roll into the great suction funnels formed by the underground waters, where they pile up. They also roll into the bears' holes, and their sharp edges must have made the animals very uncomfortable, no doubt. One can imagine, when the nest became uninhabitable, the bear moving out and digging a new one. The number of "bears' beds" at the Cro indicates a huge animal population, but it proves also that the bears liked comfort. How many journalists, when they visit the cave, appreciate the scene as it was when the tenants leaped from hole to hole, with backs bent and heads ducked?—for the ceiling was near and hard and sometimes studded with uncomfortably protruding stones.

During the first few months of his life the cub, no bigger than a large rat, was suckled by his mother, who lapped the water dripping from the walls or trickling intermittently along the galleries. At the age of one, he would spend another winter in the cave, as he cut his first set of adult teeth.

The scratching season

In the spring the bear tribe became active; the old animals exercised their claws while the young tried theirs. And in the galleries, leaping and jostling, the bears sharpened their claws. The marks remain today on the soft limestone walls; they stretch, innumerable and vertical, to the extreme ends of the deepest galleries. Claw after claw, claw against claw, the whole rock is chiselled, incised and torn. Some marks appear at levels which show where a platform, long since collapsed, used to stand. At a great fall of rock, which stretches beyond the chimney into the western branch, slabs from the roof cover the bears' floor. Smooth and perfectly horizontal sections of the vault show that the fall was recent. But

B

the bears also passed over the fallen blocks, and a second belt of claw-marks makes a sharply-cut frieze at a good height. In their thousands and their millions the claw-marks are distributed over the cave. The science of scratches, like every modern science, requires the use of cunning mathematical formulae. Science can be said to exist only where there are cumulative graphs and curves. We did not wish to leave to others the tedious task of counting these bears' claw-marks accurately. We do not claim to have arrived at the *exact* total of 13,524,978 scratches! But in a spirit of pure scientific discovery, we will allow any duly qualified specialist to repeat the count, in our presence, of course. Indeed we feel a certain diffidence in suggesting a total of 13,524,978 marks, not because we think we should have missed any—we count carefully—but because we are adding together the claw-marks of the great cave bear and those of his successor, the Arctic bear.

It is true that the diagrams in vogue among certain specialists in prehistoric science make no distinction among the stone tools left by man, between scrapers and polishers, spikes and graving-tools. All we have done is to add up scratches which were all made by *bears*. They exist even on the horizontal sides of the vaults, often deeply cut by an enormous leap or reaching up of the animal. Some of the incisions are ten or fifteen millimetres deep, and the traces of the weight-carrying claws show us the power of the leaping animal and the size of his paws. Gaps in the prints indicate a loss of balance. A bear reared up against this wall; he fell into a nest near-by, and the traces of his clumsy fall are there, almost eternal, 30,000 years old. On the floors of the galleries the clay still bears deep scratches filled with the fine manganese dust that drifts in the air underground: even more filled with it than the scratches on the roofs, dark though these are. And often, a few inches away, a prehistoric graven drawing, the outline of a rhinoceros, is similarly dusted. Were these marks and the bears contemporary? Some of them certainly were. Later, studies will be made of these scratches and of the question whether they belong to *Ursus speleus*, the Cave Bear, or *Ursus arctos*, the Brown Bear. These researches are complicated by the scratches made by young bear cubs; it will be difficult to distinguish between the print of a little great bear and that of a big little bear! Great days in prospect for new and solemn controversies. . . .

However that may be, bears' claw-marks lie over graven or painted lines, while some graven or painted lines lie over claw-marks, clear proof that the prehistoric artists and the bears were more or less contemporary. One would like to think that this co-existence does not imply that man and bear lived together; but many animals are shown in their winter coats—those of the very season when the bears sought shelter in the Cro du Cluzeau. Several potholes in the western gallery, too large for a bear to "nest" in, show signs of long, vertical scratches, that is, of long sliding on the clay.

Phosphates and human or animal occupation

The clay which lines the great galleries of the Cro is enriched by large quantities of phosphates of animal origin. These phosphates come from the decomposed corpses of animals or from their secretions. In some corridors even the bones have rotted and left phosphates of lime. Quite provisionally, the quantity of bear-earth at the Cro may be estimated at about 30,000 cubic yards. Allowing an average of 200 lb. of phosphates per cubic yard of earth, the phosphates concealed in the cavern would amount to 2,000 tons. It has been calculated that the cavern at Mixnitz in Styria (Drachenhöhle), one of the best-known bear-caves in the Alps, contained only 50 tons!

By analysing the phosphate content of the soil we can identify the most highly impregnated galleries, which must have been those most densely populated by the bears.

A more detailed examination will contribute to a solution of the question, once greatly discussed but practically settled today, "Did Palaeolithic men hunt the cave bears?" There are large deposits of crushed and broken bones which appear to be bears' bones. But these discoveries are exceptional today. A narrow corridor in the great branch of the Cro, about 1,500 yards from the entrance, yielded an exciting discovery: along the left-hand wall were claw-marks deeply scored in the brown clay, the claw-marks of a great cave bear; and opposite them, along the right-hand wall, the intact canine tooth of a great bear, still lodged in the clay. This clay, when carefully detached, provided a negative moulding of the tooth.

When foundations were made in July 1956 for the new wall at the entrance, which was built to prevent trespassing in the cave, the digging down to the rock yielded two teeth of *Ursus arctos*—the present-day bear. At present we have no sign that bears were hunted in the galleries of the Cro du Cluzeau. There are no bears among the animals drawn or painted in the cave; but man, no doubt, was not completely absent.

Here is Man, the Neanderthal

The entrance to the cave, which was open at the last Ice Age, was slowly filled by human detritus, the litter and cooking refuse of the many occupants of the porch or outer cave, and by the natural débris slipping down from the higher levels. When the entrance was enlarged in 1938 a sort of trench was dug in this embankment, giving the Rouffignac porch its present appearance. And the diggers, working under the direction of M. Charles Plassard, the landowner, were certainly puzzled by the remains of bones, innumerable flint implements and many fragments of pottery they turned up with every spadeful. They were disturbing prehistoric layers, never suspecting that they were destroying the material archives of their distant ancestors in Périgord! The most deeply buried flints gave proof of the earliest human occupation. The surface layers yielded fragments of large urns and relics of the various Bronze and Iron Ages as well as huge pieces of Roman amphorae, turned on the potter's wheel, with their deep, regular and beautiful grooves.

There were still many things about prehistoric archaeology that M. Plassard did not know. But he had a keen desire to satisfy his own curiosity and to understand. Very carefully, he had all the flint chips, all the bone fragments and all the potsherds gathered. Packed in boxes, these relics awaited the discovery of Rouffignac.

In June 1956, for the first time since they were put away, the specimens were unpacked with more care than they had known when they were first unearthed, some eighteen years earlier. In the turf-covered yard of the farmhouse of l'Egal we laid out these treasures, which had miraculously escaped when a traffic platform was built up in front of the cave. Artificially, no doubt, but with fair accuracy, the stratigraphy of the Rouffignac remains and the successive stages in the occupation of the porch were traced.

The place was inhabited almost without interruption from the Ice Age to the Roman era. Moving back through the ages we found fragments of amphorae identical with those at Vésone, the black pottery with Greek decoration of Tena and Hallstatt, brown, hand-made fragments decorated in relief from the Bronze Age or Chalcolithic ware ending as it does at the Roque Saint-Christophe. Finally, we found the cutting instruments used by men in the Reindeer Age, and the flint implements of Neanderthal men, who were contemporaries of the great cave bears. These medium-sized fragments are still rough. Few among the pieces we have kept have been polished. Scrapers and blades of thick triangular section are not very strong evidence from which to identify definitely a human occupation belonging to what is called the Moustier civilisation, which is displayed in two cave openings above the Vézère, between Montignac and Les Eyzies. The Mousterian culture at Rouffignac will no doubt be linked with the near-by deposits at La Ferrassie. New excavations in the future will furnish useful details, obtained with all desirable care. A digging deeper than the present entrance may even reveal still older archaeological levels. We shall see.

For the moment at least, these Neanderthal men, with their "strong, heavy frames, bony heads and powerful jaws showing the priority of purely vegetative or bestial functions over those of the brain" are the first discoverers of Rouffignac.

ROUFFIGNAC AT THE TIME
OF THE MAMMOTHS

A Lord of Ages past

Even more than the reindeer, the mammoth has remained the symbol of vanished weather conditions. His great size, his long hair, his trunk and long, curving tusks have fixed his place in our imaginations and he suggests Prehistory and the climate of the last Ice Age as the camel suggests sand and the burning desert. The mammoth has become a creature of legend, to be found in prehistoric iconography for over 20,000 years. The first known drawing of a mammoth came from an engraved ivory found in a cave in the Dordogne by Lartet and published in 1865. Forty years later Abbé Henri Breuil, by his admirable records, made known the mammoths of the Combarelles, which became classic from then on. The mammoth can also be reconstructed from his bones, and there are very few small provincial museums which do not proudly display in their show-cases, or built up on a base and held together with wire, some precious osteological specimen. The museum at Foix, in the Pyrenees, has three-quarters of a mammoth standing against the end wall of its main hall.

Knowledge of the larger bony parts of the mammoth, such as tusks, molars, femurs, etc., is very old, and popular credulity has attributed strange origins to some. Often these respectable bones, thanks to their size, were taken for sacred relics. In 1789 the monks of St. Vincent carried a mammoth's molar in procession to bring down rain, calling it a "bone of the Holy Lord". But the alleged origins were usually more profane, and mammoths' bones passed for those of the giants of legend. It was not until the 17th and 18th centuries that they were recognised as the remains of vanished animals which once lived on our soil. Some southern archaeologists (and by no means the least among them) occasionally took them for skeletons of Hannibal's elephants, used by him in the great invasion of 218 B.C. But the discovery of "real mammoths", preserved in ice, the natural cold storage of Siberia, brought

Europe its most detailed knowledge of this fabulous extinct quadruped.

The frozen Mammoth

As early as the 17th century, at the time of the first emperor of the usurping Manchu dynasty, descriptions could be read in China of Siberian mammoths which described them as "underground rats of the north" but made it clear that these rats were as big as elephants. In 1692 Witsen published an account of his "extraordinary and adventurous journey to Tartary and the north-east", in which he described the discovery of complete mammoths' bodies. The first discovery of a mammoth to be exploited scientifically was made in 1799 on the banks of the Lena river delta. Here an enormous block of ice enclosed the entire body of a mammoth.

A botanist named Adams learned of the discovery through the sale of the tusks in the market at Irkutsk and decided to go to the spot. He only just managed to recover the head, with one eye and one ear, and "the lower parts of two legs still sunk in the frozen earth". Dogs and beasts of prey had devoured the rest. The skeleton, almost complete, was sent to St. Petersburg in 1806, mounted there and shown in the "cabinet of curios" founded by Peter the Great, which was the precursor of the Zoological Museum of the Academy of Sciences. It was only in the 20th century that a new discovery at last yielded a mammoth's body in good condition.

In April 1901 the governor of Irkutsk notified the Academy of Sciences of the discovery among the fossilised ice of the Berezovka, the right-hand branch of the Kolyma, a river flowing into the Arctic Ocean. An expedition, of which E. W. Pfizenmayer has left us an attractive account, was organised. The mammoth's corpse lay on a slab of fossilised ice on the river bank, which had crumbled, partly exposing the well-preserved body. The ice of the exposed surfaces was brownish and pierced by long-shaped air bubbles, but the deeper layers were more compact and transparently clear. This was the true fossil ice of the great Ice Age. The mammoth had fallen into a deep crevasse, and the permanent sheet of ice had kept it intact until our time. No doubt the crevasse had been hidden under a surface layer of earth which had yielded under the mammoth's weight. Wedged between smooth vertical walls of ice, the mastodon had tried in vain to get free, and his forelegs were outstretched in a last effort. But he died of suffocation, with several broken bones, buried under masses of earth brought down by his fall.

A Mammoth's menu

His death was sudden, for unmasticated fodder was found on his tongue and between his molars. "The imprint of the edges of the teeth could be clearly seen on the scraps of vegetation wedged between the molars."

Among the remains of food in the stomach, 30 lb. of "prehistoric plants" were recovered. By identifying them it was possible to establish the exact diet of the Siberian mammoth, and it is likely that it hardly differed from that of the western mammoths, including our mammoths at Rouffignac. Now that we know what our mammoths in the cave had to eat, they seem nearer to us and more living.

The plants the Siberian mammoth grazed on along the banks of the Berezovka are to be found today in the same place. There are several kinds of sedge, the yellow Alpine poppy, the bitter *Ranunculus* or buttercup, a gentian and an orchid.

Many of these plants have found refuge in the west, on the upper slopes of the Alps and the Pyrenees. They are residual flora, once the food of animals now extinct. A plant is more tenacious of life than an animal, less hunted and less destroyed by man. And the Alpine gentian takes on a new scent when we know that it was once cropped not only by M. Séguin's little white goat but, long before that, by some mammoth of the Ice Age. I keep pressed in a heavy archaeological tome some blossoms of *Dryas octopetala*, gathered on the heights of the Wildkirchli, above the Alpine bear-cave at St. Gallen. These two are precious relics of the glacial flora that reached this place.

The Mammoth is revived

The animal was soon laid bare, with little damage from beasts of prey and dogs, though its flesh was still appetising. "The well-preserved meat of the forelegs, haunches and hind-quarters was interlarded with thick layers of fat. As long as it remained frozen it had a fresh and appetising dark red colour, like frozen beef or horse-flesh, but with much coarser fibres." But the explorers dared not taste mammoth steak. This was a pity, for we should like to have had their impressions of the taste, even if they found the dish horrible. There is no reason why a man of the 20th century should not eat the three roasts which were choice dishes in the far-off prehistory of 20,000 years ago: mammoth, reindeer and bison. This would call only for a journey and a good digestion—a trip to Siberia, if another mammoth is found there, as it is bound to be; an excursion to Scandinavia to taste reindeer and a crossing of the Atlantic to end up with roast bison. Up to now I have tasted only reindeer: a reindeer killed in north Norway, frozen and sawn into pieces before being sent to market at Bergen. It had a pleasant flavour, like a chamois of the Pyrenees. Hunters along the Berezovka had much less far to go to enjoy the "game trinity of the quaternary age", if it is true that hunters reached those parts. Not far from the mammoth, the explorers found a bison and a reindeer.

The carcass was so well preserved in the ice that a large quantity of coagulated blood was recovered and a laboratory analysis established "the blood relationship of the mammoth with the Indian elephant".

A second mammoth, discovered shortly afterwards on the banks of the Sanga-Yurak, fortunately yielded parts complementary to those of the Berezovka mammoth, giving a picture of the lord of ages past.

Portrait of the Lord of Siberia

Though he is the great elephant of the cold lands, the mammoth is no monster in size and he has a balance of form and dimensions resulting in an animal completeness not without beauty. The mammoth's skeleton found at Steinheim in a quaternary layer older than our specimens at Rouffignac, stands about 12 ft. high from the ground to the top of the shoulder-blades. The Siberian mammoths, though nearer to ours in time in spite of the geographical distance that separates them, are also about 12 ft. tall and 13 ft. long from the tips of their tusks to that of their tails. But as in the case of the human race, there are great differences between individuals and between the sexes. It is interesting to note that the basic measurements of the Berezovka mammoth are closely related to those of some of the Rouffignac specimens. In the Henri Breuil gallery the great frieze shows eleven mammoths majestically lined up in two groups, seven facing left and four facing right. Owing to the fading of these paintings, which were made 20,000 years ago, it is not always possible to take *all* the measurements. The upper part of the rock, which is very damp, has preserved the pictures in detail. At the middle level, which is dry and very chalky today, many features have disappeared. Fortunately the mammoths' legs have been preserved at the lower level, and this makes it possible to measure their height.

Mammoth No. 5—we must number them, since there are so

many—is 56 cm. (22 in.) high, or 59 cm. (23 in.) from the top of the
skull to the lower end of the foreleg, and 82 cm. (32 in.) long, from
the tips of the tusks to the rear edge of the thigh.   The tail no longer
shows, or it lies flat against the rump.   If we multiply these basic
measurements by 5 we shall get 2 m. 80 cm. (9 ft. 2 in.) and
4 m. 10 cm. (13 ft. 5 in.), exactly the dimensions of the Berezovka
mammoth.   Thus mammoth No. 5 at Rouffignac is an exact one-
fifth scale model of the Siberian companion!

All the mammoths of the balanced Rouffignac frieze are not
identical, but it may be supposed that the differences correspond
with natural variations.   The "portraits" in the frieze, no doubt,
have no absolute anthropometric—or may one say "mammotho-
metric"?—value, but their excellent drawing, their firm and accurate
line, their intense life and the happy proportions of No. 5 are so
many arguments in favour of the unknown artist and so many
reasons for placing implicit faith in his work.   There is no reason
why the great mammoth frieze of Rouffignac should not be accepted
as a one-fifth scale reduction of a group, recorded for all
time.

Mammoth No. 6, who comes before the prototype, is distinctly
larger.   The tusks have faded, but we have enough detail to reconstruct his true dimensions: 3 m. 80 cm. (12 ft. 5 in.) high and 4 m 50 cm.
(13 ft. 1 in.) long.   Mammoth No. 9 may have measured 2 m. 85 cm.
(9 ft. 8 in.) high and 4 m. 75 cm. (15 ft. 7 in.) long.   The solitary
old leader who sadly ends the great frieze must have been over 16 ft.
long.

A Mammoth's head

The mammoth has a large, powerful head, emphasised by a thick
neck springing from a massive body.   The head forms a regular
hump, rather higher than that of the shoulders.   The latter is prolonged and supported by the long, sharp flanges of the dorsal
vertebrae.   This hump must have been covered with fat in the
autumn, when the animal was well fed.   In winter it enabled him
to live on less food when snow covered the ground.   The eye was
small—it is often cunningly drawn in the paintings—and was hidden
under definitely jutting brows, which were very characteristic.   The
line of the forehead continued towards the trunk only after the
swelling brows.   Painters and draughtsmen always note it carefully.
The trunk has a thick pelt along its hinder surface, though the front
seems smooth.   At its tip are prehensile lips, clearly shown on a
mammoth painted on the "great ceiling" of Rouffignac.

Finely curved, spiral tusks give the mammoth his majestic air. Here again the Siberian mammoths bring us valuable data, for their tusks are much sought after for ivory-work. "Harvesting" mammoth tusks is one of the traditional resources of the primitive Siberian economy. At the beginning of summer, in the great thaws, river banks are undermined and washed away, and mammoth tusks and rhinoceros horns are uncovered. Then mammoth teeth are traded from market to market, and sometimes bones as well.

China and the Dragons

In China it is the custom to buy dragons' teeth and dragons' bones in the chemists' shops, for everything is traced to the dragon, which is the national symbol. As G. H. R. von Koenigswald, the man of the Pithecanthropus, humorously tells us, you can buy these precious "medicines" wherever you have a prescription and plenty of money in your pocket. "Everything that comes from the body of so powerful an animal is bound to be a very potent drug and to fetch a high price."

But these "dragons' teeth" are not those of the legendary monsters at all. They are the fossilised teeth of all sorts of mammals. More than 100 species have been counted. Among the chemists' jars of Pekin and Hong Kong you will find the teeth of "Sinanthropus" and also mammoths' tusks which are admired as dragons' bones. As long ago as the 12th century, the Chinese encyclopaedia *Ta-Kuan-pen-tsao* spoke of the medicinal properties of dragons' bones. The bones were brought down by the Hoangho river in the spring floods. The Ordos gorge, a defile dug by the river in the mountains north of the Great Wall, was known as "the Dragon's Gate". This was where the "burrowing rat" lived: that rat, as big as an elephant, which was no other than the mammoth.

More intensive "harvesting" of mammoth tusks began in the middle of the 18th century, and complete expeditions were undertaken which discovered islands like the Liakhov Isles in the Arctic Ocean, north of Siberia. Liakhov pioneered the wholesale trade in fossil ivory. During the summers of 1882 and 1884 a mission led by Dr. Bunge brought back 2,500 tusks.

The finest tusks examined by E. W. Pfizenmayer at Bulun, near the mouth of the Neva, at the beginning of this century "described an almost perfect circle, with a slight spiral tendency, for two-thirds of their length. Each tusk was 2 m. 79 cm. (9 ft. 1 in.) long, measured along the outside of the curve, and 38 cm. (just under

15 in.) in circumference at the base. Each of these specimens
weighed 32 kg. (70 lb.)."

If the reduced scale of one to five is accepted as constant, the last
mammoth on the great frieze at Rouffignac had tusks 4 m. (13 ft.)
long on the outside of the curve. This figure approximates to the
size of the finest and biggest-known mammoth tusks. The same
author reports an exceptional tusk from which a fragment 35 or
40 cm. (14 to 16 in.) long was missing at the base and another small
fragment at the tip. "Although it was incomplete, this tusk
measured 3 m. 74 cm. (11 ft. 2 in.) and weighed 109 kg. (nearly
240 lb.)." In any case, the outside length of the tusk was greater
than in the "lone mammoth" of Rouffignac. In his two tusks the
Siberian giant carried at least 250 kg. (550 lb.) of ivory!

The Mammoth's Fleece

The discoveries of frozen mammoths and prehistoric drawings
and engravings confirm one another and help us to give the hairy
picture of the mammoth which is now classical and popular. He
had a heavy fleece formed of long, stiff, coarse hairs (the outer coat)
and a woolly layer of hairs which were shorter and finer but much
denser. The whole formed a double protective coat which retained
air. The long hairs measured as much as 45 cm. (17 in.). Generally
rusty brown in colour, they varied on different parts of the body
and also in different seasons.

The outer hair was longer on the chest and neck, back and flanks.
This appeared in the mammoths drawn or painted at Rouffignac.
When we examine the one-fifth scale drawing of the lone mammoth
on the great frieze, it is interesting to note that the long hairs on his
chest, enlarged to their natural size, would be, at the most, 48 cm.
(19 in.) long, compared with 17 in. for the Siberian animal. This
no doubt confirms the accuracy of the prehistoric artist, as he well
deserves to be called.

It confirms the truth of his proportions, but does it not do much
more? The vertical streaks of manganese only suggest the fleece,
for the artist has painted but few, but they are in exact proportion
to the creature's body. Is not this minute sense of proportion—
accurate to a mammoth's hair's-breadth, one might say—the sign of
a complete art, of unrivalled sureness and accuracy in drawing, of
a deep power of suggestion with the simplest possible materials: a
rocky wall, a thick stump of manganese, a small oil lamp? . . .

For precision does not destroy "life", and our mammoths at
Rouffignac are living things.

Art and Accuracy

They certainly represent a very high level of art, perhaps the highest ever reached. But above all they remain human works. They are rendered personal and reveal the hand and touch of the artist. If all the mammoths of the great frieze are by the same hand, like those in the end chamber of the west branch at Rouffignac, others have different qualities. Those on the "great ceiling" aim much more at effect. Their lines are less pure, and they are sometimes overcharged with detail. No doubt they are of a more recent school. And the most spectacular are not always the most accurate. One mammoth on the left, a little before the "great ceiling", makes a striking effect, but according to Professor Grassé he has not the rightness and precision of his brothers of the great frieze. On the other hand, a mammoth to the right of the "great ceiling", who might be considered rather naïve from an aesthetic point of view, is scientifically accurate. This is the one who has a clearly-drawn two-lipped tip to his trunk, and—passing to the other extreme —a remarkable formation of the anus, like a sort of lid for protection from the cold. This opercule is a fundamental feature of the mammoth; the Cabrerets mammoths have it, and this is one of those minute and little-known details that might easily escape the attention of a forger. Now, the Rouffignac mammoths, whenever the drawings are sufficiently detailed, wear this feature with elegance. We shall long remember the admiring, joyful and exultant exclamations of the great anatomists: "Oh, have you seen his anal opercule! Wonderful! Marvellous! How can it be a forgery, with such a feature?" Ah, anal opercule of our Rouffignac mammoths! You protected them from the cold and you protect us from wounding scepticism. Thank you!

The real Battle of Mammoths

The rhinoceros has his family life, but the mammoth's life is communal. Like his fellow-pachyderm and near relation, the elephant, he lives in powerful groups under the guidance of his "old leaders". The glades which run today from Manauric towards the Vézère valley must often have echoed, in the past, with the heavy, slow and methodical passing of the herds. A painting or a drawing bears witness to the existence of an extinct animal species just as well as the presence of bones, but the two kinds of evidence are not of equal value. The second is natural, while the first is the result of human choice, but both are equally subject to the chances of discovery. It would be vain to argue the point whether it is more arduous or more praiseworthy to discover a mammoths' "cemetery" or to find a gallery with mammoth paintings.   Alluvial deposits and even caves in the Dordogne have yielded mammoths' tusks, or at least fragments of them, and molars either whole or often divided into natural chips.   Artists and artisans of the upper palaeolithic period worked on mammoth ivory as the Samoyeds of Siberia did thousands of years later.   Traditions persist.   Not only did the mammoth live in the Dordogne: he had a large place in its life.   And here the graphic evidence of Rouffignac is vital.   It would be, as it always is, risky to draw conclusions about these distant civilisations, but the mere number of mammoths in the Rouffignac galleries can only show the considerable part played by this animal in palaeolithic life, at least for the tribe that inhabited the Cro du Cluzeau.

People thought in terms of mammoths at that time.   That, no doubt, was because they saw mammoths and lived among them. And the painted herds are only a reproduction of the living herds, and perhaps they were painted only that the herds might live. Often the valleys must have echoed to their slow, heavy, deliberate passing.   Like the elephant, no doubt, the mammoth followed his nose.   He might be a symbol of conscious rectitude, though rather in vain, for nature has taught certain animal species, including man, the advantages of a devious path.

It must have happened very often that two herds met, and each wanted to push ahead.   Then each leader would overthrow any obstacle in his path, whether it were a native hut, a thicket or the living bodies of other mammoths.   And then the fight began.

The valleys of Manaurie rang with these battles of giants; with long, shrill trumpetings, the loud clash of tusks and heads, the wet, heavy sliding of flesh on the soil.   But the curving tusks interlocked and would not be freed.   Crouching face to face, pushing with their hind-quarters, butting with their short brows and brandishing their trunks, for minutes on end, the great beasts matched one another, staring with their small, round eyes.   The real battle of the Rouffignac mammoths is recorded in the caves.   It is still impossible to say how many times we can find the theme of battle suggested by mammoths in single combat.

The Great Frieze

The most spectacular encounter is that depicted in the great frieze in the Henri Breuil gallery: that of seven against four.   Seven mammoths face left, marching on the four who face right.   They

come one behind the other, close together near the head of the
column, more widely spaced towards the rear, where, even among
mammoths, the least brave will be found. Near the centre, the
right-hand group, which is the larger, includes some mammoths
side by side; their features overlap. One is in the second row,
passing others as he hurries to the leaders' point of contact. The
duel will become unequal.

As you emerge from the Sacred Way, the light of your acetylene
lamp reveals a new mammoth at every second or third step. Slowly
—for the bear-holes, flints and slippery clay will reduce your pace
—slowly you light up one as another disappears into the shades.
The new beast vanishes also, yielding place to a third, and so on,
until the fight appears. And the frieze goes on, with these com-
batants, until the magnificent lone mammoth is reached.

Fifteen yards of mammoth frieze! You draw back now, taking
care of the holes, and try to illuminate the whole scene, waving your
heavy lamp, but you do not succeed. You may direct your quivering light on this section or that, or on the clash depicted in the
centre, but some part of the picture is always in shadow, and that
is as it should be. The mammoth frieze of Rouffignac passes into
the shades and marches on, as though infinite and eternal.

In the raw, white light of the cinema operators' floodlights the
whole wall and ceiling are illuminated, and the two herds meet as
one. There is no more mystery, but the splendid vision will remain
for ever graven on your memory. You hold your breath in religious
awe, in intense communion with those fellow-men of 20,000 years
ago who seem to come to meet you. Your blood throbs faster and
more loudly in your temples, and you seem to hear the deep galleries
re-echo to the mammoths' heavy tread.

The Battle Theme

The struggle of mammoth against mammoth is not always shown
on such a scale as in the great frieze. The large panel of mammoth
drawings on the right-hand wall of the Sacred Way, beyond the
Breuil gallery, shows only two groups of two. The leader of the
left hand group is admirably preserved and not disfigured by
sacrilegious modern scrawlings. He is one of the finest mammoths
in the cave.

With his high, rounded head and sloping back, wrapped in his
long, stiff hair, and his hairy trunk rolled up, he gives you a melancholy look. With wrinkled brows and curved tusks pointing to his
forehead, he awaits the enemy. A band of wavy lines crosses his

carcass from head to belly like a French Town Councillor's sash. Is he a mammoth chief?

Between him and his opponent is a baby mammoth, with a lumpy forehead rather out of proportion, like those children who seem to have a long head, shaped like a sugar-loaf. His eye was clearly defined under the arching brow, and there is plenty of hair on his trunk. The scene lacks violence and rather resembles a family group. In any case, it makes a perfect picture. The two opposing leaders leave an empty, triangular space under their curving tusks, and the young mammoth fills this space. The whole is a wonderful example of pyramidal composition.

There are many more opposing groups on the left-hand wall of the Breuil gallery.

"Charlotte" and the Patriarch

At the end of the gallery we find Charlotte—a sweet name for a robust and powerful mammoth, given to her no doubt by some underground Werther longing to fix his passing human feelings for eternity.

Charlotte faces left, driving another mammoth, happily anonymous, before her (or before him). And this mammoth meets another facing right. Farther on, towards the Sacred Way, three mammoths facing left (one in the background overlapping the two in the front row) meet two more facing right. Still farther on, the theme is treated systematically. Here the "Patriarch", an old male with powerful tusks, is on the move. His features are deeply graven. His body is 70 cm. (27½ in.) long, and the span of his tusks, from his eye to their points, is 40 cm. (nearly 16 in.). Keeping the same proportions, a "patriarch" 3 m. 50 cm. (11 ft. 6 in.) long, in the natural state five times the size of his portrait, would have had tusks about 11 ft. 6 in. long, and a mammoth 4 m. 20 cm. (13 ft. 9 in.) long would have had tusks measuring 3 m. 75 cm. (12 ft. 4 in.). The data found in the case of the "lone mammoth" hold good.

Claude Barrière, who took part in the minute inspection of the gallery, made an interesting observation. The wall is not flat but forms a series of concave arcs separated by ridges which may be described as "ribs". Twice in three groups two mammoths face each other from each side of a "rib".

The mammoth hunt?

Was the mammoth hunted? He would have made a choice dish

1. Entrance to the Cave of Rouffignac

2. Plan of the cave, drawn in 1759 by Gabriel Bouquier

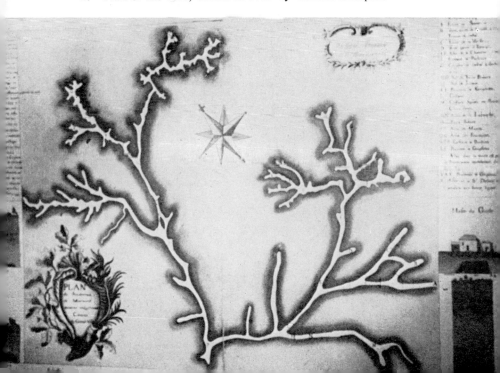

LE GRAND
DICTIONNAIRE
HISTORIQUE
OU
LE MÉLANGE CURIEUX
DE
L'HISTOIRE SACRÉE
ET PROFANE:
QUI CONTIENT EN ABREGÉ

L'HISTOIRE FABULEUSE

Des Dieux & des Heros de l'Antiquité Payenne :

LES VIES ET LES ACTIONS REMARQUABLES

Des Patriarches; des Juges; des Rois des Juifs; des Papes; des faints Martyrs & Confesseurs; des Peres de l'Eglise; & des Docteurs Orthodoxes; des Evêques; des Cardinaux & autres Prélats celebres; des Heresiarques & des Schismatiques; avec leurs principaux Dogmes.

Des Empereurs; Des Rois; Des Princes illustres; & des grands Capitaines:

Des Auteurs anciens & modernes; Des Philosophes; Des Inventeurs des Arts, & de ceux qui se sont rendus recommandables en toute sorte de Professions, par leur Science, par leurs Ouvrages, & par quelque action éclatante.

L'ETABLISSEMENT ET LE PROGRÉS

Des Ordres Religieux & Militaires; & LA VIE de leurs Fondateurs:

LES GENEALOGIES

De plusieurs Familles illustres de France, & d'autres Pays:

LA DESCRIPTION

Des Empires, Royaumes, Republiques, Provinces, Villes, Isles, Montagnes, Fleuves, & autres lieux considerables de l'ancienne & nouvelle Geographie : où l'on remarque la situation, l'étendue & la qualité du Pays; la Religion, le Gouvernement, les Mœurs & les Coûtumes des Peuples : Où l'on voit les Dignitez, les Magistratures ou Titres d'honneur : Les Religions & Sectes des Chrétiens, des Juifs & des Payens : Les principaux noms des Arts & des Sciences : Les Actions publiques & solemnelles : Les Jeux, les Fétes, &c. Les Edits & les Loix, dont l'Histoire est curieuse, &c.

L'Histoire des Conciles generaux & particuliers, sous le nom des lieux où ils ont été tenus.

Le tout enrichi de Remarques, de Differtations & de Recherches curieuses, pour l'éclaircissement des difficultes de l'Histoire, de la Chronologie & de la Geographie, tirées de differens Auteurs, & sur tout du Dictionnaire Critique de M. BAYLE.

Par Mr LOUIS MORERI, Prêtre, Docteur en Theologie.

NOUVELLE ET DERNIERE EDITION REVÛE, CORRIGÉE ET AUGMENTÉE.

TOME V.

A PARIS,

Chez DENYS MARIETTE, ruë S. Jacques, au coin de la ruë des Noyers, à S. Augustin & à l'Ecu de Venife.

MDCCXXV.

AVEC APPROBATION, ET PRIVILEGE DE SA MAJESTÉ.

---

3. Title page of *The Great Historical Dictionary,* published in 1725, in which the Rouffignac paintings are mentioned

for a palaeolithic menu, which consisted largely of meat. At first sight it seems difficult for a man to stand up to a mammoth. Even with his height of 6 ft., Cro-Magnon man was clearly overshadowed by the 9 ft. of the animal and might seem crushed by his weight. Could bone weapons such as assegais made from reindeer horns penetrate a hide nearly an inch thick, lined with a subcutaneous layer of fat 3½ in. thick? Eleven inches of "dead ground" had to be pierced before any effective penetration, and how much more before any vital organ was touched? The mammoth could be attacked only with a long wooden pike, hardened by fire at the point and perhaps wielded by several men. But then, think of the fury of the beast as it charged the Cro-Magnon hunters! Can we suppose that they used less direct methods? African native elephant-hunters use a boar-spear and, risking their lives, stalk the animal to stick it into the soles of its feet. Then the elephant, a lordly tramp, limps on for hours and days, followed by a human pack, before it finally goes mad and dies.

Other clever natives are masters of the trapper's art. On the Upper Nile they suspend a heavy wooden stake, tipped with a spear-point, over the elephants' path. The whole is connected with a cord that spans the track, and when the elephant disturbs the cord he pulls a trigger and the pylon pierces his skull—or misses him. Palaeolithic man knew ropes, as he knew many other things, but we shall never know whether he was as cunning as the natives of the Upper Nile.

In other parts of Africa a sharp stake is planted, point upwards, in a pit covered with branches through which the elephant may fall. But a mammoth-pit would have to be very large: six to ten feet deep at least, to trip the animal, and at least 15 feet wide to prevent him from climbing out. Altogether, a capacity of 65 to 95 cubic yards would be needed to immobilise the beast. Imagine the efforts required to dig such a pit! In soil which might be deeply frozen, it would be impossible; impossible in limestone, too. And in loose soil, what a task for men to scoop out the earth with their hands, or even using bisons' shoulder-blades as spades! Is it not strange that no trace of a pit this size has ever come down to us? A scene of this kind is represented in miniature in the Natural History Museum at Toulouse, in a show-case at the end of the Cartailhac gallery, using terra cotta or breadcrumbs for earth. The scene is rather picturesque. The mammoth, who evidently is destined to provide the main dish of a meal, is being harassed by a crowd of little pygmies who dance round him, brandishing spears and assegais

C

very bravely when they are at a distance and have nothing to fear. These pygmies, of course, are men. In the dust of the show-case, which obliterates details, the group resembles a scene from the adventures of Gulliver in Lilliput. But mammoth-hunting has not been proved and is hardly accepted as a fact, any more than hunting for the palaeolithic bear. Whether mammoth meat was included in the diet of palaeolithic man is another question.

Mammoth cemeteries

The loess at Predmost in Moravia contains several hundred mammoths, 300 according to some, 1,000 according to others, together with bones of horses or reindeer, thousands of stone or bone implements and even works of art carved on mammoth ivory. Predmost is a field of mammoth remains and archaeological deposits covering several types of civilisation.

Some hold that the mammoths were hunted and that Predmost was a sort of killing ground, a great hunting rendezvous. Others believe that the Predmost herds fell victims to some natural cataclysm, perhaps a terrible blizzard. Afterwards, men gathered to make use of the victims, remove the tusks, cut up the bodies for the long bones or shoulder-blades or perhaps even eat the meat.

Predmost has been described as a gigantic refrigerator on which men drew as it thawed, just as the Tungus tribes keep frozen mammoth-meat in Siberia for their dogs, and sometimes for themselves. The changes of climate of the quaternary epoch are still too little known in detail for us to form a definite opinion.

What was the "true" temperature in the Dordogne country at the time of the mammoth, and especially the "true" temperature of a given soil? The Vézère valley is open to Atlantic influence, but in Périgord local conditions have more effect than elsewhere. The sheltered valley and the plateau, the upper or lower course of a stream, each has its own climate, and to the present day the Sarladais has an average temperature in January of only 0 to 4° C. Climate, rather than soil, determines a way of life and suggests occupations.

Did the climate of that time make it possible to dig trap-pits? Or would the weighted traps depicted in certain drawings at Font-de-Gaume have been enough? We must also examine the theory that there was a natural decimation or even an annihilation of mammoth herds. Man has often benefited by remarkable chances in the course of his long development; often, too, he has failed to stand the test and has sometimes disappeared locally. The finding of a mammoth's corpse, fresh or preserved under snow, must have been

a chance in man's favour.   And man must have done all he could
to multiply such chances.

Reasons for art

Another problem is the reason why paintings and drawings were
made.   Their artistic value is undoubted, but is this art not a
supplement, a free gift added to an imperious obligation?   There
is not a vital reason for what we call by the convenient term of
"prehistoric art".   Just as the American Indian, in somewhat
similar artistic activities, draws no distinction between material life
and thought, between reality and the stuff of dreams, so palaeolithic
man sees reality and its representation with equal vividness.   For
him it would be vain and inconceivable merely to represent an object
in a picture.   That is the way of civilised man, who delights in the
appearance of reality.   That is why what we call "art" today is so
much detached from ourselves and from all that is human.   That is
why we see faces with two noses, full-face portraits with one eye
only, side views with two!   The pure profile of our Rouffignac
mammoths is more human than the humans of today.   For primitive man, dream and reality have the same force, the same presence.
He understands the act of creating an object or a being and giving
it, or restoring to it, real life through its outline.   For him "art"
is life.   For us, often, art is a game, and if some artists are talented
and "play the game" they are not always the most conspicuous.
The prize goes to him who exploits the game, giving two noses to a
man's face.

To the palaeolithic mind, the act of drawing or painting the coveted
animal on the wall is a true act of creation.   The representation itself
is not essential; what matters is the act of representing, of drawing
or painting.   And this act of creation, in the true and strong sense
of the term, well matches the eventful way of life of these Tamerlanes
of the chase.

To own mammoth, to exploit this mine of flesh and bone and
ivory, they must draw mammoth and paint mammoth.   To multiply the mammoth herds in the sunlit dales of Manaurie, the limestone walls of Rouffignac are covered with mammoths.   I remember
the first census, taken on July 17, 1956, during the visit of Abbé
Breuil.

What a lot of Mammoths!

One of us walked on the right, inspecting the walls; the Abbé on
the left, the side of the heart; the "fourth man" in the centre, facing

the damp wind of the cave, to examine the roofs, and I myself a few paces behind, finding it difficult to keep up with them, for I was writing down the count. "Two mammoths to the right, two ..." "Three mammoths to the left, three . . ." "One in the centre, one . . ." "Five to the right, five." Thus the line of counters advanced, exploring the depths, while the scribe became involved in his calculations: "28 . . . 35 . . . 42 . . . 55 . . . 61 . . . No, really, there are too many!" This lavishness had its meaning. The men of Rouffignac longed for mammoth, for they needed mammoth, they lived on mammoth, And they drew it, or rather they created it on their walls in their drawings and engravings, that their valleys might be filled with a host of pachyderms.

Did they hunt them? In pictures of the bisons and ibexes they hunted we find magic arrows and votive lines piercing the animal. There are never any arrows on the mammoths: they are always unscathed.

We have noted the frequent association of pot-holes in the Breuil gallery with the pictures of mammoths. These natural depressions lead to a lower level, to the perennial flow of waters, far below. Might they not suggest trap-pits, and should we not see in this connexion a rite preparatory to the trapping? The hollow below and to the right of the great frieze of painted mammoths, and the first hollow on the left-hand wall, which is connected with an engraved mammoth, seem examples worth remembering. One fact, however, is not explained.

The "lone" mammoth is not falling into the nearest hollow; he turns his back on it. Indeed, he seems to escape from it. The mammoth engraved opposite also gets out of the pit instead of seeming to fall into it.

In this connexion, how can we fail to recall the old legends that speak of "rats as big as elephants, rats that live underground and die directly they come into the open air, or the light of the sun shines on them?"

When they found, at the thaw, a mammoth killed by a blizzard, brought to light by a landslide, did not primitive men think the mammoth lived underground?

You may prefer to think, and this is equally credible, that there is no connexion between the starting-points of the pot-holes in the galleries and the drawn or painted mammoths. The holes are holes, and the mammoths are mammoths. That is all.

A fine bag

A shoot in the Rambouillet coverts always ends in a fine display of game. The finest, no doubt, were those to be seen at the beginning of the century in the woods at Fontenailles, when the Comtes Greffulhe had been shooting.

The biggest bag of the early palaeolithic era is to be seen at Rouffignac. The mammoth is the show-piece, taking first place both for his weight and for his numbers. The list compiled on July 30, 1956, yields these figures:

"Red Ceiling" gallery:	5 mammoths out of 5 animals
"Two mammoths" gallery:	2 mammoths out of 2
1st Section of the Sacred Way:	
—before the Breuil gallery:	7 mammoths out of 9
—Henri Breuil gallery:	25 mammoths out of 31
2nd Section of the Sacred Way:	7 mammoths out of 9
—up to the "Great Ceiling":	14 mammoths out of 43
"Great Ceiling":	
—last section, from the "Great Ceiling" to the last drawing known up to now, the "Mammoth with the Roguish Eye":	10 mammoths out of 14

And the general list gave 70 mammoths out of 113 animals represented. The percentages show the predominance of the mammoth:

100%, 100%, 77%, 83%, 32%, 71%, and 61% of the total.

For numbers alone, Rouffignac is the true mammoths' cave. Recent investigations have added to the original figures, for 91 mammoths were counted in September and more than 100 in October, scattered through five or six miles of galleries, but we can arrive at a definite total only by a systematic census, carried out gallery by gallery. For instance, the "Red Ceiling" gallery contains six, not five. A mammoth at the far end, on the left, was not noticed in the first extensive visits. Others glimpsed in a hasty exploration of the eastern branch have not yet been counted exactly. The deep gallery of the stream holds others, and so do the far ends of the Henri Breuil gallery, in which is the "mammoth of the niche". For the moment, only the Henri Breuil gallery has been completely examined. Let us recall the original figures:

Paintings: 11 mammoths.   1 horse.   3 rhinoceros.
Drawings: 14 mammoths.   1 horse.   —   1 bison.
TOTAL: 25 mammoths.   2 horses.   3 rhinoceros. 1 bison.

And here are the corrected figures after several minute inspections with the help of various experts (MM. Charles and Louis Plassard, Françoise Dejean, Claude Barrière, Jacques L. R. Nougier).

Paintings: 11 mammoths.   1 horse.   3 rhinoceros.
Drawings: 19 mammoths.   1 horse.   1 rhinoceros. 2 bison.
TOTAL: 30 mammoths.   2 horses.   4 rhinoceros. 2 bison.

The percentage of painted mammoths becomes 73%, that of drawn mammoths 82%, and in the whole of the Breuil gallery 78% of the animals depicted are mammoths.

Yes, for numbers alone, Rouffignac is certainly the mammoths' cave. This does not mean that it was reserved for mammoths only, but that is another story.

THE WOOLLY RHINOCEROS
(RHINOCEROS *TICHORHINUS*)

The Woolly Rhinoceros

Since the dawn of the quaternary era, the elephant and the rhinoceros have been accustomed to live together. The ancient elephant and Merck's rhinoceros, two "warm" species, are often found side by side, and as the climate becomes colder the mammoth and the rhinoceros are natural neighbours. Both have thick coats and deep layers of fat to protect them from the same icy cold. The Siberian refrigerators have yielded rhinoceroses just as they have yielded mammoths. The rhinoceros in this case is the "cold" species, *Rhinoceros tichorhinus*, the Woolly Rhinoceros, also called "the rhinoceros with divided nostrils" because it has a strong bony partition inside its nose to support the great curved horn. The Siberian rhinoceros reaches a height of 5 ft. 3 in. at the shoulder, with a length of 11 ft. 6 in.

If we compare these average measurements with those of the rhinoceros pictured at Rouffignac we shall find some interesting data. Thus, the third rhinoceros in the now famous (not to say notorious) frieze is in the proportion of 1 to 3.5 with the Siberian rhinoceros. On the natural scale the Rouffignac rhinoceros would measure 1 m. 54 cm. (5 ft.) high at the shoulder, with a total length of 3 m. 57 cm. (11 ft. 8 in.) from the tail to the tapered end of the great frieze. The reduction in the two cases is very exact, but different. The mammoths have been reduced more, to one-fifth full size. Deep minds might draw great and weighty conclusions from this. It may be simpler, and just as profound, to note that the rocky wall allowed only of paintings and drawings averaging 60 to 80 cm. (24 to 30 in.) high. The artists had only this limited belt of smooth wall to use; the flint "kidneys" above it and the natural concavity of the wall below it made painting and drawing there impossible. They therefore reduced their animal models, and reduced the mammoth most, because he was bigger than the rhinoceros. Even good sense could prevail in the palaeolithic age, which incidentally has been declared "superior" in an age when western art is considered supreme.

The chief feature of the rhinoceros, the great horn, is more than a metre (3 ft. 3 in.) long in the known Siberian specimens. Measuring the great horn of No. 3 at Rouffignac we find it 4 ft. 1 in. long along the outside curve and more than 3 ft. long in a straight line from base to point.

The Rhinoceros Frieze

The first rhinoceros of the group is smaller, and his great horn is proportionately smaller still. It is one-quarter as long as his body instead of one-third. Is this difference due to age or sex? Is the leading rhinoceros a young one, followed by his father and his mother?

Elephants live in large herds which have a fixed order of march when they go to their drinking places in the rivers. The calves go first, followed by the mothers, who guide them gently with their tusks or trunks. The bulls come last and the "Patriarch" or old bull of the herd brings up the rear.

Rhinoceroses are less gregarious and seem to prefer family life. They go to the water-holes in pairs. It is probable that the females had the longest but also the thinnest and sharpest horns and used them to guide the young as they went ahead of them, preventing them from straying to one side, much as goose-girls guide their flock with a long stick threatening the flanks.

In the light of this touching scene, the rhinoceros frieze becomes clear: the first is the youngster, the second is his mother, who has, indeed, the longest and sharpest horn, also the thinnest at the base. We call this rhinoceros "Dubois" after a cave-explorer from Brive who, some years ago, saw fit to carve his name on her, careless of her value and purity. Dubois, then, is the mother rhinoceros.

And father rhinoceros brings up the rear, completing the family trinity. Chance plays odd tricks! When controversy was still raging about the fabulous cave, its detractors concentrated on the baby rhinoceros and refused to recognise him. They tore him from the bosom of his family and cast doubts on his paternity. But both violence and argument were useless, for the answer was there. Opposite the two fighting mammoths, but on the ceiling and on the right, are two excellent rhinoceroses. The first (to whose fame we shall return) is also a female; she is guiding the walk of a young one just in front of her. This youngster is notable for his two horns, which are deeply graven in the limestone rock. The rest of the body is fainter, but it would normally lie partly alongside that of the mother.   Abbé Breuil spent a long time craning his neck and straining his eyes before he ventured on a theory.   Paintings and drawings of rhinoceros seem to be governed by the same family tradition: father, mother and child for the painted frieze, mother and child only for drawings.   Besides their accurate and clinical observation, our quaternary artists had sociological sense.   On one hand, they drew herds of mammoths; on the other, rhinoceros family life.

Hairy head or bald head?

Like his friend the mammoth, the rhinoceros had an ample coat: a double covering composed of long, stiff, close-growing hairs, very dark reddish brown in colour, and under them "a deep layer of black wool".

The longest hairs, measuring more than 8 in., grew on the lower part of the body and under the neck, according to the Rouffignac paintings, but the head, judging from a body found on a left tributary of the Lena river in 1771, bore hairs only $2\frac{1}{2}$ in. long.   Though his head stood well clear and was naturally closely cropped, the *tichorhinus* was by no means bald, as some have claimed.   The rhinoceros drawn on the ceiling, to which we have referred, wears a very fine, clear mane and head-covering shown by small, regular strokes of the engraving tool.   One of his plainest morphological features is the size of his hump, a reserve of fat formed on the withers.   Here the hump is enormous; it juts right out.   We find the same large lumps on the rhinoceroses in the family, especially the youngster and the father.   Mother Dubois' hump is less full, for mothers are always worried, and they show it!

Though done in a different style, the rhinoceroses painted on the "Great Ceiling" also have humps.   Once more it is confirmed that most of the Rouffignac animals are in their winter dress.   They are coming to take up their winter quarters in the cave during the hard weather, and their humps are full.

The rhinoceros of Font-de-Gaume, on the contrary, is in summer dress.   His body is long and slender, quite different from the rhinoceroses engraved on stones in the Colombière cave in the Ain department, and those engraved on flint slabs in the Trilobite cave at Arcy-sur-Cure.   These "decorative" rhinoceroses belong to the civilisation known as Périgordian and are older than the Magdalenian rhinoceros of Font-de-Gaume.   Are they, strictly speaking, of the same species?   Perhaps not, but that did not prevent the critics of Rouffignac from proclaiming at the tops of their voices in

the streets of Les Eyzies, during the sensation at the beginning of
August 1956, that the Rouffignac animals were "slavish copies of
Font-de-Gaume", insisting, of course, especially on the word
"slavish".

Rhinoceros hunting?

The rhinoceros appears very rarely in specimens of rupestral art.
From south-west to north-east, he is found at Los Casares, Trois
Frères, Gargas, La Mouthe, Font-de-Gaume, Combarelles and
Lascaux, depicted with varying technique and in different chronological orders, and often alone or only two in a cave.   Until now
we only knew of about ten.   The Rouffignac cave undoubtedly
brings us the finest specimens of *Rhinoceros tichorhinus*, and the
present count, which is still on the increase, gives the figure of nine
animals.   The mammoth gallery is also the rhinoceros gallery.
The Breuil gallery contains the three fine painted specimens forming
a complete family and one (unfinished) engraved specimen on the
left-hand wall.   In front of the "Mammoths of the Discovery" are
two rhinoceroses engraved on the roof, and finally, three more are
painted on the "Great Ceiling".

As in the case of the mammoths, we may say that Rouffignac alone
contains about as many mammoths and rhinoceroses as all the other
Franco-Cantabric art caves put together.   These figures clearly
show the great iconographic importance of Rouffignac and place it
definitely among the "Giant" quaternary caves, whose distinguished
names are Altamira, Font-de-Gaume, Les Combarelles, Lascaux,
Les Trois Frères and Niaux.

The aesthetic value of Rouffignac, though no doubt more sub-
jective, is not less.   It Rouffignac lacks the magic colouring that
blazes at Lascaux and Altamira, it does have unequalled purity of
line, both painted and engraved.   Finally, by the number of questions it raises and by its still uncounted riches, it takes its place
with ease in the front rank of such discoveries.

The world scarcity of rhinoceros is a valid argument against the
theory that they were hunted.   Their size, their violence and their
furious charging must have made them awkward game.   And if the
rhinoceros engraved on a stone at La Colombière does have some
curious, weighted arrows planted in his belly, these arrows may
express a harmless wish rather than a real incident of the chase or a
serious determination for the future.   Palaeolithic sorcerers, like Paul
Valéry, sometimes yearned for "an impossible goal".   The three rhinos
of the "Great Ceiling" are scattered there in the huge, disorderly

bestiary, but the three in the frieze and the two in the sector of the "Mammoths of the Discovery" depict mother and child. These are family groups. Is it too far-fetched to suggest that quaternary man at Rouffignac thought of a rhinoceros family when he wanted to evoke the pleasures of the hearth?

The Paolo Rhinoceros

No doubt it is not too late to come back to him. And he doubly deserves it: for himself as a rhinoceros, and for the well-merited tribute of the learned Italian prehistorian, Paolo Graziosi, an eminent quaternary specialist, who on being invited by telegram to visit Rouffignac replied simply "I'm hurrying" and hurried faster than his cable. While the little town of Les Eyzies ignored its new discovery, the humanist University of Florence brought confirmation. A few days previously, after a working and exploring visit of twelve hours, I returned to the cave with M. C. Plassard and we went up the "Sacred Way". After twelve hours without rest, our physical and mental reflexes had become a little less effective. My companion, who scrambled about in his cave with the agility of a cat, had taken a knock on the head from a jutting flint in the roof. I heard a dull thud like that of a wood on the board at the end of a bowling alley. The red blood trickled down over a fine ivory skull, reminding me of the scarlet "macaronis" in some prehistoric paintings. I was to make the same comparison a month later, when M. Plassard, his son, Louis, and I discovered the great red ceiling with its many interlacings, serpentine mouldings and other "macaronis" traced by a finger and standing out white on a crimson ground. But the inversion was complete: here was a vault, not a globe, red, not white, bearing lines which were white, not red. . . .

While we were coming back along the left side, and facing the "Mammoths of the Discovery" on the ceiling, we saw some deeply graven lines. Holding a lamp above our heads, we followed the lines: two diverging points were very clear. And near their junction, some fine but deep strokes suggested something like a ball of hair or feathers. We turned the lamp and twisted our bodies, and our empty stomachs felt like turning, too. With our backs to the wall, we seemed to see a great bird with its beak wide open, and farther along, on the left, a second bird suggested chiefly by his beak, which was also agape.

Birds of Legend?

We scribbled "Birds?" on a slip of paper and thrust the slip into the end of a cleft stick. We would see about this later. We did see, not much later, and the explanation came with Professor Paolo Graziosi. There we were, twisting and turning, with heads in air, trying to solve the mystery of these two creatures that seemed to be apterixes, but could not be.

The outlines of the "beaks" were very deep and highly polished, and their depths were black. The lines forming the ball of hair or feathers were finer but just as smooth. They gradually faded as they drew away from the "beak", that is, towards the middle of the gallery. I must say that this fading away and this deep patina, this "dust of centuries", a very thick deposit of manganese as we knew later, aroused our enthusiasm much more than the mysterious forms we had to decipher.

These fading, glazed drawings gave irrefutable evidence of authenticity, and we filled our records with sure proofs to oppose to Périgordian scepticism. And in the middle of our discussion, Paolo Graziosi declared with Olympian calm, but with a touch of breathless excitement: "It's a rhinoceros!"

Good Lord, yes, it was a rhinoceros, a magnificent rhinoceros, and a *tichorhinus* into the bargain. . . .

For a moment, a geological silence reigned in the gallery. The soul of a rhinoceros passed by.

A baptism

Now our excitement mounted once more. "It shall be the Paolo rhinoceros!" Carried unanimously. The discovery was important. This was the first rhinoceros drawing found at Rouffignac. The assaults of ignorance had already been let loose against the painted "baby". Now, the new animal, who was engraved, had the same features: the shape and curvature of the horns (not the open beak of a bird), the massive shoulders, loaded with fat over the withers, the long, matted hair. The hind-quarters faded and disappeared towards the gallery.

The manganese patina showed that the discovery was certainly genuine. This authentic engraving helped to prove the genuineness of the painting. But, you may say, why did this magnificent rhinoceros prove so difficult to identify?

Take a photograph of the "baby". Take a photograph of the "Paolo". Turn the prints clockwise and look at them upside-down. (If the earth line is given you for upright animals painted on a wall you must find it yourself for horizontal animals painted on a ceiling.) Turn your book, and you will see the curved and threatening beaks of two birds of prey!

Far from Rouffignac in time and space, natives of Siberia, the Jukaghirs, took these fossil skulls for those of fabulous, gigantic birds with which, no doubt, their ancestors had to compete for the game in their hunting grounds. But the Jukaghirs thought the rhinoceros horns were the gigantic talons of these birds of prey!

THE COMPANIONS OF THE
MAMMOTH AND THE RHINOCEROS

The Bison

After the powerful mammoth herds and the one-child rhinoceros families, the largest animal contingent was that of the bison, though it is true they came only a little before the ibexes and the horses. Today mammoth and rhinoceros have disappeared. The bison has very nearly disappeared; a victim of mankind, he now owes to man his precarious preservation. The ibex and the horse, being less highly specialised in the "Arctic" way of life of the early palaeolithic period, are still alive, finding sanctuary in the mountains in one case and protection in servitude in the other.

Rouffignac plays the part of an underground Noah's Ark very well. It harbours mostly vanished species, just those which need a sanctuary.

None the less, the bison contingent comes far behind that of the mammoths, and that, although bison was classic game and a favourite dish with upper palaeolothic man. In his pictures the bison is often transfixed with strokes and magic arrows suggestive of the chase, as in the case of the many transfixed bison at Niaux and now in that of the bison of Rouffignac.

About one-third of the Rouffignac bison are engraved, while two-thirds are painted. One bison on the left-hand base of the great ceiling is even a curious mixture: his fore-quarters are painted and his hind-quarters are engraved. When the time comes to fix more exact dates for the drawings, he will certainly play an important part, for he will show a parallel between the "engraved" and "painted" styles.

The hunter-artist has drawn his bison with as sure a hand as that of his colleague at Niaux or his neighbour at Font-de-Gaume, near Combarelles. With the great, bulging brow, the very short neck and the large hump on the withers, the fore-quarters of the bison are always impressive; they give a sense of mass and power. This power is, no doubt, further emphasised by the artist, who often dwells on the details of the broad and bushy mane. The curved horns are often unusually and dangerously slim, ending in the sharpest of points, most firmly drawn. Both in carving and in drawing, the excellent technique is best shown in the drawing of these points. Both sureness of eye and skill of hand are reminders of an advanced phase of the Magdalenian era. The chronologies of Rouffignac (which must certainly be quoted in the plural) have not yet been worked out, and they will need years of tracing, careful examination of superimpositions, and comparative studies.

The palaeolithic bison was bigger than that of today, as many bones found during excavations have proved. Hunted by palaeolithic man, still hunted by the peoples of the Bronze and Iron Ages, by the Germans and by the Celts, the bison abandoned the plains to find refuge in the forests, while their numbers dwindled from century to century. Twenty years ago the last bison were confined to certain forest lands in Poland and West Russia: to the Bielowicza Forest in the Grodno district, for example. Even so, bison had to be brought from menageries and private parks to restock the native herd from time to time.

Slow extinction . . . by Man

The extinction of the bison has gone on slowly and gradually since the upper palaeolithic period. The European bison never formed great herds like his cousin, the American bison. In 1832, on the prairie near Platt River, Captain Bonneville saw "a countryside absolutely blackened by innumerable herds", as far as eye could reach. In 1871, at a crossing of the Arkansas River, a herd of bison was estimated at 4,000,000 head. About the same time General Sheridan estimated a herd at more than 100,000,000 head after having made cunning calculations with his officers. These calculations first yielded 10,000 million bison, then 1,000 millions; eventually this was reduced to the "more modest" figure of 100 millions. A wonderful example of scientific method applied to living groups!

These vast American herds were exterminated in a few years. The bison stopped ships as they swam across rivers, they stopped the early trains as they crossed the tracks. Yet a few years later, after the War of Independence, the New York Museum had the greatest difficulty in finding a true stuffed bison for exhibition (1887–1889).

The railways brought the hunters, and the hunters brought their long rifles, and the American bison, a new victim of civilisation, was almost banished from the continent.   The bison of Europe suffered the same martyrdom, but more slowly, on a more "humane" and very "old European" scale.   Their decimation was begun by the palaeolithic hunters in the ravines of the Manaurie and went on for the next 15,000 years.   Driven from the plains and lurking in more and more limited forest lands, they disappeared slowly but surely. The rare survivors were those in eastern Europe, where the country was less peopled, less cleared, still forest-clad and little haunted by man.   The struggle between the bison and man became funda-mental.   The latter would take the skin of the former for a shrinking profit.   Times had changed indeed since the great days of Rouffignac, when the bison represented one of the steadiest market values.

All the Bison has is good

The bison yields several hundred pounds of excellent meat, which can be eaten fresh or dried (in the form of pemmican).   His skin will make a tent for the bivouac, a bed at night or a cloak by day. Bison-skin, decorated and painted with hunting scenes—bison-hunting, of course—or pictures of General Custer hunting Indians, can be used as a newspaper or for records.   The same skin can be made into footwear (moccasins), travelling-bags, or shields, for which the shape of the hump is particularly handy.   It will make a saddle, too, or cover a canoe.   Cut into strips, bison-skin will make lassoes to catch other bison.

Bison skulls will decorate Indian heads for ritual ceremonies designed to multiply the bison herds in order to massacre them. The shoulder-blade makes a spade, and the other bones can be fashioned into whistles, scrapers, spoons, needles, skewers or awls according to their original shape and the industry of the artisan. As for the horns, when worn by the lucky hunter or the sorcerer, they are symbols of power.

The mysterious "sorcerers" engraved in the Trois Frères cave also wear bison skulls and horns for ritual dances.   More pro-saically, the horns are used as hunting-horns or trumpets, or as receptacles for liquids and finally, in the last and most modern stage, for gunpowder.

Thread and rope can be made of the tendons, the hoofs yield glue and gelatine, the bladder can be used as a receptacle and the tail as a fly-whisk.   The hair is useful for decoration or stuffings, and even the animal's droppings have their use when dried and burnt as fuel.

tire , avant le mois de Mai de l'an 570. * Gregoire de
Tours , l. 4. Valois , *de geft. Franc.*

MIREMONT , bourg de France dans le Perigord ,
eft fitué fur une petite riviere qui fe jette dans le Vezere
fept ou huit lieuës de Perigueux , & à même diftance
de Bergerac. Ce bourg eft remarquable par la caverne
le Clufeau , qui va fort loin fous terre. Les gens du pays
prétendent qu'il y a de grandes falles, des peintures &
des autels : ce qui perfuade aux plus credules , que les
payens y faifoient des facrifices à Venus ou aux dieux
infernaux.

MIREPOIX , ville du comté de Foix dans le haut
Languedoc , avec évêché fuffragant de Touloufe , eft
fituée fur le Lers à trois lieuës de Foix. Les écrivains La-
tins la nomment *Mirapicum Mirapifcæ , Mirapincum & Mi-*

4. A piece of text from an 18th century book, in which reference is made
to the cave and its paintings

5. The engraved "Mammoth of the Discovery", June 26th, 1956

6. The Great Fosse. Professor Nougier is measuring drawings which are being photographed by M. Romain Robert

The bison, a "universal" animal, was the victim of his useful-
ness. Primitive economy, sometimes called the Economy of Looting
by ethnographers, made great gaps in his ranks. But if the bison
vanished, we do at least know why. His extinction is not wrapped
in the mystery which surrounds the total destruction of the mammoth and the woolly rhinoceros.

The Ibex

The "Great Ceiling" is the real gallery of the ibex. All the
eleven specimens in the cave are there, and they are even arranged
in groups on the right-hand vault and the left-hand springing of the
vault. Is this a deliberate arrangement or a mere chance? The
features are noted most minutely; heavy bodies with strong, well-
planted legs, the neck hardly marked, the chin level with the back
and the horns elegantly swept back in a magnificent pose.

The most remarkable is the "Alphonse Dalbavie", so called after
a nobleman who lived at Bordeaux about 1885, according to a
notice finely carved with a knife over the black lines of the ibex.
Since prehistoric art was unknown at that date, this superimposition
of scribblings and other inscriptions would be another proof of the
genuineness of the paintings, if any were needed. An intelligent
and well-informed journalist in Bordeaux, Jean Guichard, was asked
to search the electoral registers of 1876, 1877, 1881 or 1885 for any
further details about Alphonse Dalbavie which would enable us to
establish that he, Alphonse, was a real person, and also, indirectly,
to prove the genuineness of the graceful ibex. For it is quite clear
that the discoverers of Rouffignac must not only prove the indis-
putable authenticity of the animal paintings and engravings, and
also prove it to a degree never before required for such a quantity
of useful or useless evidence, but must also prove the authenticity
of the thousands and thousands of scribblings and historical inscriptions that disfigure the works of art or occupy the bare walls.
It is clear, too, that such a task is superhuman and would demand
thousands and thousands of hours and many lifetimes. Is not this
just why it is desired and falsely proposed by our detractors?

A few inscriptions

The Red Ceiling, in its admirable group of five engraved mammoths, carries the date 1781, repeated several times, on the leader
of the upper rank, the inscription "Pagerie 1884" on the leader,
facing right, of the lower rank, 1872 on his opposite number and
1841 and 1884 on the beast that follows him. On this basis, and

D

from now on, we shall pursue our inquiry, and we expect in a few years to give names and publish essential details. Who dared, in 1781, at the time of the alliance of Joseph II and Catherine II to divide the Ottoman Empire, go into the Rouffignac cave and inscribe this historic date? Or perhaps we can give more details: would it not be in February 1781, and should we not see in this fuliginous inscription a distant echo of the publication of the "Report to the King" (*Compte-rendu au Roi*) of his Minister, Necker? Another date, 1841, has already set us thinking. We know that in June 1841, a very favourable month for visiting any cave, especially Rouffignac, Ledru-Rollin was elected Deputy for Le Mans by 123 votes out of 127. What were the three abstainers doing? Did not one of them, or two, or all, come to Périgord to record this historic date with a candle-flame? If we could find these three names with details of their civil status, their route from Le Mans to the Dordogne, their bill at some hostelry in the Sarlandais, and trace their halt at a shoemaker's at Bugue and the substance of their confession at the presbytery of Plazac, we might be able to prove that the mammoth engraved on the Red Ceiling and marked 1841 is authentic. Q.E.D.! And since we have only 100 mammoths . . . (Our Duty at Rouffignac —I use the capital letter purposely—is to reply intelligently to every unintelligent objection). Quaternary art? Good God, no! This is the work of members of the Underground Movement during the war! And right along the first gallery on the right we have found inscriptions by these heroes. No, come, come, that won't wash! Find something else. Quaternary art? Heavens, no! These animal drawings were made with an acetylene blow-lamp! Well, we have found some blow-lamp drawings, and there was really no comparison with our mammoths and rhinos. These blow-lamp drawings are *unquaternary*: a hen and a duck. Beyond the deep galleries known as those of the Stream we have even found the bison we call Gérin. But we will speak of that choice specimen later. . . .

The "Dalbavie" Ibex again

We have already said the "Dalbavie" ibex is remarkable. For a long time yet he might provide material for caustic comment, and he is remarkable for that, too. He shines in the rôle of the "invisible ibex", inspired, no doubt, by H. G. Wells. Firmly set on the vertical wall, with his forefeet planted on a rock, he is astonishingly drawn in black manganese on a light-coloured rock background. He stands about five yards from the Stream Pothole, that underground chimney that communicates with the lower galleries. And how many tens and hundreds of "explorations"—it seems that's the name—and expeditions have foundered in that pothole! There were forty-two expeditions between 1945 and 1949. What minute examinations, what scrupulous surveys must have been made in the course of these expeditions, since not one of them noticed the Dalbavie ibex, standing right opposite the chimney! That chimney was no doubt difficult to climb, but not difficult enough to compel the cave-explorers to go on all fours, with their eyes fixed on the clayey soil and their noses ploughing the mud. Not a man looked up. (Cave-explorers, those? Never!) And if by any chance one of them did at last raise his eyes and at last see the Dalbavie ibex, and if he did not recognise it as an ibex springing straight out of 20,000 years of prehistory, I will never believe that he was a Périgordian, not he! A real Périgordian imbibes Prehistory with his mother's milk.

Thanks to the noble Dalbavie, the little ibex of Rouffignac passes down to posterity and enters into immortality under his forgotten name. And thus he will outlive the distant descendants of his brothers. The flocks of other days grew scarce. Too much hunted on the plains, they fled to the hills. Man followed, and the flocks of ibex, less and less numerous, made for the mountain peaks. The race became divided; some climbed the Pyrenees, others the Alps. Gaston Phoebus, Count of Foix, counted herds of 500 head in the Pyrenees at the end of the 14th century. Later, there were only a few score, and even those became rare. But "Dalbavie" will live.

The Horse

The drawings of horses at Rouffignac afford excellent contributions to equine history. The horse has been called the noblest conquest of man, no doubt because it was the last. Resistance to slavery is a sign of nobility. It was only in the Bronze Age, during the second millenary before our era, that the horse was "conquered". At Rouffignac he was hunted. The kitchen refuse of our palaeolithic men is full of horses' bones, teeth and even complete jaws. Horse-meat butchers' shops existed long before the siege of Paris in 1870.

Painted horses adorn the "Great Ceiling" at Rouffignac in the company of mammoths, rhinoceroses and ibex. Most of them are on the smoothest sections of the vault, before the Stream chimney. There they can develop freely, and one of the finest is nearly 8 ft. long from tip of nose to tip of tail. Lying on a bank of clay scraped up by the bears, we gazed at him for many minutes, and it is only in that position that you can really take him in. The horse looks towards the chimney; his head is heavy and rather short, with a straight frontal line. The back is slightly curved, the legs slim and short, the tail very bushy, even at the base. The painting is done in small, neat touches; one can only admire the elegant detail and general harmony of form. Not far off, another horse, rather smaller, has the same undeniable beauty.

The zoologist will study these horses, fitting them into place in the evolution of the Equides. The horses of Rouffignac are apparently related to a horse in process of extinction, called Prjewalski's horse and found on the barren plateaux of Jungaria, north-east of the Tien-Chan mountains.

The archaeologist will study their beauty of form. The horses of Rouffignac are among the finest drawings in all the body of quaternary art, and they remind us forcibly of Niaux, the most famous horse and bison cave. Graceful heads, quivering nostrils, still moist with mucus, delicate legs and stiff, flowing manes through which the cold wind of the Steppes seems still to blow—we have all these in the horses of Rouffignac, like a soft echo of the outside world that saw their creation; like a stirring of life.

And we remain amazed at the means used to create this admirable animal art. A smooth ceiling, no doubt, based on hard limestone, but what then? A brush made from a frayed piece of wood, wetted and chewed and spreading, with extraordinary skill, a stiff paste of manganese. Where did this usable manganese come from? What were its solvent and its vehicle?

Science intervenes

Future analyses will solve these problems. Twice already pious hands have scraped these 20,000-year-old lines to shorten them by a few millimetres, remove the surface film and obtain a few necessary milligrams of colouring matter. I used my penknife with an emotion and oppression I have rarely known. Suddenly all was silence. For the sake of science, indeed, a sacrilege was being committed. With all its progress, science must destroy in order to learn; can it achieve contentment only after sacrifice? The complete and aesthetic vision of the little horse was not enough. Yet the horse seems more beautiful to me now that I know he is drawn in manganese. What does the material matter, if I can feel that he is truly "palaeolithic"?

We had thought he was, ever since we discovered him on June

26. Abbé Breuil thought so, and so did Professor Graziosi. As I was to say a few days later, "Who would dare to scrape the divine lips of Mona Lisa to prove her genuine?" Who will dare to scrape the bisons of Niaux to establish their status and fix their order? Yet we scraped one leg of a Rouffignac horse. Since he did not belong to me, I asked M. Plassard's permission to take the sample. If you had said "No", M. Plassard, rest assured I should not have insisted. I had no desire to do so.

The only success of the enemies of Rouffignac was that they forced us to remove a few milligrams of black matter. Let us not regret our forbearance; to the end of time, no doubt, there will be visitors to the cave, and these visitors will ask: "Why the scraping? Why this gap?" And the guides who pass their formulae from century to century will answer: "A scraping was taken once to make a strict analysis." In two or three centuries, when new painted caves are found, must they all be scraped, down to the last millionth of a gram, to discover the exact age of Manganese 18 or Manganese 72, correct to the nearest second? Science will be satisfied, and artists will come only to admire surfaces scraped bare. "There was a mammoth here, and three rhinos over there. . . ."

But will humanity still exist two or three centuries from now? It has existed so long that it seems eternal, especially to Man himself. Let us not forget that the human species is also an animal species. And geological history, even in recent times, shows many examples of race suicide. The mammoths have vanished, *Rhinoceros tichorhinus* has vanished, and we know nothing of their fate. No doubt some great natural cataclysm speeded and closed their story. Some huge snowstorm; some hurricane blizzard. . . . We imagine these disasters. We also attribute some extinctions to man, and the bison was certainly his victim. One hundred thousand bison were slaughtered in December 1877 and January 1878. We sometimes think of "that sort of fatal law which strikes the representatives of a species when they have reached the peak of their power and development".

Does the peak of success announce the disappearance of a species? The Ancients seem to have foreseen some such doom when they murmured to one another, in the streets of Rome, "the Tarpeian Rock is near the Capitol".

It is true that the human race has one unique quality. It alone knows how to destroy itself—wholesale. It may cherish reasonable hopes of annihilation.

The Ceiling is too low

The great 8-ft. horse raises the problem of execution. How was the drawing done? The roof is very low at this point, only about 5 ft., and there is no room to stand back and see the whole of it without lying flat on one's back, or to photograph it properly without distorting it to some extent. Still greater difficulties must have faced the artist. In a prone position, his hand could not reach the ceiling. And when his hand was at work, his head must have been very close to the roof, reducing his field of view severely. Whatever you do here, you are either too near or too far off. But the quaternary artist solved the problem. Did he sketch the outline, laying out the plan of the animal on the ceiling, and then applying his coat of manganese minutely, stroke by stroke? This would seem to be the normal procedure for a "civilised" artist, but it is quite uncertain in the case of a "primitive". First of all, there is no trace of a rough sketch, no false line, no erasure or correction. Was the sketch perfect at the first attempt? Or was it drawn lightly in a different medium, which has faded away? One might imagine a charcoal sketch, afterwards "lined in" with manganese. But are we quite sure that the charcoal line would have disappeared in 15,000 or 20,000 years, according to Moissan's rules? Do we not have excellent prehistoric paintings and drawings, perfectly preserved, yet made in charcoal? One of the first materials in use, one of the most abundant and easiest to discover, was charcoal black. Here again many analyses should be made, not at Rouffignac now, where they have been made already or are in progress, but in all the other painted caves of the West. Here are a few interesting (and perhaps remunerative) openings for archaeological chemists. Must we conclude that the palaeolithic artist made no preliminary sketch but painted his colour directly on his ground? And that from the first stroke he carried in his head the exact and precise development of all the successive strokes which, in their sum, one beside the other, would finally give a true proportion to the whole? Such sureness of eye and touch are worthy of a Matisse!

A full view of the Subject

From the moment when he draws his first stroke, such is the executive method of the palaeolithic artist. His vision sometimes shines forth like a mental lamp when a natural detail suggests a theme, a detail, an animal. Here natural detail plays the part of the first stroke. On the left wall of the Breuil gallery, a "beak" or rib of the wall separates two groups of mammoths, three moving to the left, two to the right. The leader of the left-hand file is the mammoth with the flint "kidney".

A flint "kidney", in its convex lower portion, represents the rounded back of a mammoth, the hollow formed by the curve of the skull and the start of the dorsal curve. Hence its use in the drawing.

In the right-hand mammoth of the two who are charging each other in the "Discovery" frieze, another rounded flint, projecting from the limestone wall, forms the creature's eye. Here again, the "kidney" is the basis of the drawing, and the natural detail is the starting-point of an aesthetic vision. There are many examples at Rouffignac alone. Sometimes a shell embedded in the limestone has caught the palaeolithic eye and formed the starting-point of an animal drawing. The most exciting example of this artistic conception is certainly the "Bison of the Cups" in the cave at Niaux.

The Bison of the Cups at Niaux

Innumerable little natural cups have been worn in the clay floor of this cave by the dripping of water from the roof. Each drop slowly digs its little hole, and the floor is covered with hundreds of them. The feet of modern visitors have obliterated many more, but some have been preserved along the walls and in the least accessible margins of the gallery, where a man would have to bend double or crawl.

The bison, engraved in fine lines on the clay, faces right; he is precise, clear and real. Detail photographs show the fineness and sureness of the smallest stroke, lightly but skilfully placed on the clay when it was soft. Precise detail goes hand in hand with a perfect vision of the whole and a general perfection of form and proportion. Unfortunately the engraving, being carved on a low, overhanging wall which is difficult to reach, does not leave enough space to take a perfect photograph of the whole picture, as in the case of the great horse at Rouffignac.

Three "natural" cups lie on the bison's body, where they are cleverly used for magic ends. These three cups are underlined by three arrows whose tips rest exactly on their edges, in the middle of the carcass: one arrow depicted in two lines and abutting on the central cup, and two arrows at the sides, each represented by three lines joining at the extreme edges of the outer cups. The exactness of the lines which join the cups is interesting. It shows that the cups were already fossilised when the drawing was made and the magic rites were performed. If the clay had still been "live" and subject to the repeated and intermittent action of the water, the natural edges of the cups would have been enlarged and they would have cut off the sharp points of the three arrows.

The "live" cups corresponded with a damp period in the evolution of the cave. The bison was drawn later, and fuller knowledge of climatic conditions in the cave—which may have differed from conditions outside, for we are nearly a mile from the entrance—might bring forth evidence which would help us to fix the exact date of this Magdalenian drawing.

A simple method of creating this work would have been to engrave a bison on the clay and then pierce him with three ritual wounds. The real method was much more complicated: the three natural cups must have suggested the future wounds even before the bison was drawn, and the bison was engraved around these cups and in relation to them. The cups, forming inverted bas-reliefs, were no doubt particularly suggestive. If a rocky projection can suggest the hump of a bison, the belly of a reindeer or a mammoth's back, a hollow basin may also suggest an animal form and a small cup may mark a wound. The use of these natural cups as "ritual wounds" affords remarkable proof of quaternary creative intelligence, which was quick to grasp the suggestive value of the cups on the clay floor. Three of them were chosen and invested with the magic meaning of wounds, and the drawing of the bison was built up around these cups, neglecting others, which were left in their natural state. On one hind-leg and one fore-leg and above the animal's body, near the withers, are other natural cups which have been ignored. Careful examination of the bison's eye reveals another fact, even more full of meaning. The pupil, ringed by the oval outline of the eye, is "natural" and also formed by a small and regular cup, smaller than those which were used as wounds. This cup, then, is the real pivot of the work. The Niaux bison is based and composed on the pupil of his eye. The fact that there is not the smallest mistake in proportion, that the eye is in its proper place and the animal's limbs are equally well placed, shows that the artist had a clear vision beforehand of the bison he was to engrave. In the same way, some Japanese artists begin their drawing with a tiny point and proceed, step by step, to a vast design of impeccable proportions.

This bison engraved on the clay of Niaux is loaded with rich data on his origins: the suggestive value of the cups as hollows used to represent wounds, the exceptional value of one regular but deeply sunken cup suggesting the bison's eye, and especially the preliminary composition of the subject, before its execution, in the mind of its creator, followed by its perfect and harmonious execution, starting with the eye.

The Ceiling is too high

A low vault makes painting or drawing difficult. A vault which is too high creates another problem, and it was solved here, though we do not quite know how. The end part of the Breuil gallery has on its roof two excellent mammoths, one following the other towards the exit. They are over 6 ft. and 9 ft. long respectively. But in this part of the gallery the roof is at least 9 ft. above the edges of the bears' sleeping-holes and 12 ft. above their centres. How could the artist make these drawings? His line is perhaps a little less firm than in the drawings on the walls. This is notably the case with the curves of the heads and bodies, which overlap, as they do with the mammoths on the side-walls of Combarelles. Is this because the lines were drawn with a long stick, held at arm's length? Such a theory has already been advanced to explain a number of roof-drawings on clay at Pech-Merle de Cabrerets, on a roof which is also rather hard to reach. Or must we suppose a scaffold was used? This also must be considered in the case of the paintings in the great hall at Lascaux, in the "rotunda" of the well.

The modern visitor does not always realise the technical difficulties that beset the marvellous feats of the quaternary artists. He is content to admire them as the guide tells him, following the lines. "Here is the tail, here the belly, here the legs. Look, *Mesdames et Messieurs*, at the poor little gutted one!" the guide at Combarelles tells you conscientiously. Poor, poor little bovid, to be emptied of his substance! Only too rarely, the visitor wonders. We should do the wondering for him and answer his questions when necessary. Everything, from the paint-brush to the colour, from the creative thought to the conditions of elaboration and creation, is often mysterious in prehistoric art.

What about light?

The most crying need in the depths of the palaeolithic painted caves is light—light more essential to painting and engraving than it is even to daily life. "Beside Rouffignac, with more than six miles of galleries," says Abbé Breuil in his report to the *Institut* in Paris, "what are the 1,500 yds. of Niaux or the 750 yds. of the Trois-Frères and the Tuc d'Audoubert?" And he continues: "Even more than these great recesses, Rouffignac required a reliable source of light which could be quickly renewed." Inhabited caves sometimes yield actual lamps among the relics of their Magdalenian strata. They are either natural cups, made from flint "kidneys" for instance, or fragments or plates of limestone fashioned with a scooped-out bowl and a handle to hold them by. These Magdalenian lamps are the true ancestors of the so-called "Roman" lamp or *calel* of our grandparents. I still remember those lamps, filled with oil and with a little overhanging wick, which adorned a smoke-blackened chimney-piece in old Vivarais. The best had a long stem ending in a hook and could be fixed to a ledge of jutting stones or to a mantelshelf.

In the dark days of the German occupation I found the old *calel* and filled it with colza oil. It gave a poor little flame, very ill-adapted to illuminate a work of art.

Then, there were other devices, such as wooden torches, especially those made of resinous woods. Pine, no doubt, gives a bright light, but as it burns it pours out thick smoke. Very soon the air would become unfit to breathe, and it would be impossible to see. The filming of some parts of the cave, especially in the sequences showing the more distant parts of the Breuil gallery, needed an intense light which could be supplied only by magnesium flares. For some time their smoke floated at a good height, but gradually it filled the gallery, spreading in coils far beyond the points of combustion.

The next day, patches of smoke could still be discerned by a practised eye. Fuliginous flames would soon have darkened all the light. You need a good hour's walk to reach the tiny terminal rotunda that shelters the two last mammoths. Multiply this distance by two for the return journey, and a single trip with a pine torch would have darkened the cave for hours. . . .

Though a "sanctuary" is not inhabited permanently, it is certainly not used by a single occupant. Processions were formed, and there were regular underground pilgrimages to see the mammoth frieze on the "Great Ceiling" or the engraved mammoths of the "Great Fosse". And these journeyings needed light. Even for a Magdalenian, a bear-hole full of broken flints with sharp edges is not a nice place to tumble into.

Did not the great mammoth frieze require a great, fine light? Its monumental size suggests that it must have been thoroughly illuminated.

Juniper torches

Tests have suggested the use of juniper stems as torches. Owing to the formation of the internal channels of the juniper stem, when the branch burns, the flame reaches innumerable little stores of resin, one by one, each in a separate cell.   With each cell the flame receives fresh fuel, but so little at a time that combustion is complete and there is a total absence of sooty smoke.   "The light produced in this way," reports Professor Malvesin Fabre, "is strong and brilliant, and there is nothing to dim it. . . .   The only drawback is that the wood burns rather quickly and you must take care to feed the flame attentively.   The artist using this source of light must have been accompanied by an assistant carrying a juniper torch, which was easy to light, and lighting a new torch as fast as an old one was consumed.   Palaeolithic man could quickly produce fire in the cave by rubbing a piece of hard wood on dry moss or birch-bark.   In the Limousin juniper branches are still lit under falling snow or heavy rain by setting fire to birch-bark as a primer."

The birch and the juniper flourish in hard climates.   The little black, bitter berries of mountain junipers are often found at over 3,000 ft. altitude, and stunted junipers climb to nearly 6,000 ft.

Fragments of juniper-wood charcoal have been found in the cave at Aldène.   "One of them was buried in stalagmite clay under the footprint of a cave hyena."   Charcoal found at Lascaux also seems to have come from this resinous wood.   In many parts of Rouffignac, with very different chronologies, extending from the palaeolithic to the present era, ash-strewn hearths are still to be found.   Many of these hearths are and will remain undatable, but we may hope to find some with precise archaeological evidence.   Identification of the wood essence, which is always possible, will enable us to determine which wood essences were most used in a given period.   And the order of deposits and the list of essences may produce many suggestions when they are compared.   A chronological scale may even emerge, for the era of the birch and that of the beech are definite time-factors in the succession of flora.

From one bone, the great Cuvier could reconstruct an extinct animal species.   From one piece of charcoal, nowadays, we can reconstruct an entire vegetable growth.

So many hearths, so many hearths!

Our hunt for charcoal will be all the more exciting as there are hundreds of hearths at Rouffignac.   You will find many at the entrance, in the first 100 yards of the galleries.   You will find them in the eastern galleries, with black shards which may well be fragments of burial urns broken by visitors in the course of centuries.

Some galleries abound in heaps of grey soil which may be ashes of various origins. These must be analysed, too. There are hearths in the great landslide after passing the sea of mud, and here also are fragments of pottery. These are more recent, not more than 2,000 or 2,500 years old: 3,000 at the most.

"Pure" hearths are often found in the bears' nests beyond. They can hardly be dated. Finally, there are hearths beyond the "Great Ceiling", sometimes connected with the stone-fashioning workshops of which we shall speak later. What a lot of hearths! The first impression becomes a certainty. The World of Rouffignac—for it was a world in itself—was continually overrun, frequented and used but not exactly *lived in*. We explore miles below ground, we spend hours there on a given task, painting or drawing for a palaeolithic, chipping flints for a poor Celt, examining fissures to discover a lower gallery for a cave-explorer, discovering and authenticating paintings and drawings and decorated walls and ceilings for archaeologists, but we do not live there; no one has ever lived there. Better than Niaux, Trois-Frères or Cabrerets, Rouffignac shows by its very vastness that the palaeolithic sanctuary-cave was not inhabited. One does not live in a cathedral. One goes there to pray and to meditate.

THE MISSING ANIMALS

The Ark is incomplete

In spite of variations in style and differences of skill and touch, all the animal figures belong to the same palaeolithic period, suggesting a single School of Art. Paintings and engravings correspond closely both in their style and in their arrangement. In the Breuil gallery, on the right-hand wall, paintings and engravings alternate in a sublime order. The Paolo rhinoceros is of the same workmanship as the "baby" in the frieze, though one is engraved and the other painted.

Hence, the animals represented suggest the Noah's Ark of the period—a period, of course, long before that of Noah himself. But this fauna is incomplete. The mammoth holds the place of honour, and the rhinoceros enjoys his due, which is an important share. Numbers are eloquent. The herds of horses and bison are meagre; so is the flock of ibex. But where are the rest?

Since even the exploration of the cave is not yet complete, it will be well to leave a door ajar on the future. Up to Thursday, 11 October, 1956, at 5 p.m., we could affirm that a certain species was not shown at Rouffignac, and specify which. Then, in a long annexe to the Breuil gallery, we found the species in question, represented by curiously coupled specimens. Was this not the first *tête-à-tête* in the world—Adam and Eve? Rouffignac has so many priorities, so many world *premières*, that it may well claim this one. We need not fear the envy of others; their cup overflowed long ago.

Perhaps, to conclude these reflections about Rouffignac, we shall one day make a list of its "records", but let us not anticipate. We found two more examples of this same species on Saturday, 13 October—St. Edward's day!—in the great red dome of the serpents and streamers, and we know very well that there are still a few more kilometres of galleries, though not many. That is a pity. Acknowledge that the thick sealing wall and the armour-plated door put up in July 1956 were very necessary! Can you imagine the wild "rush", the treasure-hunt, as though in response to a radio advertisement?   What a crowd and what a hubbub, what incessant and perpetual filing through the galleries! Without the wall and the armoured door people would have crowded in, trampled one another under foot, killed and devoured one another, for ancestral instincts would certainly have reappeared.   They are dominant in the human race, and they do not wane.

All the "prehistoric experts" in Périgord would have joined in the rush. If the cave had remained open, it would have been "their" cave, not "ours".   And on the paintings, with the yellow clay, and on the engravings, with the points of knives, people would have inscribed their names indelibly, to assert their ownership and establish the priority of their discovery.   Would they not, M. Dubois, or Brive, who gave your name to a rhinoceros?

Would they not, Merlaut, you who own a mammoth?   Dalbavie, possessor of an ibex?   Boutillier, you marked down another ibex for your own—not the same one, of course.   Rouffignac was not spared.   Without the wall and the armoured door, all the little cave-explorers would have rushed to mark, for the world of science, the genuine mammoth and the false rhinoceros, as though scientists needed the opinion of these striplings.   Without the wall and the armoured door, we should have become rich in unsuspected fauna, for we should certainly have seen a great multiplying of "hens" and "ducks" drawn with the blow-lamp!   And even pseudo-bisons, eh, M. Gérin?

Yes, but there were a wall and an armoured door, not merely a bar to prise out.   If the rush had taken place, we should have had macaroni by Tom, streamers by Dick, serpents by Harry and scratches by Robinson.   We should have had, we are sure, an absolutely and totally authentic Rouffignac.   But we should no longer have—and of this we are sure, too—we should no longer have a Rouffignac still pure and wild, in spite of past outrages, the Rouffignac we mean to save.   Even with the "interesting additions" of the 20th century, the fauna of Rouffignac is incomplete.   We do not find the great primeval bull, or the stag, or the reindeer.

The primitive Ox

Originating somewhere in Asia—like many animal species, no doubt, including Man—the primeval bull lived alongside the bison. He was tall, with very long horns, slightly curved outwards, and he became more and more common towards the end of the early palaeolithic and the Magdalenian ages.

He rarely appears in prehistoric engravings or paintings, and this omission is certainly not due to chance. We find him, however, at Pech-Merle de Cabrerets, in the "mammoths' chapel", where he freely mingles with them. We can admire several fine specimens in the black portraits of the Lascaux cave. The great and admirable black bull of Lascaux, facing left, is the striking image of a wild bull of Camargue, who might have escaped from the Baroncelli ranch. And he bears useful witness to the very probable relationship between these great primitive oxen (*Bos primigenins*) and the bulls of Andalusia or the Vaccares. Why was the great bull in such disfavour that he rarely appears in art? His wildness, which made him unfamiliar, and his fierce and bellicose habits, which made it difficult to hunt him, have been advanced as reasons. In the Cantabrian woodlands, a century ago, herds of wild bulls spent the summer in the mountains, above the 2,500-metre level. "They shun the villages and will attack passers-by without provocation," we are told.

The Stag

He also, though well represented at Lascaux, with his fretted antlers, is absent from Rouffignac. We refer, of course, to the present species, the archaic stag, or Irish Elk, being extremely rare. Of him, the only known specimen is his portrait at Cabrerets, with enormous antlers, longer than the animal's body and spanning over 12 ft. The *Megaceros* stag of Cabrerets is traced by a finger on the clay, and he belongs to an early phase of the art represented in this cave. In the centre of a large panel, 3 yds. long and 1½ yds. wide, barred by many vertical "macaronis" traced with the fingers, the great stag stands out clearly. He measures 1 m. 20 cm. (nearly 4 ft.) from muzzle to rump and is overshadowed by his antlers, which are 4 ft. 7 in. long. "The maximum width of the horn branches is 60 cm. (24 in.), and the antler resembles a huge hand, formed by a pointed thumb and a forefinger and ring finger rather longer than the middle finger."

The panel of the Cabrerets *Megaceros* recalls many panels at Rouffignac by the frequent superimposition of an animal on vertical "macaronis" which form a systematic groundwork for the drawing. This is the case, also, with the mammoths of the "Discovery". Here, the mammoth was drawn after the macaronis. Elsewhere, the mammoth may have come first. Other sections show a sort of alternation between drawings and "macaronic", or striped, panels, as for instance in the inner part of the Breuil gallery and on the left-hand wall. The animal figures, generally those of mammoths, play the part of ornamental metopes, and the vertical macaronis form the "triglyphs", or more exactly the "polyglyphs".

These various superimpositions and alternations are phenomena which enable us to attribute a similar chronological value to these finger-tracings. They are more or less contemporary with the drawings; only a few minutes separate them, or at most a few hours or years, but they are and must remain inseparably associated in the same artistic phase.

What of the Reindeer?

He is absent from Rouffignac. The reindeer is missing from the artistic representations of this period, though it has been called the "Reindeer Age" because he was then the universal animal, as universal as the bison, and was daily hunted as game and regarded as decorative everywhere, with his anxious air and spreading antlers. In any case the reindeer cannot have been missing from the fauna of the great days of Rouffignac. And the archaeological excavations of the coming season will certainly yield reindeer bones, either in the deposits at the entrance to the cave, or (perhaps) in certain secondary deposits in the cave itself.

Let us say, however, that these deposits will very likely have no *direct* connexion with the paintings and engravings. The decorators and squatters in the cave were no doubt not the same men, but we shall be in the same era and in the same climatic surroundings, with the same fauna, chiefly of the cold-resisting types. With the mammoth and *Rhinoceros tichorhinus*, the reindeer haunted the valleys of Manaurie.

As Abbé Breuil most excellently notes, these crushing presences— the mammoth and the rhinoceros—and these surprising absences— primeval bulls, stags, reindeer—"would be inexplicable facts if we wished to see in the animal paintings of Rouffignac an exclusive record of surrounding fauna". The Rouffignac galleries are not a natural history museum, and the pictures are not lined up on the walls to take the places of stuffed animals. Even specimens of food are not an exact record of fauna in an archaeological layer. Without mentioning bones which may be lost, like those which may have been carried off by cave hyenas, the bony scraps from meals give us an idea of the "menu", of the culinary tastes of palaeolithic man, not of the entire animal world around him. Care and attentive examination must always be the rule. And it is interesting to note, as Leroi-Gourhan did when he studied the

7. The Abbe Henri Breuil under the Great Ceiling

8. Under the Great Ceiling: the Abbé Breuil with Louis-René Nougier
and Romain Robert

9. The Great Mammoth Frieze. Left to right: Professor Nougier,
Romain Robert and Professor Graziosi

fauna of Arcy-sur-Cure, that "the more fragile parts of the skeletons of game hunted by man have high survival value and are the most likely to come down to us. Fragments of bone stripped by man of their meat and their fat have a considerably better chance, both because they are less attractive to animals and because an important part of their acid-forming constituents (which are most destructive) has been removed".

In any detailed analysis of a palaeolithic dustbin the part played by man, by his likes and dislikes in the matter of food, remains essential. Prehistoric archaeology is always a science of man and of his thoughts and actions, even in its most advanced and technical branches.

Art Gallery or Temple?

If the Rouffignac cave is not a museum, is it an art gallery? Not at all. No doubt, the dadoes are sometimes deliberately orna-mented with friezes, and the artistic aim is undeniable. But some-times, indeed often—we are thinking of the "Great Ceiling"—the animals are placed in an order which, for once, is not art. They are mixed pell-mell, as when a rhinoceros floats in the air above two mammoths. Sometimes they are superimposed, and the ques-tion arises whether such-and-such a line is part of a horse or the horn of an ibex. Or is it a mammoth's tusk? We agree, finally, that it represents the trunk of a second mammoth which escaped us at the first examination.

After several hours of this exciting and undeniably original puzzle, how can we be surprised to find, in an interview with *Europe No. 1*, a glib mention of "mammoth's horns". Many apologies, dear readers. Over the "great fosse" the graven mammoths are set in artistic groups, but the ceiling is barely three feet high, 4 ft. 6 in. at the most, and to admire it you must crawl on a bank of clay that slopes steeply towards the fosse.

The Louvre, the Prado and the *Offices* are more convenient. We must therefore attribute a religious meaning to the galleries. They are ambulatories leading to underground crypts, to the altar-panels dedicated to the mammoth or the rhinoceros for some magic intercession. And the good people of the 17th and 18th centuries were much less mistaken than the little cave-explorers of today when they spoke of the "altars" in the Cro du Cluzeau or the Miremont cave, where they discovered "vestiges and paintings of all kinds of beasts".

E

"The Sacred Way"

That is why the Stream gallery, dear to the little cave-explorers, has changed its name and is now called "The Sacred Way". Delphi spreads its ruins at the feet of the glorious and splendid Phaedriades, and the pilgrim on its Sacred Way walks between the treasures of Sicyone, Gnidos, Siphnos or Athens. Each city offers its *ex-voto*, its tribute to the gods. And the modern pilgrim to palaeolithic Rouffignac must wend his way along a sacred path, leaving the red-ceilinged Hall of Mammoths on his right, the gallery of the two fighting mammoths on his left, then again, on his right, the Breuil gallery—and his will be a true religious journey among animal offerings, in a shadow steeped in ancient mysticism.

The pilgrim to Delphi at last reached the Temple, at the spring among the limestone rocks, from which the subterranean vapours that would illuminate the Pythian oracle were exhaled, as when she confronted Xerxes to pronounce the doom of Greece! The palaeolithic pilgrim to Rouffignac came to the "Great Ceiling", to the vault loaded with animal creations and realistic images, painted at his behest in order that he might follow the chase and bring down his prey with a surer hand. The sorcerer demanded payment for his services, a joint of bison or a haunch of ibex. He also could pursue the living image, but no doubt he found it safer to insist on the offering. And below the great ceiling, among the limestone rocks, gaped the underground crevasse leading to the spring. Celtic springs before the springs of Rome, neolithic springs more ancient still, all water that emerges from the depths has been the object of human attention, of an interested veneration amounting to a cult. The mysterious stream at Rouffignac lies at its earliest beginnings. Most of the animal paintings are along the Sacred Way, which leads to the Stream.

Just as Delphi sprang from a cleft in the rock, so Rouffignac may have originated from an underground tunnel, coiled in the darkness of the earth, that earth that gave life to game, mammoths and bison, that earth still hard, but which men already saw, perhaps, as Mother Earth.

This underworld played its part in exploiting the fears of quaternary man. To deploy his rites, to strike and stir credulous imaginations, the sorcerer needed mystery and darkness at noon. What a terrible setting lay in the tunnel and the Great Fosse! Let us dwell for a moment on the scene.

Introduction to the Mammoth

Imagine the slow procession in the great gallery. An underground walk of one kilometre takes half an hour, but it is possible to multiply the "cave atmosphere", and the palaeolithic procession may wander through the galleries for hours before reaching the great fosse. Since the right-hand galleries often end in a rotunda, it is easy to lead the flock to one of these, to turn about at the *cul-de-sac*, to return to the Sacred Way and to continue the round in the next gallery. A clever man can wander in Rouffignac for half a day without passing the same place twice. A march by torchlight for primitive beings allows of all kinds of effects. The tribesmen feel their way along walls which also serve as guides, and it is often from the borders of the galleries that the tunnels leading to the lower levels spring, and that the steepest clay slopes and the most spectacular bear-slides are to be seen. It is on the borders that walking is most difficult, and the borders are followed, in pitch darkness or half-shadow. Add to this clever lighting at the most difficult points, the lights of torches shining into yawning gulfs, and your future initiates, full of humility and trembling with fear, follow one another almost bereft of the power of thought.

During the mass visits of last summer, our journalists knew these feelings. And when they sank into the sticky mud, when they lost their shoes and walked on in their socked or stockinged feet, or sometimes crawled on all fours like flies caught in jam, when they clung to the right-hand wall, thickly plastered with miry clay, we used to give them much-needed advice: "Keep to the right! keep to the right! There's an abyss on the left!" And mercifully we would direct the beam of our torch along the tunnel, revealing steep slopes leading to unplumbed depths, a little after the sea of mud but still before the great shaft.

The human reactions were always the same. You would see heads bowed for a furtive glance along the slope, and quickly bodies were pressed against the right-hand wall, and the procession slowed down.

We can imagine how a torch lit by an accomplice at the bottom of the lower tunnel would have increased the impression of depth and terror. You must go in single file when you reach the Great Ceiling. All the properties of a ritual march are present. There comes a time when it is easier to crawl. A horse cut in the clay, perhaps for visitors of the 17th or 18th century, provides an outrageous landmark. Now three-quarters of this calvary are passed.

Brows run with sweat and sterns are smeared yellow. Like his modern descendants, palaeolithic man had his "stations" at which he watched the performance of certain rites, heard incantations and spent a little time in meditation before pressing on. Today only the privileged—the representative of the French Press Agency, for instance—reach the Great Fosse at the farthest depth, like a great hunter of palaeolithic mammoths, a hunter who needed sorcery to support his exploits.

The tribe arrived at last, exhausted, at the edge of the chasm. (We refer to the ancient hunters, of course, but our journalists were just as tired; some thanked us for having fixed an early hour for their visit. At the painful hour of difficult digestion in Périgord, they would never have got farther than the Red Ceiling, and that would have been a pity.)

Now, since we have your permission to enter the land of dreams, imagine the sorcerer drawing mammoths on the rock, compelling the favoured ones to crawl under old mammoths already drawn, while some hoarse, guttural song rises from the depths of the abyss, punctuated by hand-claps that resound and re-echo under the vaults, dying away in black infinity. Then, in the light of the flickering juniper torches, roofs that seemed bare are peopled with mammoth herds. . . .

How slow will be the pilgrims' return, exhausted as they are by songs and visions of the chase and bent more than ever by fatigue after their ordeal! The young men came in by day: they will emerge late at night, and the continued darkness in the open air, the confines of the cave still forcing them to bend their backs under thickets, this last impression will not be the weakest or least durable. Every time we spent many hours at work in Rouffignac, every time we came out after dark, we felt the same influence: the cavern seemed to go on for ever; heavy with clay behind us, it stretched, still crushing, before us, in spite of its immaterial form, which now prolonged it to the stars. Rouffignac is truly a timeless world. Under the porch of the cave, a ray of moonlight sometimes shone between the chestnut trees, over Fleurac. And directly opposite the cave, the great red globe of Mars drew near the earth. By a daunting coincidence, Rouffignac the Prehistoric entered the present under the auspices of the God of War!

An underground sanctuary, like its fellows, Niaux or the Trois Frères, Combarelles or the Tuc d'Audoubert, Rouffignac seemed nearer and more comprehensible simply because it was still more exceptional.

The Victims of Ostracism

One hundred mammoths and no reindeer! A definite contradiction calling for an explanation that no other cave requires. If the reindeer never appears on the walls and ceilings of Rouffignac it is because he was deliberately shunned. And naturally, another ostracism, even more striking, comes to mind: the absence or rarity of the human form in quaternary art. Alongside hundreds or thousands of animal paintings or drawings there are only a few human figures.

This disparity in subjects treated, the frequency of animals and the rarity of human beings, is accompanied by a disparity in artistic treatment. While the depiction of animals achieves perfection of form, harmony of composition and richness of detail, human representation is usually caricature. The drawing is a grotesque, never a portrait. The animal is really drawn and made lifelike, and his expression is proper and personal to him.

This contradiction can only have a psychological and sociological explanation. The palaeolithic artist was quite capable of depicting his own species and conveying its qualities and its many shades of expression. He could feel the mobility of human expression, and even with his rudimentary equipment he could have produced lifelike portraits and fixed on the rock all the sentient mobility which is never seen but once.

Think of that last bison in the rotunda at Niaux, the one facing right, who gives you, from whatever position you may see him, a gentle, human look, recalling that of Mona Lisa. Think of that finely engraved bison in the Trois Frères cave, also gazing kindly at you, for, strange to say, the bisons of the quaternary artists have the eyes of men. This Trois Frères bison reminds me (I say it with all respect) of the noble face of our Pyrenean master, Count Henri Bégouën, leader of the three discoverers of the cave. But am I not inverting the problem when I claim to see a resemblance between the doyen of French Prehistory and a bison in his cave? It would be more logical to suppose that the Count, by some mysterious mimetism, began to imitate his bison. Let us hope the millenary influence of this impregnation will remain confined to the Pyrenees. But have we not declared that Rouffignac is a Pyrenean cave in Périgord? We shall anxiously examine any uncomfortable tooth or spot on the nose which might be the first sign of an evolution towards the mammoth state. Well, the palaeolithic artist-sorcerer could have drawn men, but he did not do so because he was not allowed to.   It was forbidden by his social environment, just as the religion of Mahomet forbids representation of any living thing and condemns itself to the art of interlacings and "macaronis", historically known as "arabesques".

Palaeolithic religion or belief—the former term smacks too much of a "system"—some organisation, anyhow, may have forbidden only the representation of the human form.   The day-to-day animal world implied not only permission, but an obligation to depict the animal, since painting an animal subject meant creating meat. Social laws did not allow the image of man.   Was man still, or already, too near the gods to be portrayed?

And if by any chance one did not strictly obey the rules, one only half disobeyed them.   One stopped at the half-way house of caricature and the grotesque.

The Anthropomorphs

The sorcerer, as an intermediary between Gods and Men, profited by this compromise.   And many disguised figures are nothing but religious caricatures.   They are masks, concealing a bison-priest under the horns of a bison.   Dressed up in a bison skin, the hunter can approach the herd.   Disguised in the same skin, the sorcerer can find new power.

Masks, caricatures, grotesques, sorcerers, distorted faces, all these man-made drawings are parts of this system, sometimes singly, sometimes all together, at the same time.   "Explanatory pluralism" has never been more necessary.

On Oct. 11 and 13, 1956, we found four anthropomorphs at Rouffignac, two of them face to face in the deep extension of the Breuil gallery of isolated figures and in the great red dome of the white streamers.   All four obeyed the rules of the species, that is, of the anthropomorphic series, that is—no rule at all.   They were true "grotesques", with big noses and big mouths, like Perrault's deceased grandmother.   The finest, on the left, drawn with a finger on the clay of the ceiling in the far Breuil gallery, is enormous: a real Carnival head.   It is more than 30 in. high from the crown to the neck.   The upper lip is well drawn, and it has a certain humanity.   The opposite portrait, even more of a caricature, is rather smaller.   Is it a woman?   Adam and Eve?   But long before the birth of Adam in the Garden of Genesis!

The anthropomorph on the red ceiling of the streamers has a blunt chin, a receding forehead, a jutting nose and a lively eye. From the point of the chin to the top of the head he measures 45 cm.

(nearly 18 in.).   A companion on another part of the roof, near-by is more mysterious.   Drawn also with a finger, the head is excellent: forehead, nose, mouth, chin—then, going downwards, everything melts away in a shapeless mass.   One of us tried to pick out the beginning of a leg and a pretty breast!

These primitive drawings hardly suggest a Titian, yet they show human characteristics and a secret note which is at least perceptible. The echo that comes back to you is not your voice, that has died away, but you can still hear something.   These caricatures are not the man and woman of 15,000 years ago, but they are their shadows. They are not the man and woman; they are the presence of the man and woman, standing where you stand now, standing on tiptoe to trace a reflection of the faces on the clay overhead.

Why is the Reindeer missing from Rouffignac?

One of the chief reasons for quaternary animal art was a deliberate effort to create game by drawing, painting or engraving.   And the addition of arrows, on the bisons for instance, made the rite more efficacious.   Yet at Rouffignac, palaeolithic man neither created nor hunted the reindeer.   Why this attitude to one of the most essential   game   animals   of   the   age?   Why   this   ostracism,   this *taboo*?

Among the key elements of quaternary totemism—for we must consider this explanation—was this respect for the totem animal, which may be neither killed nor eaten.   That animal was the subject of a total dietary ban, or at least a partial one, for one must live, and man has always found some judicious compromise with Heaven. Among some American Indians, the bison might have survived if this rule had been obeyed.   They got round the ban by taking for their totem only a white-haired bison, or one that bore an arrow between its horns.   Any animal that failed to satisfy these rare and very difficult conditions was outside the taboo, to the greater profit of the bison hunters.   The totem animal was specially privileged among the tribes.   It was regarded as an ancestor, and there were strong family ties between all the sons of the common patriarch. And this ancestor worship was marked by his portraits, his pictures and the disguises which used his skin as their peculiar features.

Socially, the consequences are important. Totem links are strong, stronger than our family ties, and they are usually transmitted through the female line.   "The result is a serious taboo by virtue of which members of the same totem clan may not intermarry and must abstain, as a rule, from sexual relations between men and women belonging to the same clan."

Fear of incest leads naturally to marriage outside the clan, that is, to exogamy.

These fundamental totem rules applied to many clans which may have existed at Rouffignac. There is good reason to believe that there was a Mammoth clan, and that the sorcerers of this clan painted and drew the mammoths of Rouffignac. Is not this essentially the Mammoth's Cave, and were these people not the Mammoth's Clan? Or is this theory too simple, and was not the palaeolithic soul much more complicated? Are the mammoths pictures of reality or pictures for worship? Did they *eat* mammoth at Rouffignac? Or was the mammoth, as he should have been, the subject of a protective taboo?

With less reason one could imagine a clan devoted to the horse or the ibex, a clan who performed their worship at the far end of the Great Ceiling, a bison clan. But bison pierced by arrows are just game, no more, no less. A rhinoceros clan would be more doubtful, the creature is frightening, and to claim descent from him . . . Yet his family life was really touching!

Would such a diversity of clans fit into the real unity of the cave? There is always the mysterious absence of the reindeer.

Is not this absence the key to the most valid hypothesis? The tribe does not hunt its totem ancestor. It does not eat it. But there may be other taboos. It may be forbidden to touch the totem, to look at it—to draw it! The Moslem is forbidden to draw Life itself. . .

Thus the totem of Rouffignac may well be the reindeer, just because the reindeer is not found there. In that case, a new light is thrown on many facts.

All the Rouffignac bestiary is connected with "memory-pictures" or "reality-pictures". The walls are covered with acts of creation and illustrated *menus*. Only the great totem of the tribe, the reindeer, is absent, because he falls under the strictest taboo of all.

He is never represented because the tribe refuses to depict its progenitor. As a taboo, he cannot be eaten, except at ritual banquets in which the whole tribe takes part. Fortunately the animal is still so abundant and so varied that the tribe can easily subsist. The reindeer never appears, but he is always present in the minds of the tribe, as a skin or an ornament made from his horns, at a communal sacrifice.

Rouffignac, then, reveals the sublimation of quaternary totem-worship, a spiritual totemism so pure that any image is forbidden. Is not this "iconoclastic" feeling, applied only to the mother-species among hunters who lived more or less on the repeated portrayal of their daily prey, the germ of the idea of God? Of a single and creative God? Of our modern God already?

TRACES OF MAN

Vanity of Vanities . . .

Splendid as it is with human works which span thousands of years, though they are not eternal, does Rouffignac hold any traces of those who lived in its shadow and haunted its subterranean darkness?

If the galleries have a secret, they have not yet given it up. But the archaeologist, with his ant-like patience, is quite capable of finding it and bringing it to light.

The second physical layer of deposits at the entrance, starting from the base which yields large blades and well-marked graving tools, corresponds with an archaeological phase of the upper palaeolithic era sometimes happily named the "leptolithic" age, or that of light stones: an efficient civilisation that had a large output of small, finely fashioned flint-cutting implements and was not content to hack out a mere block or to produce a few rough chips. But the specimens saved by M. Plassard when the cave was first cleared some years ago were not yet enough to fix a period.

The main object of clearing the archaeological mound was to expose the various strata which are so many pages in an unwritten record. This was entrusted to Claude Barrière, and earlier excavations confirm a series of human phases which he will analyse for us in his next campaign.

Will he solve the problem of the human jaw-bone from the Rouffignac deposit? For the clearance of the cave entrance produced an excellent human jaw, very characteristic of *Homo sapiens*, about 6 ft. below the surface layer. If the jaw was in its right place and the depth at which it was found is reliable there would be no reason not to assign to it an early place in our chronology, associating it with the upper palaeolithic era. Other bone fragments, similar to this jaw-bone but found *in situ*, might furnish new evidence placing the jaw-bone in a definite category more than ever anonymous, for it would be outside recorded time.

Jaw No. 1 has teeth so worn that the grinding surface has disappeared. The pulp cavities are quite visible, but there is no decay, for dental caries is a modern phenomenon granted to us since the neolithic era. This complete wear and absence of decay are reliable signs of palaeolithism, but like the depth of the site, they are only signs. Sometimes a multiplicity of signs fails to establish a certainty. We label this jaw No. 1 because others follow. Claude Barrière found two more jaw-bones in the side entrance-gallery. No. 2 is broken in two and appears to have been that of a man; it has clearly visible muscular attachments and the ascending *ramus* is little indented. No. 3 belonged, no doubt, to a woman; it is more delicate, and the rising *ramus* is more indented. Both these jaws, like the first, are much worn but show no sign of decay. Two teeth were removed from the woman's jaw in her lifetime, for the bony sockets are perfectly healed. Various signs lead us to hope we shall find other human bones, associated with evidence of their dates. The palaeontologists also will have their word to say, for the "Lesson of Rouffignac" calls for much scientific team-work.

Apart from its size and the complexity of the many problems it raises, the enormous interest of the cave arises from just these questions that require collective team-work. The way was shown by the first investigations of Professor P. P. Grassé on October 10, 1956, when he was accompanied by eminent colleagues.

Speaking at this stage only of Jaw No. 1 and its probable origin in the upper palaeolithic age, there is deep significance in the marked contrast between the monumental scale of the works of art and the frail human vestiges.

Art and the fruits of labour survive; men disappear The pithecanthropian humanity which peopled the world at the dawn of the quaternary epoch and the near-by Villafranchian age has left us millions and millions of cut flints, double-edged axes, slicers and hatchets. Associated with them are only a few jaw-bones—the three dug up at Terfine, in Algeria, by Professor C. Arambourg. Along with innumerable flint chips and points and scrapers belonging to Neanderthal man, we know only a few tens of human individuals. The admirable art of the Reindeer Age has left us fewer skeletons than sanctuaries.

New Times

The fervour of crowds is fickle: they often forget today what they adored yesterday. But it is rare that nothing at all should survive in the depths of our souls. If souls disappear, they disappear less, perhaps, than their fleshly coverings. Tiny shreds of souls float, invisible, in the air. They join in a collective soul to which every man contributes without ever being able to recognise it. When the age-old ice began to melt and its white cloak covered less and less of European soil, and when the damper, warmer winds of the Atlantic drove back the cold blasts from the east, willow, birch and pine intermingled with oak and ash, and nut-trees multiplied their yellow catkins. The mammoth herds had long been swallowed up, and the reindeer had slowly followed their favourite lichens, withdrawing, all unknowing, into an Arctic of their own.

The west knew its springtime after its geological winter. A kinder nature and a gentler climate came to it, and the old civilisations had vanished. This is another mystery as deep as the disappearance of our mammoths. . . .

Do great civilisations need hard physical conditions to gain a footing, develop and win the world? It is during its most severe climatic phases that the west undergoes its civilising expansion and its most marvellous artistic flowering. When the tundra and taïga of the north reign in our valleys, from the Cure to the Vézère and from the Vézère to the Ariège and the Viodessos, then, and only then, the west asserts its primacy, to find it again only in the 17th and 18th centuries. Animal art disappears with the long winter snows, and with it go rites and beliefs, magics and religions. Ease really seems to have destroyed the palaeolithic power of thought. New climates brought new ways of life. The fauna changed but remained robust and plentiful. The herds of reindeer retired to the mountains of the north, but the other horned beasts remained in serried ranks. Herds of primeval cattle found lush and welcome pasture. Wild boar thronged in the leafy forests, where acorns and beech-mast were scattered on the ground.

It rained a great deal in this "Atlantic" age, and though the descendants of palaeolithic man were hunters, too, they sometimes preferred to gather snails. In the kitchen refuse of the time, piles of thousands and millions of snail-shells sometimes take the place of the game of other days. At different times and with variations imposed by climatic conditions, the whole world took to eating snails: *Kjökkenmöddings* in the Baltic, layers of snail-shells in the Dordogne and the Pyrenees, the "snail-fields" of the Maghreb, the *sambaquis* of Brazil, masses of shells even in Tierra del Fuego, all give proof of this.

And the West, adopting this new taste, had no need of the sorcerer to collect snails in the rain. The snail killed Magdalenian art.

Plants also contributed to the extinction of quaternary art. Man was no longer wholly carnivorous, or nearly so, as he used to be. He collected the grasses, plants, roots, tubers and fruits of the rainy seasons. A digging-stick to scratch up the soil and dig up reserves took the place of the hunter's harpoon and assegai. There was no point in blessing arms when arms themselves were less used. And in the course of the 4th and 3rd millennia before our era, man owned his land, took root in the soil and built up reserves of game on the hoof. Man became a peasant and a breeder; the wild boar became a pig and sheep grazed at the door of the hut. But old beliefs were perhaps not dead, and we find palaeolithic echoes in the texts of history. . .

The Echo of a distant Baptism

The old palaeolithic hunters may have baptised their sanctuary. The rough, rude monosyllable CRO seems to spring from the darkness of a thousand years in their guttural and very simple speech. At first it meant only stone or rock, applying equally to a hole or a cavern. How can we fail to be struck by these puzzling similarities: Cro-Magnon and Cro du Cluzeau in Périgord, Cro-du-Charnier in Burgundy, Cro-Marin in the Gatinais, all sites of rocks or caves, haunted by the hunters of the early palaeolithic age?

When the railway from Périgueux to Agen was built in 1868, Cro-Magnon, a great rocky bluff in the heart of Les Eyzies, yielded five human skeletons, mingled with the remains of their homes.

Cro-du-Charnier is doubly known for the great Solutre rock which dominates it from above and for the thousands of skeletons below —skeletons of horses slaughtered or at least eaten by Aurignacian and Solutrean men of the upper palaeolithic age.

Cro-Marin, now destroyed by quarrying, was one of the few shelters in the Paris area where archaeological deposits, with fading traces of red paint, were to be found under masses of stone.

"Cro" certainly has valid claims to be regarded as the oldest syllable in the world, and the expression "Cro du Cluzeau" is perhaps the world's most ancient pleonasm. Whole civilisations have vanished, buried under successive layers and under natural and historic soil, and there may remain of them, not a memory—that would be too precise—but only a name or a syllable. "Cro" is one of these syllables, a surviving echo of the "savage" speech of 15,000 years ago, when the men of Rouffignac hunted the mammoth with his curving tusks and long hair. For 15,000 years the memory of the mammoth faded. If expeditions of the Century of Light saw him in the flare of their torches, they did not recognise him, for to them the mammoth was unknown. Though anchored in reality and perpetuated on the walls of the cave, the mammoth knew eclipse. But sprung from one mouth and then leaping from mouth to mouth, from generation to generation, from civilisation to civilisation, the word "Cro" became eternal. A syllable can conquer time for as long as there are men to say it.

Potsherds

The successors of the great mammoth hunters were very close to us, or at least to the way of life of our countryside, until a few tens of years ago. In the last half-century the means of existence have become more uniform, and the speeding-up processes of civilisation have changed more in the last fifty years than in the two or three thousand years before them.

A neolithic hut of the end of the third millennium before our era or the beginning of the second contained a little collection of domestic utensils which seems quite familiar. Some materials have changed, flint has become shining metal, but the forms are often the same. After all, a flint blade carefully fixed in its stag-horn handle was already a "stainless" knife. Wooden or bone spoons and spatulas have remained unchanged. The same applies to the shapes, and even the surfaces, of pottery. In the Charente, huge earthenware tubs for washing are decorated with strings of clay marked with finger-prints, like much of the bronze age pottery. Rural custom is always very vital and deeply rooted. The archaeological mound in front of the entrance to Rouffignac yields many sherds of more or less red eathenware, usually undecorated, suggesting the rural civilisations of the end of the neolithic and the beginning of the metal ages. The galleries also contain many fragments which are often difficult to date for lack of other material among them. In many places, sometimes under limestone slabs, often between slabs and blocks, we find cinders and potsherds. Three vases have already been reconstructed by Claude Barrière. One, almost complete, is part of a large receptacle with a flat bottom and straight sides. Most of the fragments were found lying close together, after the great landslide, between the wall and a huge block of limestone fallen from the roof. The space was a useful hiding-place. One detail is striking: the bottom was carefully cut out and perfectly regular. Was that some rite? The same thing was noticed when we excavated the neolithic cave at Bédeilhac, in the Ariège. Layer II, corresponding with the end of the chalcolithic (the beginning of the metal age) and the beginning of the bronze age, yielded a carefully cut-out vase

bottom. Périgord and the Pyrenees have many ancient features
in common, and so has the whole of the west, ever since the upper
palaeolithic era. Intermediary links are not lacking, and here is
one more. In the Red Ceiling hall a large cup, more than 8 in.
across, was reconstructed. A long way off, in one of the eastern
passages, a small cup was found among ashes. And there are many
indications of this kind. After prospecting the walls and ceilings
we must sound the floors. Certain galleries may very well have been
used as catacombs to deposit funeral urns containing ashes, as was
the custom at the end of the bronze age.

The Iron Age

The next period, at the beginning of the first millennium before
our era, which was marked by the use of a new metal, iron, is also
well marked by pottery. The vessels are made of a grey clay with
fine incised decorations, and these geometrical patterns represent
varied "Greek" figures in the purest Hallstatt style. The owners of
this pottery and their successors, the Celts, who used pottery of the
La Tène type, seem to have recommenced exploring the many
galleries of the Cro. These peasants, warriors and Gaulish black-
smiths feared only one thing, it is said : that the sky might fall on
their heads; and they ventured very far. It is to them, apparently,
that we must attribute the tens and tens of flint-chipping workshops
that we find at a depth of about 1,500 yds., near the Great Fosse,
near the "mammoth with the roguish eye".

There, blocks of flint from the horizontal strata of the walls or
sometimes from the roof are collected in dozens, and these "kidneys" bear many traces of flaking. Well-formed tools are very
rare, and it is true that only a cursory inspection of these workshops
has been made, but the chips are typical, with fine striking surfaces
and broad faces to the larger chips, and powerful hammers. The
most varied techniques have been used in this work, splitting with
the stone hammer or splitting on the anvil, and also splitting after
preparing a striking surface, as is usual in the well-equipped shops
for the later stages where all the processes were repeated—in a word,
every device of flint-flaking. But the large, heavy chips, the deep
notches and rough, strong graving-tools are not enough to date
these workshops. It would seem that the good blocks, once roughed
out, were taken away for finishing, and that many tools made on the
spot were also carried away. We find only "rejects" or pieces of
raw material which were unsatisfactory or could not be used. An
earthenware spindle, picked up by Abbe Breuil at his first visit,

suggests that these workshops came late in the prehistoric ages: bronze or iron. They may not have been far from historic times. And we note an interesting theory of the Abbé: he thought he saw traces of the systematic manufacture of flint spikes for the *tribula*, or large planks furnished with regular rows of flint spikes, used for pricking out wheat. In the whole of Mediterranean Europe and in Morocco and the Near East these agricultural implements were found a few decades ago, accompanied by small worked flints. These were the "teeth" of the *tribula*.

The "workshops" of Rouffignac are intact, absolutely *in situ*, as though they had been abandoned only a few minutes ago. These deserted working-places, alive with human presence, make a strange impression; one is almost surprised not to see some Celt come round a bend of the gallery. Is it not one of the charms of Rouffignac that one feels this influence to be so warm and permanent?

At Lascaux, one's contact with human work is too sudden to allow this feeling. To become impregnated with it, one needs a long journey through dark galleries, as at Niaux. You must deserve it, as you must deserve access to the clay modelling at Bédeilhac. At Rouffignac, according to the hour and your mental processes and researches, a presence is always strong: that of upper palaeolithic man as you pass before the friezes, that of bronze age man when you find the pottery, men on the edge of history when you get to the distant flint-cutting workshops, and how many generations of history when you search the story of Rouffignac itself? These workshops mark the end of one world and the dawn of another. Proofs and passions are not far off.

10. The Abbé Breuil and the two authors before the Press Conference
at the Musée de l'Homme

11. In front of the Great Mammoth Frieze: Professor Martin Almagro, of
Madrid University, with the authors

12. Professor Almagro examining the last mammoth in the Great Frieze

II
THE HISTORY OF ROUFFIGNAC

F

From FRANÇOIS de BELLEFOREST (1575) to LOUIS MORERI (1725)

A Gap of 1,500 Years

History seems to have plunged the Cro du Cluzeau into obscurity. Since the very far-off time of the Great Cave Bear, the main prehistoric periods had accumulated traces of their existence. The sight of the flint-cutting workshops, at the very depths of the western galleries, rounded off the picture of these four millennia of prehistory, dark, laborious and nameless but illuminated briefly by such marvellous revelations as the great friezes of mammoths or rhinoceroses. In the early centuries of the historic era we hear nothing of the Cro, that *grottesque* whose name goes back to prehistoric times.

The cave sleeps, and the débris of former civilisations blocks its entrance. A narrow passage, no doubt a hole made by a man and hidden by broom and oak trees, would enable a bold spirit to plunge into the underground darkness, but are the spirits there? Yet the dark entrance is known. Access to it must be forbidden by fierce legends, and the cave is believed to shelter mysterious and fearful Chtonian gods, rising from Hell. As the ancient cults of Mother Earth grew more obscure, they became evil in the eyes of the early Christians. Crosses were carved on menhirs, which were christianised and became part of a new iconography. The Cro, on the contrary, became infernal.

Some serf or clodhopper, pursued by his lord, perhaps feared the cave less than he feared his suzerain and sought shelter there, to be known later as a "croquant" in Périgord. As for his master, such people abounded, living in little castles behind turrets and posterns. The fugitive took refuge in the cave as in a holy place, and perhaps felt safer there than under the domes of Saint-Front. No one knows, and surely no one ever will know.

By the light of his tallow dip, the outcast found the traces of a very distant past. He too drank at the spring, slowly finding his path along the Sacred Way. His feelings were very like those of his palaeolithic ancestor. The tradition was being carried on.

In happier times, curiosity, more even than laughter the peculiar property of man, led villagers to explore their underground domain. Some sudden invasion may have brought them to the Cro, which they entered at their leisure. And do not suppose that these premature cave-explorers were insensible to these underground scenes! From generation to generation, "guides" prospected the domain and performed its honours. If that village elder, the black-smith, wore a halo of prestige, the "guide" to the Cro must have enjoyed an enviable reputation. History itself relates his exploits.

1575 ...

François de Belleforest, a Gascon nobleman, was born at Sarsan, in the shadow of the Pyrenees, in 1530. He was the protégé of Marguerite of Navarre, the sister of François I, and he devoted himself to immense learned works, including the *Great Annals and General History of France*, which appeared in 1579. Less well known is his *Universal Cosmography of the Entire World*, compiled largely from the famous Münster Cosmography, but (he says) "fuller, more ornamental and more enriched". This Cosmography was published in Paris by a M. Sonnius, in two volumes *in folio*, with maps and diagrams, in 1575.

At the present stage of historical research concerning Rouffignac, the *Universal Cosmography* of François de Belleforest brings us our oldest text on the Cro du Cluzeau. We owe our knowledge of it to J. Boucereau, who is carrying on fruitful research at the National Library. The Thévet (1575) and Münster (1555) cosmographies only mention the fortress of Rouffignac and say nothing of the cave. Texts dated 1516 and 1527 speak of the Miremont estate but not of the underground world. The information given by François de Belleforest is therefore very important, and it is full enough to carry our complete knowledge of the "fabulous" cave back to the middle of the 16th, and perhaps even to the 15th century, for the details given by Belleforest are due to several generations of persevering and courageous explorers. He writes on p. 198:

"Near Miramont, a small town in Périgord, may be seen a cavern or *grottesque* known to the natives as Cluzeau, about which those who have entered it relate great marvels." Sure enough, this is the Cro du Cluzeau, known at various times as the cave of Miremont or Miramont, and now returned to history under the name of Rouffig-nac, for this is the name of the commune and we have chosen it for many and good reasons, as will be related in due time. And the "marvels" described in the 16th century are very suggestive, very complete and well worth pondering. We quote again from Belleforest:

"Those who have been inside say there are several springs and streams, including one from 100 to 120 feet wide, which flows very fast and strongly and yet is very deep and steep-sided, so that none dare cross it, though it extends for a long way in the cave."

Thus the underground stream frequented by palaeolithic men is brought to light. It grows in the imaginations of the peasants who haunt the Cro. A width of 30 to 40 metres may have been rather exaggerated by the darkness in which the stream flowed so hard and fast, but we must excuse a little boasting by the first historical explorers of Rouffignac.

The little 20th-century explorers claim to have had "the privilege of making astonishing discoveries" such as those of "active internal streams". They discovered their system of internal streams exactly 370 years after François de Belleforest. Let us restore to François his prestige as a cave-explorer. His account has more surprises in store for us!

The cave, he says, is so large that "it can be entered only in force and with many torches and lanterns, for there is light only near the entrance". These expeditions must have been quite picturesque, though less amusing than modern ventures. Think only of the journalistic junketings of the summer of 1956 . . .

François, Creator of Prehistory!

Shepherds' leggings must have been a better protection from the "sea of mud" than the stockings of persons of quality, and one can hardly imagine the flowing skirts of the time of François I in the Rouffignac galleries. Yet the nobility must have struggled through as best they could and done their "five to six leagues" underground. They admired the "fine halls and chambers" and appreciated their variety, for some were paved with "small, variegated stones in all the colours of Mosaic". In other rooms they admired "a few altars and PAINTINGS IN SEVERAL PLACES, and the traces or marks of LARGE AND SMALL ANIMALS".

What a precious and capital record! Here, rediscovered, described and published in 1575, are the paintings of upper palaeolithic man, paintings of mammoths, rhinoceroses, horses or ibex, paintings executed 20,000 years before. And these paintings are reported by François de Belleforest "in several places". How can we fail to recall all the points in Rouffignac which bear witness to this priceless art of the mammoths' time: the red-roofed hall to the right, the two mammoths' gallery to the left, the Sacred Way, the Breuil gallery, the Great Ceiling, and the long extensions as far as the Mammoth with the Roguish Eye? Well, there they are, these several places, already noted in the 16th century! Decidedly, François de Belleforest may add the title of First Archaeologist, very well-versed in prehistoric art, to the coveted title of First Cave-Explorer. The little cave-explorers of Périgueux are dispossessed of the fruits of their sporting exploits underground! So much for their 48 expeditions to Rouffignac between 1845 and 1949. And we ourselves bear the strange (and rather annoying) title of "discoverers" of Rouffignac! François de Belleforest steals away our crowns, for his exclusive profit. Really, the little cave-explorers ought to have joined in forming some permanent syndicate to defend us against the encroachments of this upstart François! How easily we should have come to terms! But perhaps we could agree to find some effigy of the noble protégé of Marguerite de Navarre and to set up a large replica in bronze at the entrance to the cavern: "To the Memory of François de Belleforest, Gascon Nobleman, First Cave-Explorer and First Prehistorian of France, Discoverer of Rouffignac."

François de Belleforest was a scientist already; he sticks up for his facts and he suggests the experimental method to prove the truth of what he says. "Those in foreign lands who describe marvels invented by themselves will mock at this and say we are trying to tell tales of fairyland, but we name the places, which are not far off, and EXPERIENCE will give you knowledge of them." And good-naturedly, a few lines earlier, François de Belleforest advises explorers to take provisions with them "to use in case they lose their way".

François' science does not go so far as to offer us comparative graphs of the various paintings and the "traces of large and small animals". He was not tempted by the task of counting, repeatedly and systematically, the mammoths and the bears' claw-marks.

Sacrifices to Venus and the Infernal Gods

Three centuries before Boucher de Perthes, the distinguished creator of Prehistoric Science, Belleforest attempts an explanation of Rouffignac. "I think this underground place is where our idolatrous fathers once went to sacrifice to Venus or the Infernal Gods, liking these cavernous depths, in some cases because they suited their mood, in others because 'the larcenies of love require darkness'."

This text forges a precious link between an unknown past and centuries of history which become progressively more familiar. The Celtic or Roman cavern was haunted by subterranean deities, whose memory survived into the Renaissance. Tradition, also, has always sanctioned, all over the world, the use of the caves and caverns for "larcenies of love" which call for darkness. We remember the mischievous phrase our master Abbé Breuil invented once, when he spoke of the "pre-nuptial" rites in the Niaux cavern. . . .

Sacrifices to the Infernal Gods were more brutal and certainly less agreeable to participants and officiating priests. They were the echo of a strong and persistent tradition, for François de Belleforest finds the same memories in his native countryside, "in our Comminges and not far from the Pyrenean Mountains". And he tells how an underground place was found there, too, "but not as big or as dark as this (Rouffignac), where there was still the idol of Venus, and innumerable members of Priapus and other indecencies". Where could this underground place in Comminges, consecrated to the cult of the earth and the fecundity of the soil, have been? There are many caves. Among them we cannot avoid recalling the Cave of Gargas, not far from the "navel" of Comminges; Gargas the mysterious, with Aurignacian painted hands, horribly mutilated for bloody rites of which we know nothing. Gargas is also full of limestone formations, stalactites and stalagmites, all suggestive shapes apt to call forth or sustain some phallic image, an idea which is found elsewhere, deeply and deliberately cultivated, in the ithyphallic anthropomorphs of the cave of Portel, north of Foix. Here the palaeolithic artist-sorcerer has picked out a particularly suggestive stalagmite shape to draw a human figure around it. The procedure is the same as for the bison of the cups at Niaux, engraved with the eye as starting-point. The same creative idea is used for the eyes or humps of mammoths at Rouffignac, and it governs the carvings of the "three Venuses" in the great frieze at Angles on the Anglin, in the Vienne. These female torsos are carved around natural cups which suggested their navels and were arranged accordingly.

Western humanity is very old and no doubt more stable than in many other parts of the world. It is more perennial, too, since only our west knew the flowering and the life of Franco-Cantabrian art. In its dark depths this humanity keeps its traditional memories, which rise, often distorted and difficult to decipher, from the millennia, but rise they do, none the less.

André du Chesne

Saved from oblivion by François de Belleforest, the Cro du Cluzeau was thenceforward quoted, compiled and distorted in all the great learned works. Thus the Cro became the most described

cave in history, as well as the oldest known prehistoric cave containing paintings. It was three centuries earlier than Altamira.
What a distinction!

At the time of good King Henri IV, in 1608, André du Chesne, a
King's Councillor, published *Antiquities and Researches in the most
remarkable Towns, Castles and Places in all France.* Under the
heading of Miremont, he noted, in the Cluzeau cavern, "altars,
remains and paintings of several kinds of beasts". He seems to
have condensed, but also distorted, the excellent text of François
de Belleforest. The latter had reported two discoveries: paintings
and the traces or spoor of several kinds of animals. André du
Chesne lumped two categories into one, speaking of paintings and
traces of several kinds of beasts.

Then came Canon Tarde . . .

At the château of Cosnac, in the district of Brive, lay a chronicle
of the 17th century by Canon Jean Tarde, of Sarlat. He was born
in the middle of the 17th century and studied deeply in Rome and
at Florence, where he became a disciple of Galileo. As a scholar
and a Sarladais, he too described the Cro du Cluzeau, at Miremont.
He lived near the cave, and as a well-travelled man in his time he
may have had the curiosity to visit it. Yet his impressions are
strongly marked with the stamp of François de Belleforest, who was
certainly a great pioneer. He writes clearly and decisively. He says
he saw "paintings in several places, showing traces of all kinds of
animals".

Curiously enough—it would have seemed miraculous but yesterday—this phrase from a dusty text, drawn from the records of a
château in Périgord, was picked up by friendly ears at the Paris radio
transmitter, "Europe No. 1". We should have liked to hear it.
What a valuable confirmation of the Rouffignac paintings—an
historical confirmation, all the happier as we were not in possession,
then, of the writings of François de Belleforest! A telephone call,
a friendly word, and a few minutes later we were at the transmitter
in the Rue François I. There a metal thread lay silent, carefully
wound on a flat spool. The spool was fixed on its axis, contact was
made, the spool began to turn and we heard a voice: "paintings in
several places." Twice we heard Molteni's voice give this useful
information, which we noted. Today the phrase used by Canon
Tarde no longer slumbers in the archives (now carefully dusted) of
the chateau in Périgord. It rests in audible form, in a wire wound
on a spool.

"*The Delights of France*"

From this point, the texts come thick and fast. In 1670 Savinien d'Alquié published *The Delights of France* at Amsterdam. In the story of the Miremont cave as he tells it in his book *Underground Périgord*, a young cave-explorer, Bernard Pierret (he was just over twenty-one in 1953) quotes this admirable extract from Savinien: "There is a cave near Miramont which is called Cluzeau, extending for five or six leagues under the earth. . . . In it are halls paved with mosaic, altars adorned with fine paintings, springs, a river . . ." What a pity Bernard Pierret did not read through the text he quoted, or realise how important it was! He was in possession of one of the best historical proofs. He did not know what a trump he held in his hand.

The psychological explanation of this "accident" may be quite simple. Exploring caves from 1945 to 1949, at the age of fifteen or sixteen, Pierret took no interest in historical records. For him it was more exciting to venture into dark, deep holes. And it was only much later, when he wrote out his observations, that he added historical notes. He mentioned the "paintings" of Savinien d'Alquié without connecting them with those he had had a glimpse of some years before.

Louys Moreri

In 1699 "this foreign nobleman travelling in France" published at Amsterdam and The Hague the *Great Historical Dictionary of Louys Moreri*, repeating the same text on p. 609 of his third volume.

Louys Moreri mentions and describes "Miremont, a French town in Périgord. It stands on a little river that flows into the Vézère, seven or eight leagues from Périgueux and the same distance from Bergerac. This town is remarkable for the Cluzeau cavern, which runs very far underground. The country people tell various stories. They say there are great halls in the cave, paintings and altars. They even convince the most credulous that the peasants used to make sacrifices there to Venus and the Infernal Gods . . ."

This *Great Historical Dictionary or Curious Mixture of Sacred and Profane History* is the monumental work of a priest, Louys Moreri, who gave up preaching to give all his time to the Dictionary. The first edition dates from 1674, and the twentieth, published in 1759, comprises ten volumes.

It was the edition of 1725, edited by M. Maury, a respected member of the Historical and Archaeological Society of Périgord, that enabled Jean Guichard, a reporter on the *Nouvelle Republique de Bordeaux*, to fire the first historical bomb-shell under the title: "The Rouffignac Cave was known two Centuries ago" in its number of August 9, 1956.

The industrious Jean Guichard started the hunt for parchments and ancient cosmographies. And this search, so happily begun, continues still.

JOSEPH de CHANCEL, 1730, and
THE MARQUIS de MIREMONT

Follow the Guide

In the 18th century, more and more people visited the cave of Cluzeau at Miremont. It became the scene of organised expeditions. We have definite accounts of these expeditions from 1721, 1746 and 1759. The last included about forty people, among them a Corresponding Member of the Academy, two barristers and six priests. Bruzen de la Martinière, Geographer to H.M. Philip V, King of Spain and the Indies, also refers to the paintings at Miremont, Miramont or Miraumont, in the Cluzeau cavern, on p. 316, Vol. IV, of his *Great Geographical, Historical and Critical Dictionary*, which appeared in Paris in 1768.

Joseph de Chancel has left us one of the best accounts of one of these historic visits in the 18th century.

He was born at the château of Antoniat in Périgord in 1677, and his beginnings were most promising. At the age of fourteen he wrote a tragedy, *Jugurth*, in which his characters were the King of Numidia and his cousins Adherbal and Hiempsal, whom he was to murder. Racine had the play acted in 1694 under a new title, *Adherbal*, on the pressing recommendation of the Princesse de Conti.

Joseph de Chancel became Honorary Butler to the Duchess of Orleans, composed many tragedies and hatched a few plots, too. After being a prisoner on the island of Sainte-Marguerite, escaping and taking refuge in Holland, he returned to France in 1728, decided to lead a quiet life and devoted himself to research. After having "made" history for a time he found it wiser and safer to write it.

For his *Journey from Paris to Poitou, the Angoumois and Périgord* (1730) he returns to the sources of his youth. And he gives a very pleasant account of his visit to Rouffignac on April 2, 1730. He writes:

"We came down from Fleurac, a steep mountain whose summit is covered with vines, and reached a small valley containing a field watered by a little stream. Then we climbed another mountain, opposite the first, so steep and rugged that we had to make a great effort to advance. The summit is covered with chestnut-trees. Two-thirds of the way up you can see the mouth of the cave near a clump of two wild fig-trees, a walnut and a young oak. The entrance is overgrown with brambles and thorns; you must stoop very low to get in."

The place has hardly changed in the last two centuries, and it is, indeed, from Fleurac that you would get the best view of the entrance to the cave, or rather of its surroundings, for the leaves of the chestnut-trees hide the opening. The wild figs have disappeared, but other young oaks have taken the place of their predecessor, and a frail cherry-tree grows near them. And until 1938 you had to bend your back and push aside the brambles to get into the depths. But let us follow the guide—of 1730.

At the Time of the Calvinists

"After passing the entrance, we find ourselves in a very wide corridor, with a roof as high as a pike; at first there is some light, but the floor consists of sand so sticky that it may pull off our shoes. Using our lights, we are led along various paths wide enough for two coaches to pass, under a high roof. Here we are shown, at intervals, stone walls built up by Catholics who took refuge there with their goods, their wives and children, their grain and their arms during the civil wars, when the Calvinist party ruled the province. They built a bridge inside the entrance that could be held by a single man against many enemies. Thus," says Chancel, "it was difficult to force such a dark stronghold."

These stone and clay ramparts are still clearly visible today. One, very high, bars the right-hand gallery. Another bars the gallery on the left. Some rooms show clear signs of adaptation, among them the great hall with the red ceiling, on the right of the Sacred Way.

At one time it communicated with the main gallery through a wide corridor 10 yds. long and 2 or 3 yds. high. Two roughly-built walls have been built out from each side of the original corridor, reducing its width to less than 6 ft.

This arrangement, it seems, had no defensive purpose, for the red-roofed hall has no other exit and forms a sort of trap, but by cutting off the draught from the Sacred Way they sheltered the hall and made it less uncomfortable. Our author pushed on, however, for he says: "As it is dangerous to lose one's way among the various corridors to right and left, we asked our guides to be careful."

The Gargantuan Hall of Rouffignac

"After the first gallery," he continues, "we turned to the right towards a rounded rock that rises to a point almost touching the roof, from which water drips into a hole on the top of the pointed rock. This has been called the Old Woman's Seat because of its shape." Lagrange-Chancel does not use inverted commas, but the friend of the Princesse de Conti and the Duchess of Orleans did not fail to notice the highly Rabelaisian resemblance of the finest stalactite in the cave to the Old Woman's fundament. He wondered, too, who the "Old Woman" was. "Is not this," he asks, "a distant memory of the very ancient owner of this subterranean spot, the mistress of the place, the 'Mother Earth' of our ancestors, a personification of the subterranean deities who haunted Rouffignac?" The names go back to a very distant past; ages of History flow from them for those who seek enlightenment. And the next underground place is quite as significant.

"To the left of this long gallery we came upon a great, flat stone, 100 ft. long but only 6 ft. wide, about half a league from the entrance to the cave, which is known as the Tomb of Gargantua, and on which inquiring travellers have carved their names. Among them is that of a Bishop of Périgueux." Thus the cult of the worthy giant Gargantua is found in the heart of Rouffignac. The cave was a prehistoric sanctuary. It is also the exciting repository of a whole body of folk-lore, itself rooted in Protohistory and Prehistory. Rouffignac, a complete temple of Archaeocivilisation! Why not?

Every step taken in this darkness may be lighted by an old and rich humanity. A pilgrimage to Rouffignac is a meeting with many shades, who have left material traces of their passing from the age of the Great Bear to the present day. Our acetylene lamps have often shone upon the long limestone rock of Gargantua. It is not 100 ft. long, but it stretches far into the darkness of the straight-sided gallery. And since I have known it for the "tomb of Gargantua" I find in it a symbolical and funereal quality. It is the nameless cenotaph of all those who lived in Rouffignac, all who came there seeking peace and asylum, all who used it to celebrate their religious rites, palaeolithic or pagan, Calvinist or Papist, all who longed to live in the present and still more in the unknown Beyond, even those who came to Rouffignac only because the larcenies of love require darkness. . . .

I hope a day will come when we may lay aside our archaeological mission and spell out some of those names carved with knives on the soft limestone, and decipher those surnames, also darkened by the centuries. Perhaps we shall find the name of that Bishop of Périgueux who came this far hoping to reach the crypt of Saint-Front, as legend invited him to do. Unless, of course, a presentiment drove him to ensure the continuance and permanence of the religion of Rouffignac.

The Pillars of Hercules

But our guide of 1730 tells us to follow him and not linger in the shadows. "We walked on through thick, sticky mud, and after some distance we found a shining chamber, all of rock crystal, naturally cut out of the rock but icy cold." Still following our guide, "we come upon a stream or torrent, flowing with a fearful sound; it is bottomless, and farther than that the curious cannot go".

The whole cave is bathed in the dim light of mythology. Is it not curious to find in these words of Lagrange-Chancel a direct echo of the inscription once carved by Hercules on Mounts Calpe and Abyla, the two pillars that bear his name, Gibraltar to the North and Africa to the South, the ends of the earth and the limits of his gigantic labours? The deep stream of Rouffignac also marks the end of a world like that of Hercules, past which no man could go, for there was nothing beyond.

"But what is most surprising," declares our Chevalier, "is to find in these underground places, printed on the sand, the tracks of all sorts of animals, such as dogs, foxes, wolves, badgers, tigers, oxen, buffalo and even horses, which would seem incredible if several gentlemen had not been eyewitnesses of it." In spite of many excursions, these tracks are still clear, though they have been rather fancifully explained. No doubt it was the bears' claw-marks that suggested the intrusion of a tiger.

Having brought us about two leagues from the entrance, our guide is getting short of breath. He thinks it best to turn back, "though it is thought certain that the cave leads to the crypt of the cathedral church of Saint-Front at Périgueux, that is to say, for a distance of at least five leagues, passing under the streams and rivers it may encounter on the way". Let us, then, go back to the light of day, luckier than two Dutchmen whose fatal venture the same author now describes.

"Here is a story of a few years ago" (1730)

"Two foreign travellers, thought to be Dutch, wishing to push as far as possible into this subterranean place, provided themselves with all they could need, including food. With a single guide, they entered the hole called the Mouth of Miremont, but when they reached the stream of which we have just spoken, the guide refused to go any farther and turned back. After exploring the underground passages for a long time and making their observations, they noticed that their lamps were dying down and tried to get out. But it came about that they lost their way in the strangely formed passages and turnings of the cavern and found themselves lost in a maze, far from the exit. Having no light, they burned their clothes and shirts in spite of the cold ; when these were consumed, panic seized them in the dark and they could not find the exit after long wandering among stones, mud and wild animals. One stayed behind and died in a state of frenzy; the other reached the mouth of the cavern after nine days. When he saw the light, he fell in a swoon; peasants carried him to the village of Miremont, where the two men had left their carriage, and he died there two days later."

All the expeditions did not end so tragically, or there would not have been so many in the 18th century. In 1721, 1746 and 1759 there were visits to Rouffignac, always "in large parties and with many torches, flares and lanterns". The underground expedition of 1759 included about forty persons, among them a Correspondent of the Academy, two barristers and six priests. With such leading lights they could hardly lose their way.

Text follows text, one copied from another : is not that how history is written? And we shall never be grateful enough to the poor Prehistorians, who could not copy from others, yet wrote Prehistory! Men of science, who are sometimes rather unkind to men of letters, will accuse them of having drawn on their imaginations. Let us say, then, that the Prehistorians were poets—and accept the compliment.

A fine Subject for Study and Meditation

A profusion of historical writings, very explicit writings covering the period from the 16th century to our own time, definitely confirm the innumerable inscriptions which obliterate some of the prehistoric drawings and often overlie the inscriptions of an earlier century. It would be childish to cast doubt on their chronology. Some joker may have signed himself "Charlemagne" or "Jeanne d'Arc" on the wall, but jests in such doubtful taste are rare. The great cave-explorer Martel will quote a spicy specimen later on, in Greek at that! Already a superficial examination of these thousands of inscriptions seems to show that those which bear dates can be grouped in lengthy periods. Some centuries, or some portions of centuries, are rich in inscriptions, such as the second half of the 18th century or the end of the first half of the 19th century (1840–1850), and again the last quarter of that century from 1875 to about 1900, with more precise datings up to about 1906. These active chronological sequences are not without interest. The first, in the 18th century, corresponds with a general thirst for culture, a taste for natural science and the vogue of "cabinets" of natural specimens which preceded the Revolution.

The second active sequence coincides with the quiet reign of Louis-Philippe, when the taste for science was again very strong. The third corresponds with a period of flourishing provincial "learned societies" and of a new zeal for instruction and inquiry, when the Deputies voted for free, compulsory education. This was also a time of communal monographs, often produced by self-taught schoolmasters and very interesting. It is the time when one of them, in the Pyrenees, mentions the paintings in the "Black Room" at Niaux, prehistoric paintings which also were mentioned before the birth of prehistoric science and the official discovery by Commander Mollard and his sons in 1906.

A Task for a Historian

A complete list of all the historical inscriptions, together with the mere mention of a name or surname, is of historical value if accompanied by a date and would enable us to make a useful subdivision of material. It would be still more interesting to mark these inscriptions in their exact places on the plans of the cave, and to have a plan for each chronological section. Then we could see which sections were favoured or ignored at different times. There are 18th-century inscriptions in the deep galleries of the stream, which confirm the stories we have read. Just when was the great Eastern Gallery known and frequented? About what century did "tourists" habitually go beyond the Great Ceiling to wander in the further depths beyond the "Mammoth with the Roguish Eye", seeing him, perhaps, without realising what he was?

For the first time we can make a record of exact knowledge of the cave—and what a cave!—spanning nearly four centuries. It is possible to discover at Rouffignac what intellectual periods favoured underground exploration in spite of troubles, the wars of the Austrian or Polish Succession, the reversal of alliances or the American War of Independence. It is possible at Rouffignac to lay bare the landmarks of underground knowledge and even those of cave-exploration before it became a science.

13. An excellently drawn mammoth, particularly the prehensile extremity of the trunk

14. A mammoth under the Great Ceiling

15.   Professor Grassé taking a sample of clay.   On the right is M. Charlot, professor of the School of Physics and Chemistry

16.   Serpentine drawings on the Serpents' Dome

And the counter-test, the study of the periods when the cave was neglected, is equally significant. At the end of the 18th century and the beginning of the 19th the cave seemed abandoned. Inscriptions like "Lalande 1810" on the ibex below the right-hand side of the Great Ceiling, and "Dalbavie" on another ibex, are exceptional in this period. The turmoil of the Revolution and the Empire did not encourage exploration underground. Yet the cave was so well known, particularly as a gigantic rat-run with a single exit, that it was bound to be used as a place of asylum by rebels against the First Empire. What a pity, for half a century ago they were being accused, in the Les Eyzies district, of being the prehistoric painters of Font-de-Gaume and of the drawings at Combarelles!

The first years of the Third Republic do not seem to have favoured underground excursions. Attention was concentrated on the MacMahon régime. The lack of inscriptions is striking after 1906. The cave was deserted then because a competitor had appeared. A few miles away, in the Vézère valley, Abbé Breuil, Dr. Capitan and the great Peyrony, a schoolmaster at Les Eyzies, had discovered Combarelles and Font-de-Gaume. They discovered Prehistory and Man. Public interest, no doubt, switched to the new eaves.

Fifty years later, almost to a day, Abbé Breuil authenticated the marvellous paintings and engravings of Rouffignac, and a new era began for the cave of François de Belleforest. But its guardians kept sharp watch to prevent any new inscription from being added to those already innumerable. From now on Rouffignac is "fixed" and must keep the status of a prehistoric temple, an art gallery, an historical stone age museum and a collection of petrified records of earlier centuries. It is a world fixed since its origins and halted for the first time in a continuous process of evolution.

We can only feel proud of this, for "evolution" means transformation, change and adulteration, and Rouffignac must remain from now on as it is and what it is. Rouffignac is Rouffignac. That is sufficient claim to glory.

French and Foreign Travellers

The 18th century was a great time for letter-writing, and it yields us long and instructive epistles about the Cro du Cluzeau. The collection founded by Abbé de Lespine contains interesting manuscripts published in the Périgord series under the auspices of the Historical and Archaeological Society of Périgord. (National Library, Paris, Périgord Collection.)

G

A letter dated 1721, from D. C. A. D. S., speaks volubly of the cave, now decidedly fabulous, though it produced a few elementary truths. It says: "Most of the French writers who have given us descriptions of France until now have been content to compose them in their studies without taking the trouble to travel about the kingdom and see for themselves the marvels of nature and art in the provinces, towns and villages about which they write. What they have given to the public is merely a series of extracts from authors who wrote before them." We must recognise that many writings of the 18th century were singularly dependent on those of the 17th or even the 16th! And it would seem that as early as the 18th century one could say, as we say now, that a Frenchman was often a man who knew very little about geography, at least that of his own country, while foreigners appreciated it greatly. Listen again to our correspondent: "Foreigners who travel in France are not like this: they want to see everything with their own eyes; they inform themselves about whatever is singular and most remarkable in the places they visit; their curiosity leads them to inspect mines, mineral springs, those whose flow waxes and wanes each day, Roman roads and an infinity of other things of which they give observations and accurate descriptions in the journals of their travels; and when one asks to see these descriptions, one is surprised to find peculiarities that Frenchmen who have described the same things have not observed."

The Marquis de Miremont answers

One of these travellers' journals, written by a foreigner, Mr. de Wilde, of Amsterdam, gave the author of this history his first knowledge of the cave of Cluzeau, "obtained by reading the manuscript diary of a journey made in France six years ago" (that is, about 1715, at the death of Louis XIV). And the author's curiosity was sharpened, but not satisfied. He therefore wrote to the man who seemed most likely to give first-hand information from a reliable source, to the owner of the cave, the Marquis de Miremont, then commandant of a cavalry camp. (The oldest records of Miremont date from 1516 and 1527, the time of Marignan and Pavia.) "I asked the Marquis several questions," the writer says; "questions calculated to produce the most enlightenment. He took the trouble to answer them, point by point"—as follows:

"(1) The Hole of Cluzeau, otherwise of Grandville, is the entrance to a cave or long vault that passes under a very high mountain called Chantepit. This entrance is so low that you cannot enter it without stooping, but it can be enlarged as much as you like by removing the earth that has collected in it.

"It is a tradition in the countryside that this tunnel was made by early men to pass under the mountain from side to side, as a short cut.

"(2) You cannot go in without good guides and a good supply of torches or bundles of straw, and lighters to light them again when they go out."

The technical details are new. It is a wise precaution to go underground not only with many lanterns, but with the means to rekindle dying flames. Tinder and steel, striking on a stone prepared for the purpose, must be used. A spark will ignite small tufts of straw, and the straw will light the torches and the lantern wicks.

A well-informed judgment

With these means of lighting, the beauties of the cave cannot escape notice, and the Marquis de Miremont says in his fifth paragraph: "All the vaults are very fine, but they are not of the same height. There are SEVERAL FINE PAINTINGS on them." The aesthetic judgment of the commandant of a cavalry camp should be taken seriously, for it is certain that he often saw fine pictures in the *salons* of the period, and he must know what he is saying. Many other paragraphs in his long letter give excellent pictures of "his" cave, describing it accurately and also with a great deal of intelligence and moderation. The owner knows his property, and his cave is known to him, well known, though not perhaps as familiar as it is to its present owner.

The Marquis speaks with pleasure of "quantities of statues formed apparently by drops of water, which drips unceasingly, from which it appears that they are all natural and show no sign of human workmanship".

Distances are always badly stated and greatly exaggerated; the letter estimates the distance to the stream at "eight or nine leagues", so long must time have seemed underground. For the first time, on the other hand, the underground stream is correctly described: "This stream is only two feet wide; it does not flow fast. You see it below you from above, and if you went down to its bed, you could not get up the other side without a ladder. Beyond this stream is another underground chamber, very large. We do not know whether anyone has had the curiosity to go into it."

The Truth about a Ceiling

The tenth paragraph—they had time for their scientific correspondence in the 17th century!—corrects the opinion of those who say "all the paths are paved". The Marquis de Miremont explains that for a great deal of the way you walk on rock which seems like paving, and "that is why several people have made this mistake". And indeed, that is the character of the ground near the Great Landslide, where huge slabs of limestone fallen from the roof make a natural pavement. The detachments from the roof are still very visible, both by the clean whiteness of the new ceiling and by the cracks, still in the vault, heralding new falls of rock. Some of these slabs are several metres long, with a volume of at least 350 cubic feet and a weight of 20 to 30 tons. The sight of these enormous blocks always reminds us of a remark made by one of our modest but very faithful helpers in the Pyrenees. One day when we were digging in the great cave at Bédeilhac, in the Ariège, we knocked off for a moment to stretch our legs. And we passed near one of these enormous blocks, detached from the rock in geological (or perhaps more recent) times. The mass weighed at least 30 to 40 tons. Our companion asked:

"Where do these big rocks that lie in the chambers and galleries come from?"

"From the ceiling. They are rocks that have fallen from the roof. Look at those cracks beginning up there—and over there—here's another block getting ready to fall!"

The sight was, indeed, rather impressive, and it made our companion think. "Ah, yes," he said, "I understand." And we congratulated ourselves on having explained the thing clearly and understandably to him. But he went on slowly, half aloud, pursuing his reflections: "Now I understand why the boss 'wears a helmet'" (or in French slang, "has a hang-over!"). As for the Marquis de Miremont, he always answers questions conscientiously. He answers No. 10, No. 11, No. 12.

The Mud and the Duck

This last question refers to the sticky clay in the south gallery, the "sea of mud", a sort of "Armenian bowl" (?), reddish in colour, known in the countryside as *Baljarmeno*, and supposed to be a sovereign remedy for broken arms and legs when it is kneaded with white of egg. This mixture is even better for cuts, closing the wound in no time at all. It is also used for making moulds of graven stones. "What a marvellous clay! It helps to make you break your limbs on the rocks by gumming up your shoes, but it furnishes excellent plasters to mend broken bones!"

The Marquis answers everything. Here is his reply to question No. 17: "As for the stream that bars the road through this long vault, it would not be possible to take a small boat along it, for it is neither wide enough nor fast-flowing enough to carry it. It is said (and here we find one of the best modern fables about the Rouffignac cave) that a duck was put into this little stream with a ribbon round its neck and came out some time later under the bridge at Périgueux, which is a good four leagues away."

History does not relate what colour was the little duck's ribbon, and that's a great pity. How could you recognise him? Decidedly, Monsieur le Marquis, we have taken you too seriously! This man, too, dabbling in "spelaeology" before its time, indulges in very far-fetched stories, telling us tales about "boats" and "ducks" in Rouffignac. Unless, of course, the Marquis de Miremont had a presentiment of the solemn journalistic junketings in the summer of the Year of Grace 1956, on the Rouffignac stream and even on the Dordogne, when Press "boats" (hoaxes) and *canards* were not lacking, and ducks wore many-coloured streamers round their necks.

History does not tell us what happened to the little duck who came out under the bridge at Périgueux. At least he was lucky to come out on the water. Can you see his face, with his ribbon round his neck, if he came out one day in Lent in the crypt of Saint-Front of Périgueux?

"Take the trouble . . ."

We cannot close these learned remarks better than by repeating the personal conclusion of M. de Miremont: "There is all that the Marquis took the trouble to write to me about it. He added that he knew of all the circumstances partly from the report made to him by his father, who went as far as the stream, and from guides who habitually took strangers into the cave, partly from what he saw with his own eyes. If you want to know more, set about it; go and see this marvel for yourself."

Before we ever knew M. de Miremont and his writings, we had followed his advice. In our easy-going century the Marquis's lesson has its uses. The lesson applies not only to the marvel of Rouffignac. It is the custom to inscribe certain proud sayings on the walls of our schools: "Education comes next after bread. . .

A well-filled head is better," etc. May I suggest M. de Miremont's rule, laid down by him in 1715:

> If you want to know more about it
> Set about it . . .

But educated people in the 18th century were not content with mere idle touring. They knew how to set about it; they knew how to draw up plans of the great cavern, each vying with the other.

THE PLAN OF 1759 AND THE
CHEVALIER DE BARRY

A Plan of 1759

Gabriel Bouquier, of Terrasson, a large village seven leagues from the cave of Rouffignac, made an excellent plan in 1759. Gonthier, of Miremont, drew up another in 1765 and discovered a new chamber "which seemed to be lined with diamonds. It has the finest crystallisations, and every part of it is intact, but it is to be feared that when this place is better known, the walls will soon come under the chisel. . . ." A painful and, alas, a prophetic vision.

Bouquier's plan of 1759, of which there is a fine copy in the museum at Périgueux, has a picturesque and very detailed caption. Thus, it notes at a point "y" in the cave: "Alley where M. de Barry lost his way for an hour."

Is it not the strangest thing to find today, on the left-hand group of mammoths in the great frieze, the inscription "Barry", traced in smoky characters with an oil lamp taken out of a stable lantern, or with a candle? The black lettering is much thinner than the "modern" 19th and 20th century names, but the name "Barry" quite obliterates the firm and precise drawing of two excellent mammoths painted in manganese!

Professor P. P. Grassé paid particular attention to this important problem during his second visit, on Wednesday, Oct.10, 1956. His minute examination with a magnifying glass was decisive. "Two painted lines, the trunk and tail of a mammoth in the great frieze, one of the group on the left, obliterated by the first 'r' of 'Barry', have at their intersection with the writing a dull grey colour which is quite different from the appearance of the lines not obliterated by the writing and can be explained only if the writing lies over the line."

And the eminent member of the Academy of Sciences straightened himself smiling after his long examination and pronounced the conclusive formula: "Q.E.D."

Who, then, is De Barry?

When M. de Barry wrote his name on the mammoths of Rouffignac —perhaps without seeing them!—about the middle of the 18th century, with an idle, mechanical and human gesture, he authenticated those mammoths for the future.

If François de Belleforest is the "first discoverer" of the Rouffignac paintings, M. de Barry is the first expert on their authenticity, before ourselves, of course, before Abbé Breuil, Professor Graziosi, Professor Almagro and many others. After having broken many a lance in defence of François, we need not break such long ones for M. de Barry.

But who is this M. de Barry who "lost his way for an hour" in a gallery at Rouffignac but, luckier than the two Dutchmen at the beginning of the 18th century, managed to escape from its shadows?

Is he that too famous Gascon nobleman Jean du Barry, born at Lévignac-sur-Save in 1723, who was a well-informed collector and also the lover of Jeanne Bécu, whom he gave in marriage to his brother Guillaume, a modest predecessor of Louis XV? Jean du Barry would have been less than thirty-six when he had his adventure in the Cro du Cluzeau. Afterwards he turned respectable and retired to Toulouse, where he spent his leisure in adding to his collections, filling his "cabinet", in the manner of the time, when there was a craze for natural curios, rocks and fossils, plants and pebbles.

In front of the long frieze of mammoths barred with the Barry signature I found it pleasant to recall the gracious shade of the Comtesse du Barry. To a just tribute of gratitude for the evidence supplied by Jean du Barry I added a warmer feeling for his partner, the protector of Art and Letters, the friend of Marmontel and d'Alembert and Voltaire, and an agreeable person to boot. It seemed possible to add a very suggestive chapter to this book: "The Shadow of the Du Barry glided over the Mammoths." And the whole frieze, not only the two mammoths on the left, took on a new charm, adorned with an intoxicating and distant femininity. Had not Madame du Barry come here, too, into Rouffignac, after the explorers, the Academician, the two Dutchmen, the priests of Périgord, the Calvinists and the Bishop of Périgueux? Perhaps she came with Jean du Barry, or perhaps some other partner, for the sake of a few of love's larcenies. . . . What a beautiful and marvellous chapter! The best in the book, for it will never be written. And it will not be written because it seems that M. de Barry was not the lover of Jeanne Bécu!

The real De Barry

At the end of October, a letter shattered this sweet dream. J. Bouchereau, one of my precious research workers, reported new information, received from Bugue, a few kilometres as the crow flies from Rouffignac. The real De Barry was an engineer and a geographer, Pélissier de Barry, agent to the Barony of Limeuil. So do we fall back into the banalities of every day! In 1765 he drew up the inventory of the domain of Miremont and settled at Bugue. This Pélissier de Barry took a great interest in the underground caves of the district and had the cavern at Proumeyssac sealed up for its safety and to avoid wilful damage.

Gabriel Bouquier, the author of the plan of Rouffignac, had family connexions at Bugue on his father's side and he must have known and appreciated M. de Barry and sought his company. We can understand that he did not feel inclined to write a more complete description of the "lost man" on the plan, but we can understand, also, why he took the trouble to record the incident, which occurred, perhaps, during an exploration that they made together. Eighteen years after the plan was drawn, we find another trace of M. de Barry. François de Paule-Latapie, Inspector of Manufactures at Guienne, came on a visit to Bugue, and he had high praise for M. de Barry. "He is a Judge at Bugue and a very intelligent man, well-informed on feudal and mathematical subjects and even on theory. All the strangers who pass through Bugue on their way to the cave at Miremont are delighted with his politeness, and I am far from wishing to belittle his reputation in this respect. His son, M. Pélissier, is a young lawyer like his father, not without wit and very well-mannered. He took me wherever he thought I might see something interesting (to the Proumeyssac and Cocagne caves) and he would have accompanied me to Miremont if I had wanted to go there tomorrow."

The Inspector of Manufactures at Guienne was to see his dream come true and visit the "famous cave"—the description is his— on May 1, 1778. At the end of his story he again mentions M. de Barry and says he "has not done much work on the plan of the cave he gives out as his own" and there is "a map of the Cros de Granville better than the one M. de Barry showed me". The inspector varies in his judgments, but his story does reinforce the identification of the De Barry of the cave as Pélissier de Barry, engineer and geographer, agent of the Barony of Limeuil and Judge at Bugue.

An Inspector of Manufactures at Miremont in 1778

On Friday, May 1, 1778, François de Paule-Latapie, Inspector of Manufactures at Guienne, saw his dream come true. He had mobilised the whole countryside: M. de Lostange, whom he met at the cave "in spite of the bad weather", Abbé Tilly, the servants of these gentlemen and M. Fournier, "the agent of the Marquis de Fleurac, who knows the labyrinths of the cave fairly well and was most useful to us. The ordinary guide who takes people there is at the point of death, and there are no others in the country, so that until the very moment of our departure I was sad to think I should not see the famous cave for the sake of which I had travelled such difficult roads. . . ."

Was this visit due to purely intellectual and disinterested curiosity, or was it an official inspection? We do not know, for all this happened in 1778. We may, however, ask one question. Does the present-day successor of François de Paule-Latapie, who is an Inspector of some administration or perhaps a Prefect, know his territory as well as François de Paule-Latapie knew his? It is true that the roads today are no longer difficult, and we can roll along them at sixty miles an hour. And it is just because we go too fast that we know nothing any more!

Courageously the Inspector made his way to the Stream, "the entrance to which," he says, "is very difficult to find when you don't know it, and that was our case, so that we wandered about in the twists and turns of a horrible crevasse which seems the most natural path and the most used". And he admits that to get to the Stream "you must have three qualities: courage, slimness and agility". The visit took 4½ hours, and it was "only a glimpse" as the Inspector of Manufactures notes, adding with pleasure that "the most beautiful features of the cave are the vaults, the crystals, the stalactites, the masses of rock fallen from the roof, the miry clay and the inequalities and widenings of the corridors". He says nothing of the paintings. Were they too much defaced, at the end of the 18th century, by the numerous inscriptions, often very large, which had been added in the last 200 years?

The History of Rouffignac covers nearly four centuries, 1575–1956. Eighteen years from now (1957) we shall be able to celebrate the fourth centenary of the "first" discovery in a worthy manner by unveiling a medallion to François de Belleforest. And if some new text is laid bare, very well, we shall celebrate the half-millennium! Who can say more?

Now, throughout the first half of the History of Rouffignac, until the middle of the 18th century, original writers and copyists testify to the existence of the paintings. They must have been obvious to the least seeing eye. During the second half of that History, from the middle of the 18th to the middle of the 20th century, the paintings were forgotten or misunderstood. Humanity, perhaps, does not develop its powers of observation as fast as it develops its means of locomotion. But the scrawlings must have helped to cause this forgetfulness by obscuring the Great Ceiling and covering the bestiary with names and surnames. These natural curiosities of the cave, known by the new names of Cro de Granville or Grotte de Mire-mont, as François de Paule-Latapie most accurately locates it, became its great attraction.

Revolutionary Silence

It would seem that it was in times of war or civil strife that the caves fully played the part of places of refuge and were most fre-quented. They gave shelter to those who were preparing for their own election and the downfall of others, to those who were cast down, to those who wished to vanish without going away and to those who wished neither to go nor to stay. The makers of new laws came there only a little before their victims : former lawmakers, stripped of power, mingled for a while with new despoilers. Never did such a sealed vessel as a cave contain so much upheaval and unrest, so much agitation and social conflict! But all this called for darkness, and the texts are dumb. All through the Revolution and the Empire the cave of Rouffignac lay silent and aroused no comment.

Inscriptions, traced in smoke or cut with a knife, are more common at the end of the 18th century. After that they are few. Rouffignac is no longer a place of pilgrimage, dreams or discovery. Sometimes, as in the days of the Great Mammoth or in those of barbarians and cave-dwelling fugitives, it was a place of asylum and became once more a cathedral. It harboured the outlaws of the First Empire, young recruits wanted by the "Corsican Ogre" Napoleon, youths destined for the sad fields of Bautzen or Dresden, hiding in the depths of their native soil. But tragic circumstances such as these left no time for scribbling on walls and ceilings. Young "Marie-Louises" lacking Empresses had not the heart to carve their names or those of promised loves who might no longer wait for them.

The only dated name picked out by chance during our pros-pectings is that of a certain "Lalande", preceded by the date 1810.

It is cut in clear characters over the "Dalbavie" ibex on the right-hand edge of the great ceiling. This man Dalbavie certainly got himself talked about, and after his example it will be difficult to dissuade visitors from leaving their names on the walls for some glorious posterity! Dalbavie stands alone, heading the list of proper names. We know nothing yet about M. Dalbavie. No doubt he was some worthy, stolid tradesman, who enjoyed a little leisure because of the economic crisis caused by the blockade of the Continent. Perhaps the future will enlighten us.

ROUFFIGNAC IN THE YEAR
SEXTILE XI OF THE FRENCH ERA

"Sextile Year XI" (*1803*)

Rouffignac remained, however, on the list, and more prominently so than ever, especially as the new régimes of the revolutionary era were fond of calculating riches they did not create. The *Annual of the Dordogne Department for Sextile Year XI of the French Era* (1803), edited by A. Delfau, gives us the most important and accurate description of the cave. This very long account can still serve as a basic text for an exhaustive analysis of Rouffignac. Many details are known to us from earlier reports, but it is from Delfau that we can get the most details and the most lively and colourful terminology. Many sections which today are nameless, obscure and unclassified come to life in Delfau's description and regain their suggestive names. The dynasty of Rouffignac guides is extinct. Some day, perhaps, it will revive, and Delfau's *Annual* will be the bedside book that ensures its permanence.

His discussion of the "visit" begins with a question of pseudo-scientific measurement. The depth of the cave, from the opening to the end of the longest branch, is 1,067 metres (545 *toises* or 1,160 yds.). The new metric system permits of greater accuracy, and we must take care of the last 7 metres (22 ft. 9 in.). I confess without the slightest shame that we are still far from placing our paintings and engravings accurately to within 50 metres. But is it not a mistake, and a serious one, to admit this so naïvely? Does not this expose us to criticism by those who would be full of praise if we stated that Mammoth No. 79 is 978 m. 502 mm. (1,017 yds., 16 ft. 9 in.) from the entrance? This adds nothing to the fineness of the engraving or the suggestive power of the mammoth. But we need not complain, it takes nothing away.

The total length of the galleries is about 2½ miles. But "if you consider all the angles you have been unable to evaluate, and if you consider that the visitor does not follow the median line of the plan but hugs the curve of the ellipse in order to examine objects fixed to the walls, you must increase this distance by at least a quarter and the total covered, going and coming back, will be 1 mam. 571 m. (5,424 *toises*: 10,571 metres or 11,557 yards). But in spite of this great depth, the whole cave can be safely explored with the help of a guide who lives on the spot."

Delfau describes the "Cake Room"

Like most writers on Rouffignac, Delfau begins his visit with the right-hand or eastern branch. This is much the most sensible route. After a few tens of yards you come to the first bifurcation, and it is an important one, for the highest and most easily accessible gallery is on the right. At a second fork you feel the need to be systematic, and you inspect the galleries opening to your right, one by one. But this is the longest way to the paintings on the Great Ceiling.

In the right-hand branch "the first curious object you come across is a stalagmite the people call the 'Old Woman's Seat'. Here you will see a great many rather small, nipple-shaped stalactites. Generally speaking, congelations of this kind are rare in the cave. The roof also carries glittering stones of various shapes and sizes, but they are too high for you to reach them or examine them carefully.

"Farther on is a fine chamber called the 'Cake Room'. This chamber is elliptical, about 30 ft. long and 9 ft. high, and is adorned shoulder-high with ridges of flint that make a double row of interlacing branches all around it. These branches are very elegantly and symmetrically placed, and they make an agreeable effect, rather like complicated pastry." The culinary image happily describes these red and ochre flint "kidneys", writhing and twisted, lying in two fine horizontal strata and standing out vividly on a floury ground of white clay. They are very like those peasants' cakes, made of thin, narrow strips of pastry, which are cooked in boiling oil or fat and are sometimes called *roussettes*. The ceiling of the Cake Room "is extremely smooth, adorned with little domes filled with similar shapes. Some distance from this chamber you will enter another, smaller and lower, whose walls are covered with beautifully transparent trihedral fluorspar. These stones shine like diamonds, and when the chamber is well lit it throws off glittering reflections. This is how Homer describes the cave of the daughters of Nereus . . ." Unfortunately this chamber, like several others of its kind, has been badly damaged. But we can still get an idea of it, since Delfau notes that "several pieces of this fluorspar can be seen in the Natural History museum of the Central School of the Department".

The Shell Room

Farther on again, the visitor can admire "the Shell Room, a rather large chamber covered with Terebratula-shells, fossil oysters and other shells encrusted in the rock, from which they fall at a touch". This "shell room", or more exactly this gallery leading into many "shell rooms", is certainly one of the most intensely curious passages in Rouffignac from the naturalist's point of view. The roofs are low, and the horizontal beds of yellowish shells stand out on a white clay background. Sometimes the whole ceiling coincides with the layer of sea shells, at other times there is a sort of doubling of the roof: the layer of shells forms a second ceiling under the limestone roof and hangs 4 to 8 in. below it. The beams of light passing through the spaces between the shells are strange, and the gallery would be truly unique if flooded with ultra-violet light. Experiments made with that special light under the great ceiling to examine superimposed paintings and scribblings revealed admirable shades of pure, deep violet on fragments of shells still clinging to the vault.

If spread over the entire vault, this would give the impression of another world, shining with colours both shadowy and luminous. You seem to have taken on an immaterial being and descended to the lowest depths of the sea, where you drift along winding corridors in these abysses, brushing beds of compressed shells with your fins, gliding over basins of fine sand and clay without settling in them, moving slowly in a liquid dream. . . . Then a sharp-angled flint reminds you that you are only a man underground, not a coelacanth straying over the depths of the ocean.

But Delfau, too, calls you back to a sense of reality and to the exact meaning of your visit. "After having explored all the first part of the cave, you will reach a large branch of it by a broad path called the Great Road, sometimes 5 or 6 yds. wide, with a roof 12 or 13 metres high." This "Great Road" is the "Sacred Way" of the old palaeolithic tribes, the great avenue of gods, totems and men.

The ceiling is pierced "at intervals" by domes "of perfect beauty; none are more regular in shape, and they could serve as models for the cleverest architects". Did the ancient builders of Saint-Front visit Rouffignac? Delfau dare not say. He is aware of the climatic changes in the cave, and he warns us that "the soil is wetter. You walk in a very sticky, muddy earth". Since reading this learned paper of Delfau's, I hardly know whether I can speak of the "sea of mud". Perhaps I should call it, as he does, *terre bolaire* (clayey earth), not merely "clay"!

The Sea of Mud

Well, no. From now on we will speak of the "sea of mud" or "glue" of Rouffignac, for the term is expressive, and for us it is a link with our Master who was the first to use this onomatopaeic and graphic expression at his first visit, on July 1, 1956. "The glue . . . the glue . . ." At the end of a hard and heavy day, twelve hours in those thrilling depths, we were coming back full of fresh knowledge, loaded with prospective responsibilities, and on our way back the clip-clop of our shoes, sinking ever more deeply, accompanied our second crossing of "the glue". How heavy it was, that Périgordian mud, that yellow clay sticking to our soles, the glue, the glue! Should we ever get rid of it and follow a straighter, lighter path? The glue . . . To us this bogging-down at Rouffignac was like Nessus' tunic. The glue: it was Rouffignac itself, sticking to us and paralysing us, too, for violating its secrecy and bringing it into the outside world! No! It was not Rouffignac; what is in Rouffignac cannot be hostile. The mud we carried out was only a foretaste of the yapping pack that would cling to our coat-tails when they heard the news! Mud, yes, that would be the mud. That would be it. . .

Towards the Labanche

Although this part of the cave is more humid, in spite of this "clamminess", to quote another expressive term from Delfau, "there are very few stalactites to be seen there". The roof sometimes rises very high, to 30 or 45 ft., and dark openings bear witness to the slow and relentless destruction caused by subterranean waters, after flowing freely for a time on the Pradelian plateau which, one guesses, is not far away. There are 20 or 30 yds., certainly not more, between you and broad daylight, measured in a straight line, but you have already followed the galleries for 500 yds., and this gives you rather a shock. And for miles and miles, as the galleries are more or less horizontal, you will still be underground, beneath 100 ft. of earth, but getting farther and farther from the light outside. Pushing on all the time but remaining at the same level; advancing all the time, and getting farther and farther from the light! These are some of the "natural paradoxes" of Rouffignac, and I sometimes wonder whether Rouffignac is not made in the likeness of our wretched humanity. Man, too, no doubt, makes constant

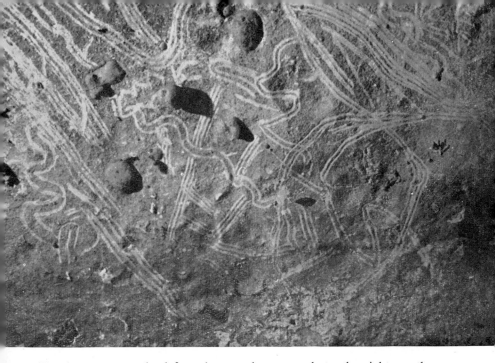

17. A serpent to the left and an anthropomorph to the right on the Serpents' Dome

18. Anthropomorphic figure on the Serpents' Dome

19. The two fighting mammoths in the Two Mammoths' Gallery

progress, moves on ever faster, multiplies his inventions and builds up his techniques: does that raise his level? I mean his REAL HUMAN LEVEL. Is Man any the better for it? Is he any nearer to happiness, peace and serenity, to real peace of soul, to a fully balanced state?

The Golden Age

We know that old legends are always founded in fact, and the very language that gave birth to them and conveyed them still reaches us in a few syllables. We know, too, that all the cosmogonies in the world dwell upon a Golden Age, a happy childhood of humanity. There must have been some such happy Age, and it is the business of Archaeology to find it for us. Two chronological periods (and neighbouring periods) have a valid claim to represent that age: the end of the upper palaeolithic era, that of the mammoths of Rouffignac, and the dawn of the neolithic era. Before that would be too early, for man was then too needy, too much burdened with the perpetual search for food and with wanderings from one place to another; after it would be too late, for it was then that the neolithic world, acquiring new foodstuffs, game tied to the land in the form of domesticated animals, supplies of vegetables also kept handy in the form of plants cultivated in a field, first acquired the idea of property, that of fixed territorial boundaries and the notion of the State rising above the notion of Man. With the help of a crazy demography the way lay open to the most numerous, strongest, richest and most all-powerful tribe.

What if the province then took the place of the plot of land, and the State that of the province? The race went on and the goal was never reached. When men thought they had reached it, it withdrew before them, and they sank even more deeply into the frenzy of rivalry and the craze for speed.

Tomorrow? There will be 3,500 million specimens of *Homo sapiens* in 1980 (*sapiens*—what irony!), 4,800 millions in the year 2,000. Will there be 128,000 millions in 2,500?

Tomorrow? Our flying-machines will use all the speed of their atomic engines to hover over Orly in foggy weather, while the earth will turn beneath them, less fast than they. And when they alight, their crews will not recognise the airport or the calendar!

Tomorrow? Some deliberately contrived and instantaneous cataclysm will make ancient history of good old natural disasters like the Lisbon earthquake, the eruption of Pelée or the explosion of Santorin. Henceforth Man must do better. But who, except

H

some old fossil of a historian, thinks today of Lisbon, Pelée or Santorin? The species will disappear, and it, too, will survive only as a legend. Already France, always in the van of progress, is reducing history lessons in her primary schools, showing the way for other grades of learning and other enlightened countries.

Civilisation and Facility

Perhaps the Golden Age of Rouffignac will sink back into the oblivion from which we have rescued it with so much trouble! Is not the Golden Age still there, still present and alive, in the depths of the Cro du Cluzeau? "The leisure of an easy life." I remember that phrase of the great prehistorian Piette; for him it explained the drawings of reindeer, bison and horses on bone scrapers, the carvings of reindeer on daggers and clubs, the drawings and paintings in the caves, the bounding or crouching bison of Altamira. Did the Arts spring from the leisure of an easy life? But life was anything but easy in the early palaeolithic era, the time of the reindeer, bison and mammoth, when ice, snow and tundra bit so cruelly into Europe. The direct effect of this hard climate on human living conditions was to compel men to live not on the flora of their time (very poor, of course, compared with the "warm temperate" flora of the earlier interglacial periods), but almost entirely on the fauna. The upper palaeolithic era, 20,000 or 30,000 years before our time, became exclusively the period of hunting, we may say of big-game hunting. In the vital matter of nourishment there was established a complete predominance of animal food. Now, any human economy is more insecure in proportion as its target becomes more restricted and uniform.

Just so, the neolithic era marked a revolutionary turning-point in human economy with its varied collective resources, both vegetable and animal, adding new products of agriculture and cattle-raising to the traditional products of hunting and fishing. This variety was a valuable protection against famine. It favoured social development. The scarcity of palaeolithic resources was dangerous and full of risks: famine, the decimation of populations and a short-lived humanity. At thirty the reindeer and mammoth hunter was an old man whose days were numbered. This paucity of resources was even more dangerous because it depended on hunting, which was still more chancy than the previous dependence on foraging for vegetables. Game varies both in its movements and in its numbers. The hunting régime of palaeolithic times was a régime of economic insecurity. Phases of plenty, no doubt, alternated with phases of want when game was scarce, but the morrow was always a source of painful anxiety.

This meant living from hand to mouth, a life of anxiety that the sorcerer would find ways to exploit. It might seem that art for art's sake would be foreign to such an atmosphere, in a civilisation of great hunters but also of fear. I do not believe this since we have found Rouffignac.

The great friezes of Rouffignac are art for art's sake. They are real picture-galleries conceived for the pleasure of their admirers and executed with love and with no thought but to create a thing of beauty.

In times of famine the sorcerer chief must have drawn the mammoth to "create" the game his people wanted, but in periods of plenty, when bellies waxed fat in the light of lamps well supplied with grease, when whole haunches of game were stored for days on end, for more days than could be counted on one's fingers, when there was a slackening of the demand for "reality pictures" to "create" game and it was good to wander in quiet galleries with a mild temperature of 60° F.—when the "feast" days came round, why should not the artist-sorcerer seek to "realise his vision and give material being to his dreams"? Why should he not paint, with broad, bold strokes, the great mammoth frieze?

No, it is not the leisure of an easy life that gives birth to art. It is rather the rare pauses in a life of hardship.

Ease has never founded great civilisations or given rise to great forms of art. Ease is a putting to sleep, a descent into the tomb, not a spur. Country life has never produced "great centuries"; civilisations bear the names of towns, never those of the countryside. The latter indeed produces men, but these men only too rarely enjoy even the pauses in a life of hardship. They are often the slaves of Nature.

In their hard, healthy and strictly ordered lives, our great ancient hunters must have known a mingling of want and plenty and painted and drawn from hard necessity and for pleasure in turn. Alternately they were artists to live and artists for love. Once caught up in his craft, the artist hardly knew why he drew. He drew as he breathed. Art was born at last, and humanity knew its real Golden Age.

Tomorrow?

The Golden Age is behind us, a little farther behind us every day, as daylight fades at every step in the galleries of Rouffignac. Does this mean we shall never see it again? The answer to this new fear lies with man, and with man alone, not with his slaves and his technicians and his machines, for these have no life. It lies, to be more precise, with the two or three thousand millions of living beings who share and dispute the world.

No, we must not go back to crawling on all fours. In any case, our mammoth hunters walked like you and I, as did all their many ancestors. We must not go back to the dark life of caves and caverns, which now correspond with the greatest perils to our species. It will suffice to think out and understand the meaning of human evolution. It will suffice to shed a few illusions.

Just as the ancient outline of a mammoth is not eternal, though it may be 20,000 years old, so Humanity will not progress for ever, though it has progressed for a million years and that progress accelerates at a crazy speed. As for man himself, has he changed? "Ceaseless progress, always at the same level; ceaseless progress, away from the light": unconsciously that phrase, the "natural paradox of Rouffignac", came to me as I followed the "Great Road" of the cave in the footsteps taken by A. Delfau in Year XI of the Republic, that "Great Road where one sees few stalactites". It is true that straw torches, which burn badly in that heavy air, do not give enough light to "enable us to examine objects placed at a certain height". Those words have both a material and a spiritual meaning.

Still underground

On this "Great Road", like many of his predecessors, our guide points out in passing "the tomb of Gargantua", calling it "the tomb of some giant like those Sons of the Earth who, the poets tell us, are buried beneath the rocks of Mount Etna".

"Near the end of the Great Road," he continues, "you enter a branch called the 'Alley of the Labanche', remarkable for a quantity of very fine cauliflowers that cover its walls and hang from its roof. These stalactites, which have a perfect resemblance to the vegetable after which they are named, make a pleasant series of bouquets in this place. But it is difficult to pull any of them off (again the same utility reflex) and to get a whole one you must use a chisel and cut through the rock, to which they adhere strongly."

"Leaving Labanche, you pass into a chamber with a narrow and difficult entrance, where you have to go down a rather steep staircase. But soon the roof rises and you find a great room known as the 'Market', whose structure is very fine. The ceiling, especially, is remarkable for the domes which are more numerous there than anywhere else and are filled with flint branches whose various shapes produce a very agreeable and singular effect. The floor is of clayey earth, still wet, and it shows the footprints of all the people who go through this place; and when you see these footprints all over the ground, it is easy to understand why the chamber is called the Market-place."

Of course, the "cauliflowers" have long vanished under the blows of vandal hammers, and the footprints are superimposed and confused, but the domes, with their pretty bunches of flint, remain. They form the ceiling with the many snake-like interlacings marked by fingers on the red clay, between the projecting flint "kidneys". Oddly enough there are very few scribblings or signatures, only two or three on each side of the ceiling thus decorated with "serpents" and figures.

A blocked Passage

"Coming out of this room, we arrive at last at the opening of the great branch, but we must stop for a few moments to look at two landslides near the end of the 'Great Road' and towards the south side of the mountain. If we examine them carefully, we cannot doubt that this fallen material, which comes from the roof, has blocked a passage." We are, in fact, just under a former chimney into which the waters of the plateau fell, and through which sand, water and gravel from outside still percolate. And our guide remarks: "The fall of rock, which is on the left, clearly shows the shape of the opening; moreover the branches of this cave get steadily narrower and slope down at their ends. Here, on the contrary, the vault is high, and there is no doubt that other underground passages lie beyond these subsidences, among them a new air shaft which is the former geological entry into Rouffignac!"

The Great Branch

"It is near this spot (continues Delfau) that the Great Branch begins. (This is the Western Branch or Sacred Way, which is as long as all the rest of the cave.) Without going into the details of its innumerable ramifications, it is enough to say that they are, as in the other branch, always very curious and varied. But we cannot resist halting for a moment under a vault which is well worthy of examination. Men have never built one stronger or more elegant. The centre of this vault is low, jutting towards the ground in the form of an inverted cone and meeting another cone that stands below. All around and towards the ends of the chamber you will find the same trick of Nature, and these cones, which are regularly spaced, leave arches between them which form so many passages leading round the dome. The latter is shaped exactly like a parasol."

This geological architecture is to be found in several parts of the Rouffignac galleries and also in the "serpents'" ceiling. Secondary domes more or less flank the central dome, like chapels radiating from a great central crypt. Was this arrangement noticed by the palaeolithic artists who engraved the ceilings? An accurate plan of the distribution of the interlacings and "serpents" in the hollows of these vaults will perhaps yield a favourable answer. A rapid and very superficial examination enabled us to note that the serpent represented is engraved along the axis of the great rotunda, FACING THE ENTRANCE. Such a privileged position seems to show the importance of this serpent, and the many little streamers that accompany him are perhaps serpent-symbols, too! Is this the "great red dome of the serpents"?

We must lay down a working method. We must study many figures, not only by themselves but in their context and in their topographical position. A figure sometimes derives all its importance from its placing, as does the "sorcerer" of the Trois-Frères cave, or the composite creature with great antennae at Lascaux, which is Figure No. 1 for present-day visitors and perhaps forms a magical representation of some disguised sorcerer and the last image to be visited by palaeolithic pilgrims.

Another prophecy for Rouffignac!

"After this chamber [says Delfau] we find several others worthy of notice. One, especially, is very curious, though it escapes the notice of most travellers; its entrance is so narrow that one can easily pass by without seeing it. Citizen Gonthier, of Miremont, who worked on the first plan of this cave in 1765, made the discovery." (Another citizen who has forgotten his predecessors, forgetting also that many others, sometimes illustrious, made a plan of Rouffignac before him. What a fine specimen of historical reconstruction!)

But let us get on to his discovery, which seems to be genuine, and that is the main point. "This room, which one could believe to be lined with diamonds, has the finest crystallisations, and every part of it is intact." We are in Year XI of the Republic, of the First Republic, that is to say, not in Year XI of the Fourth! But A. Delfau has no illusions about the longevity of these crystals. "It is to be feared," he writes, "that when the place is better known, the chisel will attack its walls."

What a fatal human law it is that destruction must so often follow discovery! So much so that the scientist is often in a cruel dilemma. The physicist cannot announce a new micro-division of the atom with a light heart, or the archaeologist a rediscovered city or an ornamented cave. They know that the newly-split atom will be the decisive step towards the annihilation of a million men at one blow, that the black swarm of greed will descend upon the city to scatter its ashes, that the cave will be invaded by those who want to claw at the paint to see if it holds and will be criticised even by those who have not yet seen it, vilified by those who ought to have seen it, to such a point that one dreams of a decorated cave somewhere in another limestone France, the position of which would be locked in the most secret recesses of one's heart.

One would tell the secret to no one, save oneself. One would go in secret pilgrimage to drink selfishly from that deep spring. No learned colleague would know of its existence, no Commission, no ministerial Department, no journalist, no sightseer, no idle tourist longing to while away his compulsory and organised leisure, no one . . .

If it has a hundred times fewer mammoths than Rouffignac, that will be enough. It will be the new Secret Cave. And it will be ours, gentlemen, for we have plenty of time to find it, and it will be even more beautiful than Rouffignac, for its mystery will be preserved.

At last, the Stream

"After having examined the main parts of the Great Branch [says Delfau] we finish with the Stream, which is not the least remarkable part of the cave. It is a funnel-shaped abyss, into which one descends by rather difficult steps." So the clay steps we still use today are several centuries old, and in spite of perpetual tramping they are better preserved, perhaps, than stone steps would be! But they are not "palaeolithic", though the men of the mammoth explored the "abyss", for at that time the crater was smaller. Subsidences and falls of clay have enlarged it since the paintings were done.

"On arriving at the bottom, how great is the traveller's surprise! He looks up and sees before him a passage running out of sight between high rocks" (lighting was very poor in 1803). "At his feet flows a stream which crosses the entrance and disappears. He enters this winding passage, which contains a remarkable series of acute and re-entrant angles, and he views with astonishment a whole cavity quite separate from the cave. It lies more than 10 metres (more than 30 ft.) below the floor of the cave, and it contains none of the features which are characteristic of the upper levels. Some great natural force seems to have made this new passage at a later date. If you follow it, you will come again upon the stream that you lost at the entrance. It winds like the Styx in these dark depths. As you follow the labyrinth, the paths multiply and become more difficult. Torches throw only a faint light on them and the road, plunging ever deeper, seems to be leading you to Tartary."

The lost Children of Rouffignac

The example of the two Dutchmen who were lost at the beginning of the 18th century did not suffice. Nor did that of Monsieur de Barry. The indefatigable Delfau tells us the story of an engineer who made a plan of the cavern in 1765, when M. de Boutin, Intendant of the district of Bordeaux, came to visit it. "The engineer nearly lost his life in these labyrinths (of the Stream) with two others who had followed him. Having gone deep into this passage without thinking much of the long journey back again, they suddenly saw that their lights were going out. Terror seized them and they would inevitably have perished if the engineer, keeping his presence of mind, had not succeeded in getting out of the galleries and bringing the guide to rescue his companions.

"It is related that three workmen who entered the cave without a guide about fifty years ago" (that is, about the middle of the 18th century) "died there, victims of their folly. A dog they had taken in with them was clever enough to find his way out, and this led to their discovery. Not seeing his master come out, the dog would not move from the entrance. The regular guide to the cave, who lived quite near (on one of the tenant farms of the plateau, known as 'l'Egal', now called the 'Shepherdess's Farm'), saw the dog rooted to the spot and was struck by its obvious uneasiness, which suggested that someone might be lost in the cave. He went in, followed by a number of people carrying many torches, and they found these unfortunates in different places, where they had collapsed from terror and despair. One of them was still breathing." Our author adds that to prevent such accidents two walls were built about 50 *toises* from the entrance, but crowds of sightseers almost destroyed them. It is much more likely that these walls dated from the troubles during the wars of religion in the 16th century. The fact that they were double shows that they were built as defences. You don't build a wall merely to prevent your fellow man from getting lost.

Rouffignac has its walls, and there are legends attached to them. The last "Wall", that of 1956, is certainly not the one which has made least ink flow or loosened fewest tongues in the country round. But it fits normally into the traditions of Rouffignac, and it does not disfigure the underground landscape.

We shall follow our guide no farther, in spite of the risk we may run in entering this cave without foresight. He has finished his story, but he spins it out with "natural" and geological considerations. We shall, however, note his conclusion: "The cave is worth seeing and inspecting carefully."

A. Delfau is the last poet of Rouffignac! His successors will be indifferent to the beauties buried underground and to their deep human meanings. They will no longer compare the Périgordian cave with that which sheltered the daughters of Nereus. They will not mention the Sons of the Earth under the rocks of Etna, and the Stream will be just a stream again, no longer Styx

IN THE TIME OF MARTEL

The Antiquities of Vésone, 1821

In 1821, in the time of Louis XVIII, the Duc de Richelieu and the Comte de Villèle, W. de Taillefer wrote his *Antiquities of Vésone*.

Druidical customs were then in fashion, and he could not resist regarding several Périgordian caves as "Druidic". The Druids inherited all the mysteries of the past, and as flint axes were "Celtic" or antediluvian the oldest customs were supposed to be Druidic. Therefore "the caves of Domme, of the Drouilh forest, of Cadouin, of Vitrac, and perhaps one (now almost filled up) near Vésone, under Ecorne-boeuf (a prehistoric site corresponding with the oldest in Périgueux) were Druidic, according to this writer. So were several of those in the Dordogne valley, in the plains of the Isle, in the Drôme, in the Vésère, etc. etc. So above all was the famous cave of Miremont, about which former cosmographers had woven a thousand dreams. In it they saw altars, mosaics and statues, all things quite foreign to the Druidic cult, which were never there at all. In the age of ignorance all those tricks of Nature which are so common in limestone caves and in all those of Périgord, were taken for man's handiwork. A few people have tried to explain these dreams by suggesting that incrustations may have covered all these marvels since that time; but for so large a cave, incrustations are very rare at Miremont. Besides, they are hardly anywhere thick enough to prevent the rock from being laid bare by a tap with a hammer". (Decidedly, the cave of Miremont lives under the hammer).

Yet all these altars, mosaics and statues have disappeared. Make way for the Druids! The intellectual attitude of W. de Taillefer is instructive; it is also a lesson in modesty. Today the Druids have disappeared; make way for the mammoth-hunters! But are we not still deep in the age of ignorance for those who will judge us fifty years hence? Let us be careful, for perhaps our mammoth-hunters will be deposed also, as the Druids, the daughters of Æneas and the Sons of the Earth have been. Dynasties change; so do the occupants of caves and also scientific theories. Cosmographers and scientists change, too, and are forgotten or will be, but the memory of Æneas will survive as long as there are educated men. Memory holds the images of poets longer than those of savants, because the works of scientists are always obsolescent, one displacing another.

Isidor Isaac Rabi, Nobel prizewinner for physics in 1944, is certainly one of the greatest physicists in the world. But I wager that in 1,000 years, if humanity still exists, very few men will know his name, though they will cherish the name of Paul Valéry as we cherish that of Homer.

Périgord illustrated

Years pass, and Rouffignac-Miremont falls asleep. The world is in too great turmoil to take much interest in the cave. Abbé Audierne, in his *Perigord* (*illustré*) (1851), quickly sketches "the famous cave" which was reported and described long ago. He repeats the old clichés. "You stop at an abyss that cannot be plumbed but reveals, at a great depth, winding passages between the rocks that lead one to suppose the cave goes farther still. But there the torches go out, and certain death awaits the rash explorer who would push ahead." Visits, then, will stop at the crater of the abyss. Abbé Audierne declares: "When I visited it with M. Romieu, then Prefect of the Dordogne, and M. Marot, a mining engineer, we found a great many bones and a bear's tooth. It took us seven hours to explore the cave."

The *Topographical Dictionary* of 1873 gives only a few lines to Miremont, "the finest cave in the Department, 1,067 metres deep". (O magic of precision! O mathematical prestige of those 7 metres!

At last Martel came . . .

The end of the 19th century was marked by the devouring activity of Eduard Alfred Martel, the originator of cave-exploring and underground science. From 1883 to 1887 he explored caves in the Cévennes before attacking the great natural caverns farther West: Dargilan, Bramabiau, Padirac.

In 1893 he was at Rouffignac and he mapped it in two days with MM. Rupin and P. and A. Lalande, plotting 4,800 metres of galleries. In its general lines and even in many details Martel's plan follows that made by Gabriel Bouquier in the 19th century. Did he have the old plan in his head? One is amazed at the work done in two days, even with two diligent assistants. The Martel plan may be regarded as a reliable working basis, especially in the general distribution of paintings and engravings. It was necessary, however, to make much more detailed sectional plans of the areas especially rich in parietal drawings, and this was done in October 1956, for the main section of the Henri Breuil gallery, by Jacques L.-R. Nougier.

Though Martel noted the peculiarity of Rouffignac, he thought the cave was fossilised and contained no running water whatever. He missed the lower level, seen and described by François de Belleforest in 1575. Martel did not undertake to explore the Stream.

Martel's "Foirail"

When the controversy over Rouffignac was at its height, our opponents often repeated one question: "But how is it that nobody saw the paintings in a cave so much visited and so often recorded by engineers or topographers? We can understand it for the drawings, but the paintings are so obvious! How do you explain the fact that nobody saw them, not even Martel?"

Our opponents demanded a proof that would be very hard to furnish: a negative fact concerning a man who was dead!

But it was not a fact. Martel DID see the paintings of Rouffignac. Proof of this was brought to us indirectly by the Comte de Chalup, President of the Syndicat d'Initiatives and a man of wide learning if ever there was one. During a visit to La Pradelie the Comte de Chalup showed Mme Plassard jr., the "young woman in a blue smock" of this sinister story, a PRINTED plan of Rouffignac made by Martel.

The word *Foirail* is PRINTED exactly at the position of the Breuil gallery, on the spot where the great frieze of rhinoceroses and mammoths is. Apart from this, Jean Bouchereau confirmed to me at the National Library that in a work entitled *The Abysses* of 1894 and in *Unknown France* (1928), Martel's plan is marked *Foirail* (fairground) at the great junction formed by the Sacred Way and the beginning of the Breuil gallery, where rhinoceroses disport themselves, with mammoths a little farther on. This is the case according to "the plan of the Crau de Grandville, also called the cave of Miremont or Rouffignac, in the Dordogne, made on August 12 and 13, 1893". Let us note in passing the use of the name "Rouffignac" for which the little cave-explorers reproach us.

Is not this use of the term *Foirail* revealing? The Comte de Chalup offered this explanation, which for our part we willingly accept: "Rouffignac is the shadow of Altamira."

Altamira

A few historic dates will throw light on the problem.

1868. A huntsman unexpectedly discovers a great cave in Cantabria (N.W. Spain), not far from Santillana del Mar. This cave will be called Altamira.

The landowner, Don Marcelino S. de Sautuola, explores this subterranean formation on his estate. He is an enlightened proprietor and something of an archaeologist as well.

1875. Sautuola makes a search and finds fossil bones of the bison, the horse and the great stag.

1879. Sautuola begins important excavations in the cave.

1879. His daughter, little Maria, discovers the Altamira frescoes. "*Papa, mira toros pintados!*" (Father, look at the painted bulls!)

1880. International Congress in Lisbon.

Archaeologists refuse to visit Altamira.

Cartailhac, the French delegate, walks out, indignant, while Sautuola tries in vain to win recognition for his marvellous discovery. "Be careful, the Jesuits painted Altamira!" he is told. Sautuola dies without getting Altamira authenticated.

1893. E. A. Martel makes a plan of Rouffignac. He notes paintings at the intersection of the Stream gallery and a gallery on the right. A dilemma faces Martel. How important and how valuable are these strange animal portraits? Is this a "new Altamira"? Should he start another controversy?

According to the Comte de Chalup, E. A. Martel dared not assume such a responsibility in 1893. He merely "noted" his observation, and that was why he marked the word *Forail* on his plan.

The state of mind surrounding the discovery of the first prehistoric paintings (and even the last; have we progressed in 1956?) being what it was, Martel avoided responsibility.

1895. Discovery of drawings at La Mouthe. This is a decisive step. Now Martel travels about the world searching for caves and deep pot-holes. Like many others, he never returned to Rouffignac.

Human Progress again . . .

So Martel, too, was a "discoverer" of Rouffignac! But after François de Belleforest, that does not matter in the least. We do not claim the title of "discoverer". We claim the scientific responsibility of having brought Rouffignac to the world, in spite of and against the Périgordians—Rouffignac in Périgord!

Besides, it is inconceivable that the same mistakes and absurdities should be committed in 1956 as in 1878! It is the more inconceivable as we have Altamira, the first in time of the painted caves, while Rouffignac is the 100th!

The opponents of 1956 have none of the excuses of the opponents of 1879. Our predecessors had at least the excuse of novelty. The "moderns" cannot even claim extenuating circumstances; on the contrary, their circumstances are singularly damning. Is this the happy result of three centuries of compulsory public education, in the Holy Land of Prehistory? What a failure!

A French teacher may be allowed to be ignorant of the structure of a Maya temple, but it is quite intolerable that he should know nothing about the rudiments of the archaeology of his own country. Yet there is no lack of goodwill. I see many signs of it around me, schoolmasters trying to inform themselves, to understand the prehistoric past that they touch every day, at every step. I always receive them with interest and with kindness. I could fill three pages of this book with the names of those who have come from the Somme or the Vaucluse, the Tarn or the Aisne, from Languedoc or Normandy.

Rouffignac nearly missed being found

The discoveries of prehistoric caves in the neighbourhood of Les Eyzies struck a terrible blow at underground touring at Rouffignac. On April 11, 1895, Gaston Bertoumeyrou, almost a child, found a bison engraved in the cave of La Mouthe and informed Emile Rivière.

The latter undertook to prospect the gallery and organised excavations. Archaeological deposits of the palaeolithic era blocked the opening. The drawings, then, must also go back to a very distant date, earlier than the deposits.

Young Bertoumeyrou's chance discovery started an avalanche of finds in that district. Emile Rivière employed local peasants to clear the Mouthe gallery. One of them, Pomarel, noticed similar drawings in a gallery at Combarelles which belonged to his parents-in-law. For a long time this gallery had been given over to rural uses. It was partly closed by a wall of uncemented stones, forming a useful stable for plough-oxen. Pomarel told his schoolmaster, Denis Peyrony, of his find.

Dr. Capitan, Abbé Henri Breuil and Denis Peyrony went into the gallery on September 8, 1901, and Combarelles came into history. A week later, to the day, the same glorious team found the gallery of Font-de-Gaume, adding the prestige of paintings to the drawings already reported.

This month of September 1901 saw the cave of Rouffignac more or less abandoned. From that time on the taste for novelty and the fascination of prehistoric art favoured the caves in the Vézère valley, to the detriment of the comparatively slight natural interest of the Cro de Granville. Tourists were attracted by Man and by the innumerable traces of prehistoric habitation and the painted caves where Man performed his rites.

Yet Rouffignac had an accredited guide, M. Massaubra, a road-mender at Fleurac, who is now seventy-six years old. From 1900 to 1926 he took people to see the "Cro-Granville". He scrambled down the slopes at Fleurac, opposite the cave, crossed into the parish of Rouffignac and did the honours of the "underground". As he went he showed all the curiosities, including the "Old Woman's Seat", that great stalagmite marked on Gabriel Bouquier's plan: "C: Old Woman's Seat." And the worthy road-maker habitually used an expression dating from before Robespierre and Danton, the lewd word already used by Lagrange-Chancel in 1730, when Louis XV was twenty years old.

Mme Massaubra, aged 72, the road-mender's wife, also conducted tourists. That summer she sadly confided to Jean Guichard, a journalist from Bordeaux who came to "interview" her, a surprise that threw a very clear and deeply psychological light on the "unease of Rouffignac": "Why was the discovery made by Pyreneans, not by local people?" Why? Because the cave of Rouffignac happens to be a Pyrenean cave, lost in Périgord. Because the Périgordians were often unlucky, seldom persevering and often ignorant.

In 1915, however, Rouffignac was near making its entry into history. Abbé Breuil, the "discoverer" of Combarelles and Font-de-Gaume, who was already well known all over the world and had exceptional experience of cave-art, arrived at the entrance.

Unfortunately he was not alone. He brought a very well-known and distinguished entomologist, M. Alluaud, who was a specialist in beetles and was anxious personally to collect specimens of a *Trechus cavernicolus* peculiar to this cave, which had been reported long before. Quickly, in less than an hour, M. Alluaud captured the insect he coveted. And the two scientists left the cave in a hurry, the entomologist never to return and the Abbé to learn with great surprise on July 16, 1956, as he alighted from the Paris express at Bordeaux, that we wanted him to come to Rouffignac, forty-one years after his first visit to the cave. The visit of 1915 had lasted barely an hour and had been confined to one gallery leading to the left.

First Prehistoric signs

The softness of the clayey limestone, with large flints embedded in it at various levels, and the great mass of sticky mud made the Abbé very doubtful of finding drawings, paintings or engravings. And indeed, the start of the expedition enabled him only to make a difficult acquaintance with the first few hundred yards of the cavern, 200 or 300 at the most. It is only beyond the "Sea of Mud" and the big landslide that the walls become fit to carry drawings and paintings, both by their substance and by the nature of their surface. Abbé Breuil noticed on a ceiling, however, a few of those traces of human fingers that we call "macaronis". "That makes me think," he said, "that we may get some results if we examine the cave more thoroughly." But he was then very busy with important work and travels abroad, and he did not come back until 1956.

None the less, he passed on his observations to one of his colleagues, Abbé Glory, who had found the paintings in the Baume-Latrone cave in the Gard, which was discovered by four schoolboys from Nîmes, Gabriel Suther, Roques, Pierre Morizot and Paul de Foïard. Abbé Glory came to Rouffignac in 1948, accompanied by MM. Vidal and Bay and Dr. F. Ed. Koby, of Basle. Dr. Koby is undoubtedly the best specialist on quaternary bears. We owe to him a series of final accounts of the civilisations known as those of the "Alpine Bear-Hunters", which have reduced great imaginative build-ups to their proper scale.

The Abbé came to Rouffignac to get a few photographs of bears' claw-marks. He was quickly satisfied. But the three explorers arrived at the cave entrance very late, when night had fallen. They explored the right-hand gallery, and Dr. Koby and M. Bay stopped short at the good claw-marks and took some excellent pictures. Meanwhile, Abbé Glory continued his prospecting. But it was now midnight, and no doubt they had a long journey to make the next day. They hurried to the surface, and discovery once more eluded them.

20. Deeply engraved mammoth on the left side of the Sacred Way

21. The Paolo Graziosi rhinoceros engraved on the roof before the
Breuil Gallery

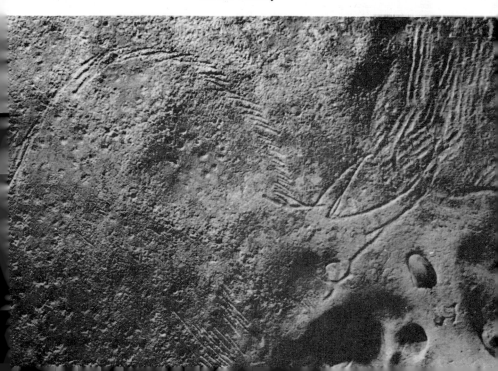

22. Entrance to the Henri Breuil Gallery

THE LITTLE CAVE-EXPLORERS

Enter the Little Cave-Explorers

The year 1945 saw a revival of activity at the Cro de Granville or Cave of Miremont. The names are interchangeable, but we are in the commune of Rouffignac.

A few very young men, delightful boys, no doubt, were seized with a fine and praiseworthy desire to explore the subterranean cavities of their Perigordian soil, which is as full of holes as a well-made Gruyère cheese. Often, in countries which have caves, tunnels and *cros*, in all "holey" regions, inquisitive and sporting youth finds in this exploring something to exercise its muscles and its wits. No doubt, too, this is a more intelligent pastime than kicking a ball that never bursts or throwing it into a basket which is holed already.

Thus, "spelaeological" zeal, as we must now call it, brought together a few young men of Périgueux. Young Bernard Pierret, aged sixteen to seventeen, was the leader, probably because of his hardihood and courage and also because he was studying for examinations. In a few years he would be a schoolmaster in a little village in the Dordogne. His troops were Robert de Faccio and Gabriel Gérin. These were his two lieutenants, of the same age as himself, whom we shall see again later, one as a master mason, the other setting up telegraph poles for the Electricité de France in the district of Oran in Algeria.

For the time being their ambition (which they achieved) was to go as far as possible in prospecting the Cave of Miremont. E. A. Martel, in his quick survey, had forgotten the lower levels, in which deep underground streams flow.

"Our discoveries," writes Bernard Pierret in his *Périgord souterrain*, "revealed active internal streams. For five years, from our first personal visit to our great final camp in 1949, in the course of forty expeditions making a total of more than 1,000 hours' work, sometimes camping underground (at first with A. Pierret, later with Dr. M. Latour), we were able to explore 2,800 metres (3,160 yds.) of new galleries, of which we did not see the end. These galleries

I

consist essentially of narrow corridors and sunken streams. Exploring these corridors and streams is incredibly difficult, tiring and slow. In the galleries you have to squeeze endlessly between jagged walls on which you tear your skin and your clothing as you hang suspended over pits into which it would not be nice to fall. In the streams, on the other hand, you must crawl constantly in icy water, slipping on the slimy clay that covers everything and cutting yourself painfully on sharp flints, always concealed in just the right places."

Spelaeological results

This fine underground adventure paid, for the young explorers never complain of their efforts. "Not one of us will ever regret the hard hours of Miremont." It also paid by its results: the mileage of the cave was increased, placing it third among French caverns, after the underground river at Bramabiau and the great labyrinth of the Dent de Crolles, which contains over ten miles of galleries and chambers. It would be truer to say that Rouffignac is the first cave of France, since Bramabiau is only the course of an underground river and the Dent de Crolles is a maze of galleries which have been connected artificially by piercing the "blind" sectors.

Finally, the expedition paid by yielding new data on the underground extent of the lower streams: a West stream, a South stream and a North stream, converging on the "Mona" chamber to form an East stream into which the North stream flows at a spot that has never yet been reached. This lower network corresponds only in part with the upper network of galleries. It prolongs them at a lower level, for the streams have sunk as they extended their course.

These explorations were not lacking in the keen and proper pleasures of discovery. "The joy of Saint-Ours and the Scouts of France when they reached the first stream, the joy of R. de Faccio, G. Gérin and M. Martin when they climbed the waterfall, the joy of H. Duroueix and G. Werner when they came out into the East stream, the joy of other teams finding the Mona chamber or the Stalactite stream, the joy of our regretted friend and colleague C. Moinot as he made his way along the South-West branches . . ." What true, deep, paying and profitable joys! Yet one regret remains. They did not complete their mission. Bernard Pierret, the leader of the team, was not as tactful with the owners of the Cro de Miremont as he was keen and courageous underground.

The cave was firmly sealed at the end of June 1949 by a double door, armour-plated below and fitted with strong bars above and mounted on stone walls. Nowadays the cave cannot be opened except with the permission of the proprietor—and above all with his key.

"Until then," says Bernard Pierret, "the owner freely allowed us to explore. Now he told us we should have to get the key from a farmer. Not finding it [or the farmer either, no doubt!] what would you have done in my place?"

We shall not yet reveal the reply of Bernard Pierret, aged twenty to twenty-one in 1949 and by then, no doubt, engaged in the noble task of an educator in the Dordogne, one of the most beautiful departments of France and its prehistoric department *par excellence*. We shall not yet reveal his reply, for with it we leave History for the Present, for Reality, the mangled and bleeding flesh of Today. . . .

Misadventures of Specialisation

Recent events have thrown light on all the visits the Rouffignac cave may have undergone. There was the visit of Abbé Breuil in 1915, that of Dr. Koby and Abbé Glory in 1948, that of Bernard Pierret's team from 1945 to 1949.

Abbé Breuil and his explorer friend Alluaud are in a hurry. They are looking for a rare beetle, and they find it.

Abbé Glory and Dr. Koby are in a hurry. They are looking for good bears' claw-marks, and they find them.

Bernard Pierret and his team of young cave-explorers are not in a hurry, but their search is a long business. They want to find new deep galleries. They ferret about, more or less on all fours, considering every hollow and every crevice worthy to receive them and prolong their journey. The lower galleries of the "stream" are what they are after, and they find them. Everyone finds what he seeks at Rouffignac, within the narrow bounds of his speciality and the time that is grudgingly allowed him. Here we find the two major obstacles to discovery at the present day: specialisation and lack of time.

Of course, all forms of knowledge grow quickly in complexity, and it becomes impossible to know all their aspects and master all their shades. Half a century ago, an historian would call himself a "specialist in ancient history", delighted to devote himself to that rich period without any care for mediaeval history or "modern" facts, and sometimes pitying some less lucky colleague obliged to teach general history and happy if he were not burdened also with geography, which should be independent. But all that has changed.

A few decades ago we had specialists on Rome and learned dis-
courses on Athens. Hardly a generation later we had to reckon
with the specialist on Sparta, while several learned men shared
Athens in the most literal sense, one devoting his life to the Erech-
theion and hardly glancing at his colleague, who was given over to a
passionate study of the Ceramic Quarter. Chronology, space, facts
themselves were so many reasons for cutting up, dividing and dis-
persing. That is an inescapable necessity of research, a condition
of progress and knowledge. And yet . . .

This extreme subdivision of subjects makes all the more admirable
certain exceptional work, such as that of Henri Focillon, to take an
example from one of my former Masters. From Pironese to
Buddhist art, from European painting in the 19th and 20th centuries
to the art of Roman sculptors, from aesthetics and the life of forms
to his admirable *Art d'Occident*, his palette was charged with colours
as various as they were distinguished.

Prehistory and Modernism

In prehistoric archaeology, which is a new school, one could
sometimes wish to be more highly trained, more highly "scientific",
one thinks, than in such a traditional school as history. And dispersed research does more harm there than elsewhere. The amateurs who still hold undisputed sway, at least by their numbers,
seem to delight in specialising in the mere dust of a subject. We
could easily find a solemn specialist on the fourth Solutreon, a rare
despiser of the second Magdalenian, an expert on gluttons' carvings
on bones less than 3 in. long, an obstinate Benedictine counting the
facet-stampings of the Seventh Levalloisian, and spending his life
at it. We must needs believe that the study of all these trees, all
these shrubs, all these plants, all these blades of grass, all these
vegetable cells is essential to knowledge and to progress. But we
cannot see the wood for the trees, and not only must we see the
wood, we must also see the plain, the desert, the ocean and the sky.

After having embraced the widest body of knowledge there is,
after having passed the test of intelligent specialisation without
narrowness, certain minds should specialise at least in non-specialisation. François de Belleforest was specialised in non-specialisation,
or else universal curiosity was his pastime.

That is why he tells so well of all the "marvels" of the future
Rouffignac, its fountains and its streams, the endless galleries and
the rooms and chambers paved with little stones, the traces of
animals great and small, the paintings here and there. . . .

Good old François de Belleforest! He is a geologist and cave-explorer of his time, an historian and an archaeologist, a tourist and a sightseer. He is a real "man", not a thinking-machine or a robot-explorer. He has time, too, that ample time the lack of which robbed hasty visitors of their discoveries. He has time to read and travel, time to make his visits, time, no doubt, to waste his time. He has time for enthusiasm about everything he has time to see!

François de Belleforest deserves to become a symbol for Rouffignac. The symbol of MAN.

Where time and specialisation were not respected

Why did we discover Rouffignac? How did that chance come our way? Why did one of us, a specialist in the western neolithic world to which at one time he was nearly confined, and the other, a fervent explorer of the Pyrenean world, escape from their specialities? One abandoned "his period" and the other "his geographical domain" because a few hours of freedom beckoned us, a few hours which enabled us to follow the old road taken by François de Belleforest or an unknown predecessor, the prehistoric road that led to the "Mammoths of the Discovery" on 26th of June in the Year of Grace 1956.

III
THE DISCOVERY OF ROUFFIGNAC

26 JUNE 1956

Consequences of an Accident

In 1946 my son Jacques had a serious accident and underwent an urgent operation. The surgeons recommended good milk and strengthening meat for the convalescent. At the beginning of August the family left for the Charolais, to stay with some good friends of our childhood. The school at Baudemont, above La Clayette, overlooking lush pastures dotted with white oxen and dominated by the wooded "mountain" of Dun, was then our retreat. The districts of La Clayette, Chauffailles, Matour and other places were under the jurisdiction of our friend the Judge, also an old pupil of the college at Nemours and the École Normale at Melun. I sometimes attended court sittings and took an interest in the life of the Charolais, as rich and calm as its fields and its horizons. Thus I made the acquaintance of local notables and found friends among them. It was only natural that I should meet M. Charles Plassard, a textile manufacturer of Varennes-sous-Dun and assistant magistrate at La Clayette, who was both the predecessor and the successor of "my Judge" when, in his absence, he presided paternally over his court. One of the daughters of the house, Janine, was preparing for an examination in the October term, and I gave her her first lessons in geographical sketching and block diagrams.

In the evening, when the many little bobbins were still and the heavy, greasy-smelling skeins no longer turned in the hot, thick air, we would sometimes talk. "You," M. Plassard would say to me, "who are interested in caves and not afraid of walking underground, ought to come to the Dordogne. I have a large estate there and it contains an immense cave."

But I had no time to accept this invitation, and also, I must confess, the requirements of scientific specialisation were then drawing me to other interests. A cave in the Dordogne could not contain traces of our earliest Western peasants! When you are writing a thesis and at the same time teaching in a secondary school, you have neither taste nor leisure for wider activities.

But my new friend became more persuasive. "There are such fine concretions. Sea anemones, my dear sir! Sea anemones in limestone!" But really, sea anemones did not tempt me, and I did not even ask the name of this huge cave, somewhere in the depths of the Dordogne.

For several years, when we went back to the Charolais, we got no further in our talks about caves. But every year we discussed them. My friend's lively and colourful accounts gave me a picture of his estate, with the tenant farms and woods above and "the cave" below —the cave of the starfish and anemones. Already, perhaps, he spoke less of the limestone anemones, for at each visit they seemed to fade away and vanish in the night. But the picture of the great cave never left me. I knew it slept somewhere, and I was sure it would wait for me. Yet it nearly escaped me, for "they" were at work there; "they" were exploring the mighty cave.

In August 1955, when my holidays took me from Paris to the Alps and from the Alps to Ampurias, I found my friend the Judge at Menton and my friend from the Charolais at Nice. For some years we had been working with Romain Robert, the founder of the active Prehistoric Society of the Ariège, in Pyrenean caves, excavating in the proto-Azilian and Magdalenian deposits in the cave of La Vache at Alliat and studying the painted caves along the chain formed by Niaux, Le Portal, Bédeilhac, Les Trois Frères, Marsoulas and Gargas. A few months earlier, together, we had "done" Monte Castillo, in Cantabria, and Altamira. The quaternary magic was beginning to work, in spite of the 20,000 years between us.

A Promise

That year, leaning on the balcony of M. Plassard's villa at Nice, I made a promise. "Well, it's a good idea; I'll go and see your cave this year. You will tell me where it is." But I never asked him. Ten months later, at the beginning of June 1956, the promise was still not kept. It was my wife who reminded me of my moral obligation. I wrote to my friend Plassard and received an address: Monsieur Louis Plassard, Domaine de La Pradelie, Rouffignac, Dordogne.

I see myself now, with his letter in my hand, consulting Michelin map No. 75 and searching with my finger for "Rouffignac". Les Eyzies, La Bugue, Rouffignac—there it was! There was a black star marked "cave" over the name of the village. Ah, I thought, there's a cave already marked; that promises well. If there's one there may be two, the limestone country must be favourable. In relation to Les Eyzies, Rouffignac was more or less a "pendant" of Lascaux. That also seemed a good sign to me.

What was more, I had permission to photograph the cave at Cougnac, not far from Gourdon, in the Lot. The coincidence was decidedly favourable: Romain and I would leave our excavating in the cave of La Vache and go and make our chief colour-pictures of Cougnac. Then we would go on to La Pradelie in the evening, and the next day we should see.

We made an appointment with the Plassards and we arrived at La Pradelie, via Gourdon, on the evening of June 25. There a warm welcome awaited us. We spoke of Nice and the Charolais, my former pupil, Janine, and our mutual friend, the Judge. And seated round a *foie gras* of Périgord, we spoke of the cave.

"I noticed a star on the Michelin map. Is your cave far from there?" I asked.

"But that's the one!"

The Cave of the Star

I seem to remember a violent nudge under the table. My friend was expressing his feelings—*our* feelings. The famous cave, for which we had come half across France—this was the Cave of the Star, a cave marked in the Michelin guide, a Tourist's Cave! We had followed a star like the Shepherds and the Magi, and the star was shining on the cave. But for us, this was not a new world coming into being, but a hope in ruins. What bad luck! "The cave" was the Cave of the Star!

Friendship is a great thing. It made us forget our disappointment.

We did not hurry to the cave at dawn the next day. Shamefully, we lay in bed. "The future belongs to early risers." But what was the use of getting up with the lark to visit a cave already marked in the Michelin guide?

We spent the morning sorting boxes of archaeological remains from the entrance to the cave, found when the opening was cleared about 1938. An examination of those flints and potsherds revealed at least four important periods of occupation. Some fine Grecian ornamentation even made me feel a slight excitement: a vague, very vague touch of enthusiasm. But the expressive pout of my companion brought me back to realities. We were not there to admire La Tène potsherds!

Early in the afternoon we entered the cave. We felt not even a faint desire to say: "At last!" That dull and joyless entry was as sour as a marriage of convenience. . . .

Discovery!

At 3.15 p.m. on June 26 we discovered the two fighting mammoths, the "Mammoths of the Discovery", drawn on the wall. It is impossible to tell the story of that day. Describing a day means living it again, and one cannot repeat such an experience. It was not even a day lived, but much rather a dream, an exhilarating procession from mammoth to mammoth. Mammoths to right of us, mammoths to left of us, mammoths above us—we knew not where to look! The great panel of five engraved mammoths on the right-hand wall jerked us out of an incredulous silence punctuated by that hackneyed word, so often repeated by the Radio: "Marvellous! Marvellous!" Was any other word appropriate?

Charles Plassard was still thinking of his anemones and starfish. "Come along . . . They're over here!" We longed to shout at him: "To hell with your starfish!" We wanted to see as soon as possible, for we were in a hurry then, that ceiling over the bed of a stream under which Mme Plassard had waited, one day, for young cave-explorers who had gone to plumb the very depths. At Menton, in the house of my friend the Judge, she had told me how bored she was that day with long hours of waiting, sharing her solitude with a smoking acetylene lamp. How, having nothing to do, she had read and re-read the few legible inscriptions, sprawling in broad smoke-trails over the ceiling. How she had thought then she could detect some finer lines, like drawings—*like animals*. She had noted them without knowing what they were, and later she recognised them with us. "Yes, I saw that one—and this one—no, I never saw these mammoths, they're too much scrawled over, but I recognise this ibex, the 'Dalbavie'."

Mme Plassard was an educated and cultured woman, but she owed her knowledge to a time when Prehistory was not taught in schools, but only the sage principles of Claude Bernard. She had a good degree dating from the last century, and I paid due attention to her remark: "There are finer lines, like drawings—like animals."

Across the years Mme Plassard had almost hit on the phrase used by François de Belleforest in 1575: "paintings in several places," and that of Canon Tarde at the beginning of the 17th century: "paintings of all sorts of animals." Bernard Pierret quotes this word "paintings" from the *Delights of France* of Savinien d'Alquié in his own pamphlet, *Périgord souterrain* (Underground Périgord), p. 105, line 16, written in 1953, three years before our visit. He must have read that word, since it is in his paper, but he did not understand it. He saw the paintings, too, but once more he did not understand.

Mme Plassard had seen the finer lines, and she had understood at least that she did not understand. That was the difference, no doubt, between her and Bernard Pierret: a difference of intelligence, that's all.

The Return

Do not imagine our return was exhilarating. It was dark already, and the crickets that chirped in the sun at the cave entrance had fallen silent. Under the pale green leaves of the chestnut trees we climbed the little path from the cave, already crushed by the huge weight of the mammoths of Rouffignac.

Two mammoths would have delighted us. Fifty were oppressive. We held a "council of war", for we foresaw what would happen. To find fifty mammoths or more, in a cave marked with a star in the Michelin guide, what a story! At first sight the fighting Mammoths of the Discovery and the innumerable finger-trails on the left-hand wall had pleased our critical spirits. And as the number of animals grew, we felt two contradictory thoughts fusing together in our minds: a more and more pressing desire for proofs of authenticity, and reassurance due to the immense number of drawings.

We realised that the "marvellous" importance of the discovery would give rise to controversy. We knew the archaeological world very well, especially its local or regional circles, from which we had already suffered elsewhere.

It was imperative that we should collect favourable proofs of the story we had to unfold. But the very number of our discoveries was already the best of proofs. As we bent over the engraved mammoths, including the last one "with the Roguish Eye", not yet so named, and lifted our eyes to the paintings on the Great Ceiling and then carefully examined the painted mammoths and rhinoceroses we found only good engraved or painted lines and well-drawn figures.

But what a responsibility, to throw such a flock to the wolves of the world of science! We had counted nothing, but we knew already that the Cave of the Star contained more mammoths and rhinos than any other cave in the world, perhaps more than all the others put together.

Poring over Martel's plan we discussed all that through the evening of that too heavy day, June 26. Through the open window blue moths and dragon-flies with soft, transparent wings flew in to flutter round the lamp. In the distance one could guess at the Vézère valley and the country around La Bugue, and we knew that Les Eyzies lay a little farther north.

We were only a few miles from it as the crow flies. In the morning, through a gap in the foliage, M. Plassard had shown us the white bluffs of Les Eyzies as we went down to the cave. What would the people of Les Eyzies think when they learned of the fabulous discovery made that very evening by two "Pyreneans" at their very gates?

First Move: inform the Abbé

Our council made one prompt decision, which was agreed to before any premise was discussed. We must inform the Abbé. Abbé Henri Breuil, Honorary Professor at the Collège de France and a member of the *Institut*, was the "discoverer" of Combarelles and the Font-de-Gaume in 1901. The Abbé had spent years and years crouching or lying in caves to make records of Altamira, Combarelles, the Trois-Frères, in a word, of everything. The Abbé had been called in at once in 1940, when Lascaux was discovered by chance, and his knowledge and experience had certified it genuine. Quite frankly, we never thought of M. Séverin Blanc. . . .

Since we were starting a record, we had to give it a title. "Cro de Granville, Cro de Miremont, Cro du Cluzeau, Cave de Miremont"—there were plenty of names. Every period, more or less, had added its toponymic stratum. The word "Cro" was the best, because it was by far the oldest, the term being "pre-Celtic" and no doubt of palaeolithic origin. But it was more a common than a proper name.

"What commune are we in?"

"Rouffignac."

"Well, then, the new cave will be called Rouffignac in Périgord."

The name rang loud and clear, with a pleasant flavour of the land. Rouffignac was born.

Our first inspection of the drawings had shown us how fragile they were. The clayey limestone that carries them is sometimes soft and crumbling all over the surface. This was the case with many drawings in the Stream gallery, before the Great Ceiling. Beyond, the limestone was harder, but it was still easy to cut. All this was 20,000 years old, and it was not eternal. We had to prevent a possible rush of tourists and sightseers. It was June 26, and the "season" was just beginning in the Dordogne. What a windfall for sightseers!

Our first care: Secrecy

The cave must therefore be guarded by secrecy as well as by its iron gate. Charles Plassard told us a few stories of the closing of Rouffignac, since so it would be called henceforth.

He had bought the estate in 1929, and the rumoured existence of a mysterious subterranean world under the plateau of La Pradelie had influenced his choice. He had spent a day with a farmer, walking through fields and thickets, inspecting farm buildings and estimating the value of the woods and the yield of the soil. In his mind's eye he would prop up a roof, straighten a building, improve a field, plant pine-trees here, a hedge there. The estate pleased him on the whole. "And then, you know, there's a cave: a huge cave underneath!" The bargain was struck.

A small metal door, with a lock that had long been forced, then protected "his" underground domain. The "protection" was quite illusory.

Every year "unknown visitors" entered the cave freely. In 1938 Charles Plassard decided to tidy up the wooded slopes overlooking Fleurac. As for the cave, he liked to walk through the great galleries alone, and no one today knows their windings better than he. He also liked to share his pleasure with a few friends, to show them the "Cake Room" or the "Tomb of Gargantua", as well as the famous "starfish", star-shaped stalagmites grouped around a flint "kidney". Had he noticed already that his stars were getting fewer?

To facilitate his visits he had the entrance to the cave widened and made a road to it from the Pradelie plateau. An oaken gate, a strong chain and a large padlock formed a new barrier against clandestine visitors, but it was still not enough. Had the work on the road aroused public curiosity? What was happening to the starfish?

War, cruel and implacable, passed through Périgord as it did elsewhere. The village was burnt.

In 1945, boys from Périgueux came to explore the cave and play at "spelaeology". They came with perfect assurance, as though they had owned the place, and no doubt behaved just as freely on the private roads of the estate as they did underground.

At the end of June, 1949, the owner, rather tired of this, had the vault narrowed by two small masonry walls, one on either side. At last a wide double door closed the cave, with a grating in its upper part.

Breaking and Entering

On July 24, 1949, the new gate was forced. Indignation was not enough. M. Plassard informed the police, and the gendarmerie at Rouffignac opened an inquiry. During an interview with the President of the Spéléo-Club of Rouffignac, a witness of the scene sadly hung his head. M. Plassard noticed him.

"It wasn't you, by any chance?"

"Yes, it was I."

"I like frankness. Since you confess, I will withdraw my complaint." And M. Plassard, yielding to his customary generosity, withdrew the charge. The assistant Judge at La Clayette told us all that in the evening of June 26. He told us of the troubles and violations of the cave. And as he had withdrawn his complaint, he did not tell us the name of the boy who had forced the gate. It was not for him to tell us, since the offence was expunged and amnestied by the withdrawal of the charge.

We did not ask him for the name. But we knew already, that evening, that the barrier of 1949 might be forced again. We knew it was too weak to guard such a treasure as the mammoths of Rouffignac.

"Let's keep it secret."

The next day, June 27, we went back to Rouffignac. We found more drawings, but we wanted specially to take a few pictures to show to Abbé Breuil, first and foremost, if he could not come at once to Périgord. We were physically exhausted by our exertions of the previous day and weighed down by the endless problems that arose in our minds and the crushing responsibility we had to discharge.

And there were too many drawings and paintings! I see us now, sitting under the Great Ceiling, tired and dumb. The day before, in the same place, we were full of the excitement of discovery. Joyfully we identified the pictures. A horse here—and two mammoths. Another rhinoceros! Two horses over here. Oh, come and see the ibexes: two, three, five ibexes! The next day, over-tired and gloomy, we had not the heart to photograph them. There were too many.

That same evening a letter went off to report the discovery to Abbé Breuil. We did not give the exact location. A letter may go astray. That night we returned to our families.

The Abbé made an appointment to visit the cave on Tuesday, July 17. We were to meet him at Périgueux station, the evening before, at the 6.13 p.m. train.

23. The Breuil Gallery: the family of three rhinoceroses

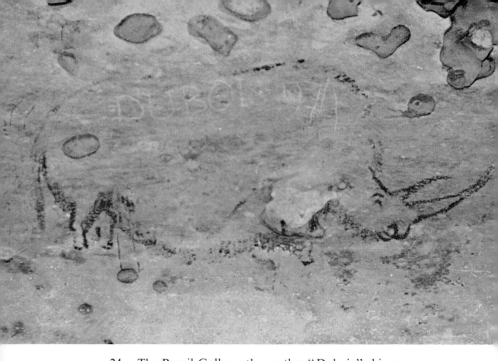

24.   The Breuil Gallery: the mother "Dubois" rhinoceros

25.   The Breuil Gallery: The father rhinoceros at the end of the frieze

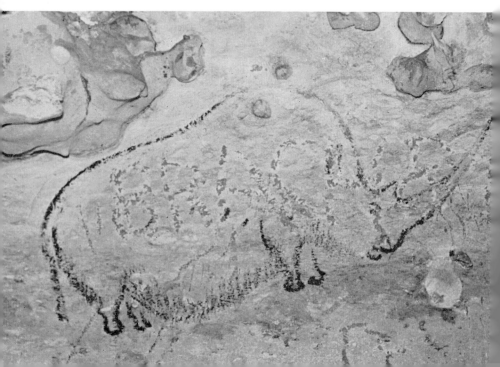

Poitiers Congress

Just then I became Secretary-General of the 15th Prehistoric Congress of France. The Congress met at Poitiers from Sunday, July 15, to Friday, July 30, under the chairmanship of M. Etienne Piatte, Dean of the Poitiers Faculty of Sciences. Between 100 and 200 delegates were to follow our working sessions, and a dozen foreign countries were represented. The first meeting took place on the Sunday, and I received a telegram telling me that Abbé Breuil would arrive in Périgord the next day. I therefore had to go, leaving the Congress which had hardly begun, and I was sorry. But the mammoths were waiting, and their authenticity was worth any Congress, however important. No one is indispensable here below, and I passed on any useful suggestions to my faithful and active assistant, Pierre Peccatier. I said to my Dean and chairman: "Excuse me, I am off to the Dordogne. I have to meet Abbé Breuil there. I will come back as soon as I can." On the Monday, without telling the delegates of my departure, which would have provoked many questions I could not answer, I settled the programme of our meetings. At ni e o'clock the reading of papers began in both the halls set aside for the Congress, and the machine was in action. It could keep running alone. At eleven-thirty I jumped into Claude Barrière's car, which took me to the station. The struggle was beginning. For already as the result of a presentiment or of long experience, I foresaw a struggle, but I did not foresee the battle that followed. In my wildest imaginings I did not foresee its future scale.

The faithful "Aronde" car (No. 9 in the Ariège Department) was waiting for me at Périgueux. It was becoming a habit with us to meet like this, at the stated hour, in any odd corner of Europe. Three weeks before, we had met like this in the station at Gourdon to go on to Cougnac together and then to "X"—that is, to Rouffignac.

The Fourth Man

We had with us an excellent friend and collaborator, M. François Denjean, an honorary lecturer in the Ariège, who was also a major in the Army Reserve and the correspondent of the Dépêche du Midi. He had often accompanied us on archaeological expeditions in the cave of La Vache in the Ariège, and we had crawled through "siphons" together during our explorations. There's nothing like it for cementing friendship.

K

During the whole Rouffignac campaign he was to support us diligently and discreetly. The big Parisian reporters were surprised to see photographs in which he and I appeared with Abbé Breuil. So there was a "fourth man" in the business, counting M. Plassard? Yes, and the fourth man was François Denjean. He was in the secret, and he never betrayed it, but that did not prevent him from being the first reporter of Rouffignac.

My last memory of Périgueux was strange. It went back three or four years. Wishing to visit antique Vésone and going to Les Eyzies for a course at the Institute of Practical Prehistory, I alighted one morning from the direct railway coach from Paris to Agen, which stops at Les Eyzies. And early in the afternoon, there I was again, in front of the station, very excited and overloaded and wanting to catch another train. There were no more trains: there had been a derailment six miles away. Motor-coaches were running a shuttle service. I asked questions. What train was derailed? The Agen express: the last coach had turned over. It was the one I had left in the morning. O mysterious destiny of Rouffignac!

Directly the Abbé got into the car he asked us:
"Where are you taking me exactly?"
"To the Cro de Granville, at Rouffignac."
His sharp eyes wrinkled more maliciously. "But I know it," he said. "I visited it in 1915—oh, very quickly!" And he told us of his hasty expedition with the African explorer Alluaud, who was looking for a beetle.

On July 17 we all went into Rouffignac, the two "discoverers", the two Plassards, the Fourth Man and the Abbé, with his walking-stick, his cigarettes and his folding chair. We rather feared the effects of fatigue and excitement on the distinguished man of science, and we had arranged to bring a garden chair, made of chestnut-wood laths, from the Légal farm where we had spent the night.

The visit took twelve hours. As we stood before the Rhinoceros frieze, we understood from certain rather emphatic expressions how deeply moved our master was. He, too, found the word we had used three weeks before: "Marvellous! These rhinoceroses are marvellous—and those mammoths—and the ceiling!"

The Abbé leapt from bear-hole to bear-hole, and we followed him with difficulty. At last, beyond the Great Fosse, we reached the last mammoth—the Mammoth with the Roguish Eye. Our return journey was long and slow. We had to recover from our emotions and our exertions. The chair was unfolded more often. Not far from the rhinoceroses which were about to become subjects of fame and "scandal" we rested, ate a few sandwiches and took some photographs.

Our return journey was difficult and the mud was heavy. We were all very tired, extremely tired, but the mammoths had won their first battle: that for recognition. Discovered on June 26, they were "baptised" on July 17. In the bowels of the earth we named the place of the great painted frieze of mammoths and rhinos "the Henri Breuil Gallery". It was a small tribute by the prospectors of Rouffignac to the man who has done so much for Prehistoric Art, and has, in fact, given humanity its earliest examples.

The Abbé, M. Charles Plassard, the "Fourth Man" and I held another Council of War the next morning, July 18. We were all rested and fresh and the Abbé was heartier and livelier than ever. He was not even stiff. Those mammoths seemed almost miraculous: he prepared a long and well-documented report for the Architectural Department of the Ministry of Education. In this he recorded the history of the discovery and declared its great importance. As we had agreed that the secret should be kept until steps had been taken to protect the cave, it was decided that only the Minister should be informed and that he should be asked to be most discreet.

Protective measures now had to be devised. The gate at the entrance was not enough. It had been forced by "X" on July 24, 1949, so that we were aware of the danger and determined to take every care. To guard against unwelcome curiosity mere bars were clearly inadequate. We feared that sticks or fingers might be used to underscore drawings or test the solidity of surfaces, and the works of art were fragile. We also had to fear graver misdeeds. Too many scribblings and smoke-signatures might obliterate the paintings. At any cost we must prevent actions which were irresponsible yesterday and would be vandalistic tomorrow. We had to preserve this new and priceless treasure. Charles Plassard showed generous understanding.

"We must have," he said, "a stone wall three feet thick and set in a rock foundation to prevent people from digging under it. It must be sealed to the roof so that no one can climb over. Then we must have an armoured door which cannot be burnt through and locks which cannot be forced. We want the work to begin at once, and until it is finished we must keep the secret carefully. That is the only way to protect the paintings and drawings."

M. Plassard gave us every possible assurance. That same evening he began a patient and secret search for cement, a door, locks and masons. But secrecy about the place need not mean silence about the fact of discovery. It was an important addition to the artistic heritage of palaeolithic man and of the human race. We had to keep the place secret for obvious and pressing reasons, but it was our duty to inform the scientific world. The Prehistoric Congress of France was actually sitting three hours' journey from Périgord. Eminent specialists were there, among them Professor Graziosi of the University of Florence, a great expert on quaternary art.

And I personally had to return to Poitiers as soon as possible to resume my duties as General Secretary.

Official Announcement at the Poitiers Congress

It was decided to announce our discovery at the Poitiers Prehistoric Congress. Our letter to the Minister would be delivered in Paris on the 19th. We would therefore announce Rouffignac at Poitiers on Friday, the 20th, in deference to the Minister, who would learn of the discovery from Abbé Breuil's report and not from the Press, which was closely following the Congress. In the evening of the 18th we drove the Abbé to the home of a cousin at Périgueux who was expecting him, posted the report in the letter-box at Périgueux station and took the road for Poitiers. We arrived at the Saint-Jean baptistry late at night, and there I found a room and the papers of the Congress at the University City.

The next morning I also found my chairman, who confided a certain anxiety to me. "We have our solemn closing session to-morrow at 10 a.m. I am afraid it will be rather thin." To which I answered with a smile: "Don't worry, my dear President, your closing session will be very full!"

The next day we furnished the closing session with the finest herd of prehistoric animals man could desire. The provisional inventory then included:

61 drawings of mammoths,
12 drawings of bison,
8 drawings of ibex,
6 drawings of horses,
4 drawings of woolly rhinoceros,

that is, nearly 100 first-class drawings or paintings, not counting innumerable finger-tracings and complex serpentine designs on walls and ceilings.

To the four "classical" groups identified during our visit of June 26—the frieze of painted rhinoceros, the frieze of painted mammoths, the panel of five engraved mammoths and the Great Ceiling, we now added the mammoths of the Red Ceiling, since discovered by Louis Plassard and recognised by us, with the Abbé, on July 17. No doubt the main body of our discoveries was then known and announced, but the paintings recorded were only about half those we know now.

By quoting a few expressions used by Abbé Breuil, such as that concerning the rhinoceros in the new cave, which he considered "the finest in quaternary art", and graven or painted compositions of mammoths "unique until now", we paid a respectful and well-deserved compliment to his very exhausting twelve-hour exploration, by which he set a fine example of scientific courage.

FIRST ATTACKS: JULY, 1956

The Press moves in

A few journalists—always an inquisitive race!—who were present naturally asked where the discovery was, and were told: "In the Dordogne." But drive out Nature and she comes back at a gallop, as we know. The departmental and administrative name "Dordogne" was displeasing to me. I have never been able to stomach a subject for a diploma or a thesis based on these unnatural and mongrel creations of the Constituent Assembly. To fix a geographical position I always use hydrographic terms like "between Loire and Seine, between Dronne and Tardoire, between Lot and Aveyron", taking the names of rivers for reference. No doubt I told these journalists "to the north of the Dordogne", meaning north of the river of that name. But my questioner understood me to mean "in the north of the Department (of Dordogne)", and that was what went out on the teleprinters.

So it happened, one fine morning, that the Sub-Prefect of Nontron woke up in a frenzy. A sensational cave had been found in his sector, in the north of the Department, therefore in the Nontron district. And the Sub-Prefect knew nothing about it (for the best of reasons)!

On July 21 and 22 the participants in the Congress went for excursions in the Charente, around Angoulême, and in the evening of the 22nd a colleague drove me to Limoges, where I took a train to the Alps to join my wife and daughter. On the 23rd I arrived at Gap, happy to find my family and hoping to get a few restful days of Alpine peace and quiet. Alas! my peace was shortlived. In the evening of the 24th I took the train back to Rouffignac. After two telephone calls between Gap and Tarascon-sur-Ariège we decided to meet on the 25th at Périgueux station, by the 3.51 p.m. train. The good François Denjean was in the party. We felt this expedition would be difficult, and we knew we could rely on his advice.

Letter to M. Séverin Blanc

In front of the station we reviewed the situation. The "secret"

was in danger.   It was only a question of days, at the most.   We
decided to send a cordial word to M. Séverin Blanc, without yet
stating the exact position of our find.   (There were still only four
of us in the secret—the Abbé, the two "discoverers" and the
"Fourth Man".)

"My dear Friend," Romain wrote to M. Blanc, "I am sure you
are one of those who rejoiced at our discovery and you were not
offended if we were unable to tell you of it by word of mouth before
you learned of it from the Press.   You will understand that from
June 26, the date of our discovery, to July 16, when the Abbé Breuil
arranged to meet us at Périgueux, we told not a soul of our secret.
On July 18, the morrow of our expedition, we should have liked to
pay you a visit, but the Abbé wanted us to drive him to one of his
relatives, and this led us to go afterwards to Poitiers. . . ."   We
intended to go, not to Les Eyzies but straight to Rouffignac, without
losing a moment except to write this letter.

What was our reason for this hasty return to Rouffignac?   A
vague, very vague threat seemed to hang over the cave, and we
hurried to it.   We were then far from expecting the powerful assault
that was to break upon us, but we felt that there were "leaks" in
the secret of the cave's whereabouts, and we were getting ready to
defend it.   The "leaks" became a flood in a long article in *Le Monde*
dated July 24.

A dangerous Interview

The young and very able reporter of *Le Monde* had succeeded in
interviewing Abbé Breuil—not an easy feat.   A very friendly conversation had taken place, and the Abbé had quite naturally let fall
a few dangerous hints about the geographical position of the cave.
And we knew that the wall was barely begun, the future door was
not yet made, the burglar-proof locks from Fichet's had not been
delivered!   If the place became known we should have to fear a
rush of tourists and sightseers; a real disaster.   Would our friends
the Plassards have enough authority to dam the flood?

The *Monde* article admitted that the "treasure" lay south of a
line from Brive to Périgueux, which was unimportant, that the cave
was closed "by a single gate", and "since depredations are always
to be feared, the exact place is a secret that the specialists have
promised to keep".   So far, so good, but the article went on: "But
this is an open secret, for the place is mentioned in every good guide
to Périgord, and the Abbé Breuil himself remembers having gone
there about forty years ago."   This was getting much more precise.

More precise still were a few lines admitting the existence of sig-natures written in smoke in the 18th and 19th centuries, and another passage reporting works of art in galleries "extending for nearly 8 kms. (5 miles)". Five-mile caves are not legion in Périgord, or even in the whole of France. Our secret would soon burst like a soap-bubble in the wind.

The next day, July 26, the first wave of reporters broke on Rouf-fignac. It was high time, but we were there. First on the scene was Max Olivier-Lacamp of the *Figaro*. He arrived in the after-noon and gave his card to "a young woman in a blue smock", Mme Plassard, Jnr.

You were not the first journalist to arrive at the estate, Max Olivier, but you were the first to be admitted. Why? You explain it yourself in your article in the *Figaro Littéraire* of Saturday, August 4:

"Though I did not know the exact spot, I had enough data to find it. All I had to do was to get into the stronghold and be received by the discoverers. I used a very old dodge, long proved infallible. (I apologise for it to MM. Nougier and Robert.) On Thursday, July 26, I signed an article in the *Figaro* on the search for the fabulous cave, adding in substance that it was time the men of science lifted the veil, for already ill-natured rumours about their discovery were going round."

Oh, yes, the "dodge" is infallible. It worked for you. If you're proud of it, so much the better. And where did those unkind rumours come from? At any rate, you saw the entrance, the gate and the wall that was being built. Yet you missed the "story" of your life, because you could go no farther. Could we make an exception, even for you? Can you imagine what a rush of your colleagues there would have been the next day?

"No one or everyone"—that was our rule with reporters, in that race for news. You were disappointed, and you made us pay for it. Now we are quits, and we are still good friends. We shall remember the lesson the next time we find a painted cave. You must find something else, and ourselves, and all the journalists if you want to be received!

Once the position of the "fabulous cave" was known, the Press would "splash" it in its editions of the morrow. But the wall was growing, and it was guarded at night. Well guarded. Directly Max Olivier was gone, we hurried to Périgueux and asked for an interview at the Prefecture. The offices were closed, but our cards opened the way for us without any other "infallible dodges".

We reported the exact position of the cave and our reasons for keeping it secret before the Press broke loose. On our way back we also warned the Mayor of Rouffignac, and we have a pleasant memory of his kind reception. He promised to have the place discreetly watched by patrols of gendarmes as long as the wall and the armoured door were not in place. But the wall was going up, and it was well guarded at night. The mammoths of Rouffignac could continue their age-long sleep!

People have smiled at our "unnecessary" precautions. Perhaps they were. But if we had taken no precautions, might they not have turned out to be necessary? And too late! So it was better to take them, whether they were necessary or not. And it was from the Press that we learned, like everything else, what was happening outside our headquarters at La Pradelie, a few hundred yards from the scene of operations, that is, from the wall of the cave, which was rising, but not fast enough.

As might be expected, the Press reports were often distorted, with exaggerated news, misinterpreted insinuations and vague allusions turned into definite and dangerous statements. "I didn't say that... I never meant that... Above all, don't give my name. ... You can publish *my* name, yes, yes, I give you permission. ... Isn't it charcoal? ... Ah, you say it's charcoal! Well, it is charcoal." So there we have drawings made with charcoal, when no one really knows anything about it. The war of the caves, the war of the mammoths had to be kept going, because the Loch Ness Monster hadn't turned up that year, and there was no new Drummond murder! The real war, that of 1939–1945, was over long ago, and paper had to be sold to holiday-making crowds at the seaside and elsewhere. Good paper, nice, heavy paper had to be sold. A few weeks later I remarked to a great reporter who had become rather friendly: "But why make this senseless campaign against Rouffignac? You had Nasser!" He answered: "No. It's not the same thing. It's not the same paper. A lot of my colleagues *wanted* Rouffignac to be a fake. *Then* they would have sold papers! A new Glozel, what luck! And then, that's amusing, it makes you smile, even laugh sometimes. As for Nasser . . ."

The Press as a Source of History

It was through the newspapers, which were historical records, after all, that we were able to form an idea of what was going on in the other camp, after making our difficult survey of the evidence. From that time on, this "very contemporary History of Rouffignac"

could be followed in the Press.   It is partly by the Press that political
or diplomatic history is created, day by day.   We have to do that,
too.   We shall refer the reader to our sources generously, knowing
personally just how much and how little they are worth.   The debit
exceeds the credit.

Let us go down, plastered with chalky clay, along the Manaurie
valley, and mingle with people in the streets, or rather the one street,
of Les Eyzies.   Tongues wag of their own accord even when
nothing is happening; if something is happening, what then?   For
fifty years Les Eyzies district has known itself to be prehistoric.
It sweats prehistory through all the pores of its many caves.   A
peasant in the Brie may know nothing of the polished flint axe-head
turned up by his plough.   The peasant of Périgord knows all about
it, and he puts it on his mantelshelf.   Sometimes he keeps it piously,
in memory of the "ancestors" or to protect his hearth from lightning.

Sometimes, too, he sells it to the passing squire, or to the foreigner
who offers the best price.   A rocky recess is always useful as a cart-
shed, but if it is prehistoric it can be leased, and it brings in more
money than the near-by field, for less trouble.   There was a time
when caves were let on lease, for fair rents, to conscientious fossil-
hunters who used honest methods of excavation, the methods of their
time, not open to criticism.   What will be said of our diggings fifty
years from now?   Today caves can be bought, but hush . . .

The Vézère valley is very beautiful, but so many of the rivers that
wind and leap in the Massif Central have valleys just as charming.
What sets the Vézère valley apart is its prehistoric caves and the fact
that as you walk downstream you ascend in time until you reach
buried ages and the art of thousands of years ago among hamlets and
villages nestling against the rock, or overflowing the valley in an
elongated fringe.

A "No" to Curiosity

How could a new cave, especially if its whereabouts were unknown,
fail to stir up minds and fire imaginations between La Bugue and
Montignac, and in the heart of that country, at Les Eyzies?   When
Lascaux was discovered, Léon Laval says "the inhabitants of Montignac and the district crowded down, though the descent was
difficult".   We could not wish for a crowd or deal with one.   The
cave is immense and difficult without being really dangerous.   At
present several hours are needed to see its most important contents.
We have seen that the walls are fragile; so are the floors.   For
centuries they have been trodden by thousands of people.   That was

natural; now it is not allowed. We have to preserve bears' claw-marks on clay, flint-cutting workshops as they stand, bears' sleeping-holes intact, and seek for and perhaps be lucky enough to find bears' tracks on the clay and human footprints like those we reported and studied in the cave at Niaux. We have to find bones, connected and correctly placed. The recent discovery of a bear's canine tooth embedded in its clay mould is more than a hope. It is a promise.

If for the purposes of this contest and to make our counter-attack effective we invited a few journalists to visit Rouffignac, they only explored galleries where there was no danger to future observation and saw painted areas well known to history. We could do no less than show them these, but we certainly could do no more.

The announcement of the discovery was made at Poitiers on July 20. "Three days later, in the charming village of Les Eyzies," writes Max Olivier-Lacamp, "two perplexed scientists met. They tried to identify the cave from the pictures in the newspapers." However, these two scientists agreed on certain details. The bed of rounded "kidney" flints appears nowhere as clearly, in that region, as in the Cave of Miremont, or Cro de Granville.

Photographic Proof

One picture in particular must have attracted the attention of the two pioneers, anxious to lay bare the secret of the mysterious cave. "Abbé Henri Breuil (on the left), a master of world prehistory, and the two authors of the discovery examining the Rhinoceros Frieze," the paper said. "I know that Rhinoceros frieze," said one of the explorers, M. Séverin Blanc. "I examined it at the request of a cave-explorer named Bernard Pierret, who made detailed visits to the Miremont cave every year and was surprised to see these animals appear on a wall he had always seen unpainted. That was in 1949. I was visiting Miremont, *which I already knew very well*, with Bernard Pierret and his team and the well-known cave-explorer De Joly, who was in the district.

"As André Breton was to do later in the Cabrerets cave, I ran my finger over the drawing and it became quite black! The rhino-ceroses were inspired by the famous prototypes in the Font-de-Gaume cave, and they were drawn in acetylene lamp-black."

The use of this extract is a delicate matter, for it is impossible to allot responsibility for a particular term, printed in italics, to the interviewee or the interviewer, or to quote either of them exactly as they play the ball back and forth to each other. "I never said that." "Yes, you did. I transcribed it!" Dialogues between deaf people must be very easy sometimes! But the text remains, and it must be proof of the errors it conceals. Blanc's second paragraph (above) suggests the prose that was to be inflicted on us by the papers, great and small, from that time on. Three monumental mistakes in three lines! Who could do better?

In imitation of André Breton

"I ran my finger over a drawing and it became quite black." The statement is incorrect. The painted lines of the first rhinoceros, and those of the others for that matter, do not come off on one's finger. Minute examinations have been made. The best specialists on quaternary art have paid even more attention to this rhinoceros than to the others. The paint "holds".

During his important visit of Sept. 12, Professor M. Almagro pointed out to Max Olivier-Lacamp that "in the upper part of the disputed friezes, especially the frieze of painted mammoths and that of the rhinoceros, which was photographed by the cave-explorers, there was an incipient oozing of the limestone which produced a finely granulated mixture of colouring matter and crystals in process of formation". The reporter expressed satisfaction at this important scientific observation. And the secretive little man confesses: "While M. Nougier's back was turned I stroked the back of one of the mammoths with my finger. The contact enlightened me, if I may say so!"

It was high time, alas, after all the harm that had been done by ill-considered words. But as some ancient evangelist, St. Luke or St. Matthew, it hardly matters which, declares: "There is more joy over one lost sheep that is found than over the whole flock."

The paint holds, and it has held very well, for I imagine more than one visitor, last summer, rubbed his finger on the spine of a rhinoceros of Rouffignac, just like the Regional Director of Antiquities. And what if the paint had not held? The case would have been neither won nor lost, according to the camp you might have joined, for the fixing of the paint has nothing to do with the genuineness or worthlessness of the paintings. Even if they are 10,000, 15,000 or 20,000 years old, these prehistoric paintings are not eternal, and it is frightening to think how little may remain of Lascaux or Altamira in only 500 years!

How to preserve the admirable frescoes at Lascaux is a problem for the public authorities, as everyone knows, and it causes painful anxiety to all humanists, justly attached, as they are, to the absolute integrity of these masterpieces. The cave is small and often crowded, the paintings are heated in the daytime by lights placed close to them and cooled at night, when the lights are turned off, and there is a harmful and insidious exudation of carbon dioxide gas. . . .

Luckily for Rouffignac, the new discoveries will never run such risks. The size of the galleries ensures a stable atmosphere; that stability has lasted for centuries, and we are not afraid of hurrying crowds and dazzling lights. Carbon dioxide gas is unknown there. Guarded by its own immensity, Rouffignac can remain the painted cave of the Chosen Few.

The fate of these prehistoric paintings is bound up with their rocky ground and the natural conditions in which this material exists. Thus, at Niaux, one overhead cornice bearing a marvellous bison is always damp. And the black paint of the bison—which, by the way, has not been analysed—is literally suspended in the oozing moisture. In the course of half a century, a visitor has sometimes eluded the watchful guide. That visitor, too, has been tempted to rub his finger, and the bison is getting fainter and fainter, paler and paler, for the paint follows the sacrilegious finger. So we hear an aphorism that is meant to be Cartesian: "You tell us these bison are 15,000 years old. It's impossible. Look"—showing a blackened finger—"the paint doesn't hold!"

For days on end Abbé Breuil noted frescoes at Altamira lying on his back, on sacks stuffed with heather. And he explains: "There could be no question of taking an impression of the great figures on the ceiling. The soft paint would have stuck to the paper, and they would have been destroyed."

In some sectors of Rouffignac the colour sticks to your finger. In fact, it is THE WHOLE WALL that sticks to it. That is not the same thing. On soft clay surfaces, which seem to be eaten away from inside and from outside, too, the mere touch of a finger will remove a scale of slimy clay. If a line in a drawing were on the soft surface, the line would disappear with the material. It even happens that the line offers a local concentration of very fine particles of manganese, and then the line resists friction while the ground crumbles. In this case the line protects the background.

"SLAVISH COPIES"

"Slavish Copies"

Mistake No. 1: the colouring matter of the rhinos does *not* come off on one's finger.

Mistake No. 2: the rhinos of Rouffignac have *nothing to do* with those of Font-de-Gaume. The straight body of the classic rhinoceros of Font-de-Gaume, popularised by Abbé Breuil's excellent record, is quite different from the rhinos of Rouffignac, with their massive fore-quarters and their fine, fat humps designed to supply energy to withstand the rigours of winter.

The rhinos of Rouffignac are related both by their appearance and in their chronology with those engraved on stones or flints in the caves of Arcy-sur-Cure and Colombière. Of course, they are all rhinos, and they never show the elegance of giraffes or the undulating pose of boa-constrictors.

Where Acetylene comes in

Mistake No. 3: the drawings are not made with acetylene soot. My daughter Colette-Françoise, at the age of six, knows the difference between a prehistoric line and a line, or rather a patch, made with the smoke of a carbide lamp. The frieze is well known to the Regional Director; his wife, Mme Blanc, found proof of it. "From under a pile of books" she pulled out a little work called "Underground Périgord" by Bernard Pierret, President of the Spéléo-Club of Périgueux. The book was published at Montignac in 1953.

"Séverin Blanc quickly turned the pages to Plate XVI, between pp. 112 and 113, and said simply: 'There you are!'"

The plate showed a white tent set up in the Rouffignac cave at a place called "the Camp". Kneeling in front of the tent were two very young men, Bernard Pierret and Robert de Faccio, watching for "the little bird who is coming out". The photograph was taken in 1949, when the "explorers" had not yet reached their majority. In the upper right-hand part of the picture "the three rhinoceros displayed themselves". This was the famous "proof picture". Proof of what?

The famous Rhinos

It is definite proof that when a flashlight picture of the underground camp was taken, the film ALSO received an impression of three rhinoceroses parading in the right-hand corner. We repeat, in the right-hand corner. The subject of the picture is the two cave-explorers on each side of the tent, not the frieze. We must even wonder whether the explorers ever saw the rhinos before they developed their picture; there is no proof of it. But with the print in their hands, they had to admit that "there was something on the wall".

Yet this was not the first time mysterious signs had struck these young people. In January 1949 there was a two-day cave-exploring expedition in the depths of Rouffignac: three young men and the owners, M. and Mme Charles Plassard, who accompanied them for the first day.

As in previous expeditions, efforts were concentrated on the lower galleries. M. Charles Plassard even followed the explorers into the maze. They left their watches with him while they went on to wet and half-blocked galleries, and he remembers a long wait, with his hands full, over mysterious crevasses, by the occasional light of a few matches, for his lamp had given up the ghost. Meanwhile Mme Plassard was wisely musing on the edge of the great descending crater, also finding the hours monotonous although she could examine the strange and delicate lines traced under the heavy inscriptions. She could not help seeing these lines; they made shapes like drawings, *like animals.*

When the others came up, they all mentioned these drawings without attaching the least importance to them. Of course, the explorers were in a pretty bad state, with their terrible and heavy loads.

This incident of the rhinoceroses led to further reflection. It was the second chance offered to Bernard Pierret and his team, after they had missed the first chance under the Great Ceiling. Of course, the young cave explorers were not archaeologists and even less prehistorians, the latter science being perhaps the most delicate branch of archaeology, though it often seems the easiest. A collector of insects or postage stamps must have some knowledge; he must know how to make an identification, how to use the magnifying glass and the forceps. It seems that a flint-fancier need not go so far. He only needs a few engraved plates in a book, on which he can lay his flints to compare. He may find that they are "Levalloisien IV". Then he can order his visiting-card as a specialist!

The appearance of the rhinos certainly moved Bernard Pierret to ask for a "consultation". They were in Périgord, a few miles from Les Eyzies, whose white bluffs could be seen from the plateau of La Pradelie, overlooking the cave. It was quite natural that Bernard should seek the expert advice of M. Séverin Blanc.

The Crux of the Drama

A sort of doom weighs heavily on all this "Rouffignac affair", a doom like that of antique drama, like that which once dogged Oedipus. "You will slay your father and lie with your mother."

Like Oedipus, Bernard Pierret sought counsel of the oracles, and the oracles were rendered in Périgord by Séverin Blanc, appointed by the Department of Architecture to be Regional Director of Antiquities. Was he not "the Sage of Les Eyzies"? Indeed, that was rather true. He had wisely taught the children of the country-side; he had taught the children of the first children who passed through his school. The master of little schoolboys became the master of the caves of his country, and he "taught" Combarelles and the Font-de-Gaume, and the prehistoric collections at the old feudal castles of Les Eyzies, to more than one visitor.

Bernard Pierret was a very shy, very young teacher, appearing before his "great senior", the Regional Director of Antiquities. He wanted to report some vague drawings recently observed, according to himself, in the Miremont cave. These drawings had been made "news" by the last revealing photograph of Pierret's camp.

"Yes, Director, I think there really are drawings."

"When did you discover them?"

"We only noticed them a few months ago." (And before that, he had questioned the Director.) "We didn't take much notice of them. But the more often we saw them, the more there seemed to be. They seemed to multiply."

(Of course, the young cave-explorers' eyes were getting used to the very special task of spotting prehistoric drawings.)

"What colour are these drawings?" the Director must have asked.

"They are black, Director."

"What is the colouring matter?" (A natural question, too.)

"I don't know; I am not a prehistorian. The lines are black, as though they were made with charcoal or an acetylene lamp."

One more question remained. It was bound to be put.

"Where is this painted cave?"

"Quite near here, in the parish of Rouffignac. It's the Miremont cave!"

I seem to hear Séverin Blanc's guffaw at that statement. "In the

26. The Breuil Gallery: detail of the head of the "Dubois" rhinoceros

27. The Breuil Gallery: horse's head, painted on a flint "kidney," using the natural relief

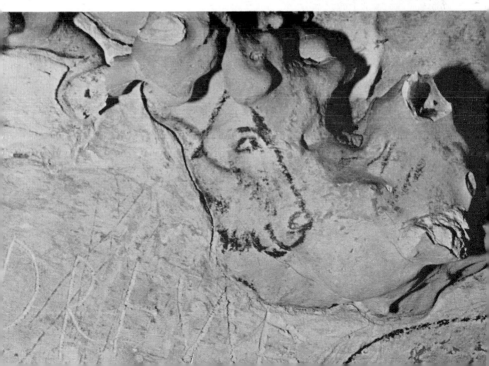

28. The Breuil Gallery: two herds meeting on the Great Mammoth frieze

29. The Breuil Gallery: the two mammoths over which the eighteenth century "Barry" inscribed his name

Miremont cave? Come, come, that's impossible! That cave is known, only too well known. If there were paintings there, you may be sure it would be known!" (Oh, yes. François de Belleforest knew it in 1575!) And I can imagine the embarrassment of the young explorer. He must have been rather vexed. I might see proof of this in the fact that he insisted, and insisted very strongly, that the Director should come to Miremont and see for himself.

The mysterious Visit

Yielding to this pressing invitation, the Director came to Miremont. He grumbled, no doubt, and thought he was wasting his time and there was nothing new to be found in this historical cave, which had been known for so long.

About July 20th, 1949, a little procession arrived at the Pradelie plateau and asked for the key of the gate to visit the Cro. (This was the key of the famous gate set up at the end of June.)

The Director was accompanied by M. de Joly, President of the Spéléo-Club of France, Bernard Pierret and M. Moineau, of the Périgueux Spéléo-Club. M. and Mme Plassard courteously accompanied the visitors.

As the procession went underground, the plot thickened. The knot of the Rouffignac drama, that drama of the future, was being tied at the moment. How far did the underground visitors go? Did they reach the Great Ceiling about 800 yards from the entrance, or only the rhinoceros frieze, after 650 yards?

M. Plassard's evidence is definite. "The visit was not long. It took an hour or an hour and a half." But as the senior member of the expedition, he did not follow the cave-explorers in their wanderings.

It is likely that the drawings on the Great Ceiling were not reached. Were the rhinos reached? We are not sure!

M. Séverin Blanc alleges, and we find this claim in accounts of the "battle", that he "reached the first rhinoceros. There he rubbed the drawing with a finger, which was blackened", and he considered the rhinoceros was drawn with acetylene soot, and he went no farther.

This allegation seems to us incredible.

It is incredible because the paint of the rhinoceros does not come off on one's finger. It is incredible because, if M. Blanc felt a doubt about the first rhinoceros, it is inconceivable that he did not examine the second, less than two feet farther on, or the third, two more feet away. It would be only human to hesitate about the first painting,

L

especially a painting found in the most-described cave in history, a cave as busy as a boulevard in the 17th or 18th century. But what the deuce, you go on to examine the second and the third! It is inconceivable that M. Blanc did not see the great frieze of eleven mammoths, a few yards distant. . . .

It is inconceivable, too (for he arranged tens and hundreds of visits to the cave of Combarelles) that he never had the elementary idea of going to the other side of our gallery and glancing at the huge panel on the left-hand side of the Breuil gallery, which carries ELEVEN large, consecutive drawings. And it is quite incredible that M. Blanc did not see the "Mammoths of the Discovery" on the left-hand wall, just before the mouth of the Breuil gallery.

If M. Séverin Blanc, Regional Director of Antiquities, did not see these things, it was because HE NEVER WENT THAT FAR. M. Blanc was a tired man; we know it and we respect his infirmity, which was painfully contracted in Nazi prison camps. In 1949, I myself still felt the effects of a captivity which could not be compared with his. M. de Joly was not interested in these galleries without concretions, without the marvellous stalagmites and stalactites of his cave at Orgnac. Why go any farther along these galleries, and why paddle in the Sea of Mud? Merely to verify the claims of Bernard Pierret, these apparitions of rhinoceroses occurring with every chance geological expedition, these rhinoceroses drawn with black paint, charcoal or smoke—Pierret himself did not know which.

Too soon, the visitors turned back. Why did M. Séverin Blanc say to Mme Plassard as he came out, taking great care that M. de Joly should not hear him: "I think I saw some drawings on the walls. I'll come back one day."

M. Séverin Blanc never returned to the cave. But we cannot believe our opponent was so incompetent that he could not recognise a painted or engraved prehistoric drawing.

On the other hand, we can well believe he was CARELESS. He cannot have seen the rhinos and the mammoths of Rouffignac, or he would have recognised them! And when, on July 21st, he inquired curiously about the whereabouts of the fabulous cave, he had, no doubt, forgotten his short, too short visit to Miremont in 1949, six years before.

But there were the photographs . . . recalling Miremont. They were as insidious as remorse! Remorse for not having gone on to the frieze reported long ago: reported by a boy and now seen to be "just" authentic. Remorse, too, for not having returned to Miremont, for though he did not reach the rhinos, he had thought he

recognised a few finger-marks on the walls. But with De Joly, of
course, there was no point in mentioning them. Why associate
him with a prehistoric discovery? "Yes, but I must go back. I
will go back one day." That was what he said to Mme Plassard.
And he never did go back.

His hand seemed to brush a bad dream from his damp brow. It
was at Rouffignac, the near-by commune, it was the Cro de Granville! Bernard Pierret had been right to draw his attention to it.
But he, so carelessly . . .

Enter Bernard Pierret

Now let us get back to Bernard Pierret and to his attitude, as
described to us by Max Olivier-Lacamp.

"Meanwhile Bernard Pierret, having at last emerged from a cave
he was exploring near Eaux-Bonnes since July 17 (three days before
the announcement was made at the Poitiers Congress) arrived at
Bordeaux and looked through the files of the newspapers that had
appeared while he was underground. "BUT IT'S MIREMONT!" he
yelled to his team-mate Robert de Faccio, who was with him in his
visits to the cave between 1945 and 1949. . . ."

We can understand that shout of rage and indignation. The
Miremont drawings condemned as fakes by Séverin Blanc were
authentic! Through the fault of Séverin Blanc, the little cave-
explorers had missed their discovery. . . .

We can imagine how they both felt when they "hurled themselves
into the first train for Périgueux, jumped into a car and arrived at
Les Eyzies. About eleven o'clock at night they descended like a
whirlwind on M. Séverin Blanc, who was being bombarded with
telephone calls from scientists and journalists all over the world".

What that night was like and what happened at the "anti-Rouffig-
nac" Council of War, we shall no doubt never know. But we know
what decisions were taken.

"The same evening," to quote Max Olivier-Lacamp again, "the
Regional Director of Antiquities issued his first definite accusation."
Rouffignac was a fake! The paintings in the Miremont cave were
FALSE. And he could never retreat after that

"It's a Fake!"

The cave-explorers, too, could not retreat. They, too, declared:
"The paintings in the Miremont cave are FALSE." This allegation,
they thought, would heal the injury to their pride and relieve their
boundless rancour at having missed the find. But the cave-explorers

154 THE CAVE OF ROUFFIGNAC

were young, and there were several of them. Little by little, they cut the ground from each other's feet, denied each other's statements, floundered and lacked boldness and perseverance in their error.

From that time on there was a step-by-step struggle, for or against. The counter-attack from Périgord was heavy. It scored some points, and the local Press gave space to the statements of the cave-explorers.

PRACTICAL JOKES

Cave-explorers at play

The details of these operations are uninteresting, but some episodes have a lesson for us. On June 29–30 a great evening newspaper carried this heading: "'I saw a young cave-explorer make drawings with his acetylene lamp', the ex-President of the Périgordian Spéléo-Club tells us." The paper then quoted from a long statement by M. William Martin:

"When I was a member of the leading team exploring the cave, one of our comrades, who had come to relieve another and was waiting for us, M. de Faccio, the son of a contractor in Périgueux, amused himself by making drawings on the roof with the burner of his acetylene lamp."

From Paris, to which we had moved our headquarters, we issued a denial of M. Martin's statement through the French Press Agency (A.F.P.). M. Martin then wisely withdrew it. A few days later, at Périgueux, an enlightened journalist, Jean Guichard, put the following precise question to W. Martin at a Press conference:

"M. Martin has stated he saw M. de Faccio drawing animals. M. de Faccio has denied it. What are we to think of this?" (*Nouvelle République de Bordeaux*, 1. 9. 56.)

Bernard Pierret: "M. W. Martin is in the room."

M. W. Martin: "I was with Pierret in the leading team in 1948. When we came up, we saw drawings. (We noticed it was impossible not to see them when coming up from the lower galleries along the Stream.) I asked: 'Who did that?' De Faccio answered: 'I did'."

M. de Faccio (also present): "I may have said that, but I didn't do it."

Several voices: "It was a joke!"

There have been many "jokes" of this kind in the "War of the Mammoths". The worst of it is that they were taken seriously.

Other "Jokes"

Séverin Blanc made a "joke" of his own. He said: "Those drawings were made by members of the *Maquis!*" (war-time underground fighters). Séverin Blanc is also reported to have said to

Raoul Cousté (a personal friend of ours and also a friend of the "Sage of Les Eyzies", who declared, without having seen them, that the drawings at Rouffignac were "slavish copies" of those at Font-de-Gaume, Cabrerets and Niaux): "I visited that cave towards the end of the German occupation, and in fact I saw a number of drawings to which I paid no attention because they were obviously fakes, made when the Maquis were using the cave." His statement to a great Paris evening paper, *Le Monde*, was even more definite: "Six years ago," he said, "I quickly recognised them (the paintings) as fakes, and on that point I am quite definite: they are faked drawings made with charcoal" (July 28).

Two days later, Bernard Pierret, making another "joke", no doubt, said: "I declare that I found new drawings every year. They were drawn, quite cleverly, too, with a carbide lamp. The rhinoceroses, in particular, are recent paintings which must have been made in 1949. A proper analysis would prove that they are fakes."

"Jokes" of this kind came from all directions. We had only to collect them.

Pre-War Paintings

At the other end of France a man from Périgord whom we did not know launched his counter-attack even before we had realised the effect of the "jokes" that were pouring in. We were then not very good at the art of "Cold War".

M. de Laurière, owner of the château de La Marzelle, at Fleurac, just opposite the entrance to the Rouffignac cave, wrote to Abbé Breuil. He also wrote in the *République du Centre*, at Orleans, on August 3: "As I take an interest in archaeology and prehistory, I visited the caves twice in the summer of 1938, and I saw the drawings then. They cannot, therefore, have been made by members of the *Maquis* during the occupation, or by more recent visitors. . . ."

So M. de Laurière saw the drawings in 1938, and Bernard Pierret says the rhinos were recent drawings, made in 1949? One witness is a serious amateur and a member of the Historical and Archaeological Society of the Orleans District and of the Historical and Archaeological Society of Périgord. The other witness is—Bernard Pierret.

The Press reproached M. de Laurière for having given no publicity to his remark "because he was afraid of making a ridiculous mistake, after the Glozel affair". It is unseemly to cast a stone at him, even in this matter of prehistory. To "launch" Rouffignac we needed the certainty we established together on June 26 and July 17. We do not claim to have seen these things before anyone else. We do claim to be responsible scientists. We do claim to have defended Rouffignac and made the authenticity of Rouffignac prevail.

Double Headlines

The most amusing thing—at the time it seemed to us particularly foolish and even odious—was the way in which "jokes" and serious statements were coupled. Of course, that method yielded sensational and very "journalistic" headlines:

"Historic frescoes, says Abbé Breuil."

"Clumsy imitations, says M. Pierret."

As though the opinion of a great and undisputed specialist could be invalidated by an assertion of Bernard Pierret!

But if we had kept silence, as we sometimes meant to do, we should certainly have been blamed. The fight was on. We had to reply with the same forcefulness, and using the same means; we had to use the Press, which seemed to us more and more like Aesop's tongues. Abbé Breuil became younger every day under such sweeping attack. Our headquarters at Isle d'Adam and at Suresnes were always in touch, but when the battle was hottest our communiqués went out from the editorial offices of the great newspapers. In the early days of August we were clawed by some, slashed by others and praised by a few, but we must acknowledge that we were kindly received everywhere and made good friends.

A Paris Conference

As a great favour, Abbé Breuil received reporters! "You can't paint with an acetylene lamp," he would say. It was then August 2. On August 3, we gave a lecture at the Musée de l'Homme to which reporters from the great French and foreign Press were invited. The hall was kindly lent by one of the Directors, and it was full of people, who were considered "neutral".

A little before the proceedings opened we were greatly surprised to see a familiar figure come forward and sit down in the front row. It was Abbé Breuil himself, whom we had left the day before in his quiet retreat at Isle d'Adam. "I feel twenty years younger," he said, "I have come to hear you." And he settled down to listen, with his hand to his deaf ear, as was his custom. And of course he did hear us. He would have had to be very deaf not to hear us, but sometimes there are none so deaf as those who won't hear. . . .

The arguments are well known. Bit by bit, we demolished the enemy's war machine—his "jokes", too. We analysed the Rouffignac "crisis" as an essentially psychological phenomenon, of local and regional origin.   The cave-explorers had seen the drawings "materially", but they had not seen them "intellectually" and they were not to blame.   A cave-explorer is not an archaeologist, much less an archaeologist specialising in prehistoric art.

They had not seen the engravings, and that, too, was natural, for though they are clearly visible, as photographs prove, engravings do not strike the untutored eye.   Sometimes we have spent long minutes in looking for an engraving, though it was noted on one of our little tally-slips.   This was so true that we wondered, as we moved our lamp close along the wall, whether we had made a mistake on the slip.   And suddenly, there was light.   Another mammoth, of course.

The battle was won by the showing of eighty lantern slides, starting with a general view of the Pradelie plateau, then a view of the bluffs of Les Eyzies seen through a gap in the woods, and ending with the last " Mammoth with the Roguish Eye ".   From the "psychological" atmosphere which explained the "crisis" and the war of the caves and the war of the mammoths, we passed to the facts themselves; the engravings and paintings, done in fine lines very different from the sooty inscriptions made with acetylene lamps.

Beauty of form, fineness of line, perfection of anatomical detail— all these were convincing.   "Work of the *Maquis*" and drawings made with acetylene lamps became absurd.

Abbé Breuil led the applause, unusual at a meeting of this kind, and the Press began to change sides, though of course there were still some reservations.   It is difficult to affirm today the truth of what you denied yesterday.   Some great papers cleverly and happily got over the difficulty by putting a new reporter on the story.   That made the inevitable pirouette less difficult.

When the battle was won in Paris, we had to exploit our success and push on with the exploration of the cave, which was far from having yielded all its secrets.

History lends a Hand

On August 8, when we returned to the Pradelie estate after a spell of work, we learned that a journalist from Bordeaux, M. Jean Guichard, wanted to speak to us.   "Bah, let's receive him: we received others before him!"   Thus we made the acquaintance of a pleasant and lively reporter for whom criticism was not solely negative and destructive, but also, and especially, positive and constructive.

At last, a journalist who asked nothing of us and even brought us something!

He brought an extract from the great *Dictionary* of 1725, an extract reporting "paintings and altars" in the Miremont cave. He had made a good beginning in the search for historical texts. He also brought the plan made by Gabriel Bouquier, of Terrasson, that 18th-century plan which had been lying in the museum at Périgueux. Light might come from Périgueux! Furthermore, he brought us the precious key to this plan, with the famous note:

"X. Gallery where M. de Barry lost his way for an hour."

And two mammoths in the left-hand group of the Great Frieze bore the inscription "Barry" in faint, smoky characters, much dimmer than the few modern inscriptions like the "F.T.P.F. 1944" 50 yds. from the entrance, made by the *Maquis* in a gallery where there was not a trace of prehistoric painting, just as, *vice versa*, there were no *Maquis* inscriptions in the painted areas.

Jean Guichard, then, brought us three serious arguments, pending the results of analyses. Above all, he started a great movement of historical research, a movement which was soon to make Rouffignac the most-described cave in history. Fired at last with a spirit of decent emulation, the Press poured out historical notes, and many well-disposed correspondents made their contributions to the history of Rouffignac. Our thanks to them all, to J. Bouchereau, G. Bourdelot, L. Deguet, Canon Bouyssonie, the Comte de Chalup, Gouvat, Jean Guichard and Maury, who spontaneously sent these historical texts or plans to Abbé Breuil or to ourselves.

"The paintings of Rouffignac were already known in 1725"! That news gave us great joy. Rouffignac claimed a new record. Bathers from Ussat-les-Bains, in the Ariège, visited Niaux and its "Black Hall" in the 19th century, before the paintings were identified as prehistoric by Commander Mollard and his sons in 1906. Now Niaux was beaten by several lengths of history. Several years later J. Bouchereau traced the record back to 1575! Meanwhile we found a mention of the paintings in the account given by Savinien d'Alquié and quoted by Bernard Pierret in his little volume, p. 105. What irony!

Professor Graziosi hurries in

The next day, for the first time, Rouffignac offered its treasures to the special correspondents of the great Paris papers. Professor Paolo Graziosi, of the University of Florence, an eminent specialist in prehistoric art who recently discovered the prehistoric paintings on the island of Levanzo off the coast of Sicily, had already made the acquaintance of our paintings and engravings. He saw our first photographs at the Poitiers Congress, which he attended, and they had convinced him.   Direct contact with the rhinos and the mammoths filled him with enthusiasm.   On August 9 we asked him to do the honours of the cave, not wishing to exercise any pressure on the journalists who had been called from Paris.

For the first time since it was built, the heavy armoured door opened for others but ourselves, who had become the faithful keepers of this priceless art.   Let us quote the very objective account of Bertrand Poirot-Delpech, of *Le Monde*.

"To tell the truth, this is more an expedition than a visit, and the privilege of inspecting rock paintings is not easily won.   It was only after trudging for more than an hour in sticky clay, sliding under vaults less than 3 ft. high and skirting grim precipices that we saw in the light of our lamps, 1,200 yds. (really half that distance) from the entrance, the first engraved or painted figures.

"Even then, you have to know how to look.   Like the many cave-explorers who have gone before him and have left coarse traces of carbide lamps on the walls, the layman, today, often passes by drawings without seeing them.   It is only when the master of that place holds his light at a certain angle and reminds you to forget the damage done by time or former visitors that the picture you are looking for becomes clear.   Then the effect is impressive.   You see nothing but that.   The forms line up, shining through the dirt of centuries.   Here are the eleven mammoths. . . .   There are rhinoceros.   More than 100 animals are assembled here, half of them engraved, half outlined in black."

Not being a specialist, the reporter very properly refuses to pass judgment on their authenticity, but he says: "Only common sense can be used, but occasions for it are not lacking.   Supposing the patina were faked (how?) and the thousands of bears' claw-marks superimposed on the drawings were artificial, too, and supposing some swindler had taken the trouble to spend months in peppering all these works with a substance exactly like the ancient dust—all of which hypotheses are equally risky—there are still two arguments which are not easy to refute.   The first is the equal proportion of painted mammoths and engraved mammoths to the total of animals represented.   If it is true, as unbelievers assert, that the former are false but the latter are authentic, a forger of unequalled skill, before painting his imitations, must have made an inventory of the engravings, though most of these are hardly visible.   A pretty piece of work!

"The second argument is also based on logic.   It is to be noted that the dated signatures which partly conceal certain drawings go back to 1870 and 1880."

A colleague is not less enthusiastic: "Speaking for ourselves, after an exhausting march through 800 yds. of corridors where the clay often glued our shoes to the ground, we do not conceal our wonder at the sight of such riches. We were struck by the similar style of the engraved and painted animals, whether mammoths, bison or horses. One is amazed by the astonishing fineness of line and the prodigious power of observation" (André Larcher).

Graziosi's Declaration of Authenticity

All the journalists agreed that they were not competent to decide on the question of authenticity, and many suggested arbitration. These were armistice proposals! But the great arbiter had already made up his mind, with the clarity and authority that we know. Abbé Breuil was "for". Dr. Paolo Graziosi, the best foreign specialist in prehistoric art, then gave his opinion, after visiting the cave on August 9, 1956. His verdict was clear, precise and categorical.

"After having examined the paintings and engravings discovered up to now very attentively for many hours, I can state categorically that these engravings and paintings are not only authentic but are among the finest and most important that the records of palaeolithic cave art have given us until the present day."

And the Florentine scientist was surprised at the controversy. "It is enough," he said, "to have a normal experience of prehistoric art, to recognise immediately not only the authenticity but also the extraordinary interest of these paintings."

After Abbé Breuil, his "partner in world prehistory" had come all the way from Florence to give his verdict! Could we hope for an end of the quarrel?

But Séverin Blanc stuck to his guns. On being questioned by a number of journalists who went to consult him at Les Eyzies strictly for the sake of impartiality, he maintained his point of view. There was, however, a shade of difference. He still made a distinction between the paintings and the engravings. Though he refused to certify the authenticity of the paintings, he did not dispute that of the engravings, which he had never seen! And M. Séverin Blanc announced the same evening that he had been asked by the Ministry of Fine Arts to make a report before October 15. "Can you make a report?" asked the journalists. "Yes, yes, gentlemen, we shall take care of that."

Raoul Cousté, the reporter from Bordeaux who acted as spokesman for Les Eyzies, was in the party. It seems he had visited the cave some years before, and had noticed nothing. "The mammoths," he wrote, "have scored a point—a great point," but according to him there was still a doubt about the rhinoceros frieze, and only that. Those were the "accursed rhinos", and we foresaw that very soon, to quote Mme Plassard, Jr., "people would be arguing about the hair on a wart on the first rhinoceros!"

Vain Quarrels over Priority

It is true that Raoul Cousté's argument is specious; it is meant to be subtle. The Périgueux Spéléo-Club, he claims, saw the Great Ceiling and the Brive Spéléo-Club saw the engravings! We may wonder what *we* saw, and if we saw so little, no doubt we shall be allowed to claim half a fragment of "macaroni". What is the reason for this campaign?

Now we make the better acquaintance of M. Dubois—yes, the patron of the Dubois rhinoceros, the man who wrote his name on the rhino's stomach, to bewitch it, no doubt, or to bewitch himself. On January 16, 1955, a team of cave-explorers from Brive descended upon Rouffignac. In the Bulletin of the Second South-Western Regional Spelaeological Congress, which met at Bordeaux on May 14 and 15, 1955, they published the following report:

"We have taken up the study, abandoned by the Spéléo-Club of Périgueux, of the Cro de Granville or Miremont cave. This cavern, which is the fourth largest in France (four miles of galleries altogether are known up to now) is very curious, both for its two aspects, consisting of great galleries in the form of a delta ending in blocked passages and a network of streams winding in deeply corroded tunnels, and also for distinct signs of human habitation."

Indeed, the traces of habitation are innumerable, especially during the various Celtic phases of the Halstattian Civilisation.

In conclusion, the cave-explorers from the Corréze, who are more "expert" and better judges and observers than their brethren of Périgueux, add: "Let us note in passing that not far from the junction of the Martel corridor a drawing of a bovine animal engraved on the wall is undeniably of prehistoric origin." The drawing referred to is not that of an ox, but that of the hind-quarters of a bison on the left-hand cornice, before the Stream crater. It is "undeniably of prehistoric origin". One good mark for M. Dubois, but a bad mark for having defaced the rhino on the frieze! To his glory and his shame, the rhino will bear Dubois' name for all time. You reach posterity as best you can. But what will the Registry of Fine Arts say to this sacrilegious inscription? But for the heroic battle of the Rouffignac mammoths, we may be sure very few prehistorians would have read the paper produced by the Brive cave-explorers. And the mammoths would sleep on, perhaps for long . . .

On this shifting scene of operations, Les Eyzies was in retreat and Brive in a state of cautious expectancy which, to its credit, it never abandoned, while Périgueux and the President of the Spéléo-Club were still in a fever.

Vain insistence

Without a pause, Bernard Pierret kept up his attack, often in the same terms. At the beginning of the month, after the Paris Press conference, he wrote furiously: "I maintain my position"—and he again attacked the rhinos. "There are drawings which I saw appear during my expeditions; I may add that it was almost an amusement for us to find new ones from year to year." But we quite agree; it is a very fine and exciting amusement! We gave a first reckoning followed on July 30 by another, more important. The third "census" is now going on and will exceed all our hopes. It is curious how a minute survey, with clever oblique lighting, multiplies these "apparitions".

But Bernard Pierret goes on: "What I demand—and I am astonished that it should be refused—is a confrontation on the spot, at which I can say: 'This drawing or that appeared in such-and-such a spot in such a year'." All very fine, my dear Sir! But when did Bernard Pierret ever ask for this "return to Rouffignac"? We say "return", for the word "confrontation" is hardly appropriate between him and us. There may be confrontation between two delinquents or between two experts. There can be no confrontation between Bernard Pierret and Abbé Breuil, or between Bernard Pierret and ourselves.

The manœuvre is too plain; it was supported by headlines in the Press.

"'Authentic', declares the Italian specialist."

"'False', maintains M. Blanc,"

proclaimed the *Echo du Centre* on August 10, 1956. Professor Graziosi and M. Séverin Blanc are put on the same footing. They are not even on an equal footing, for one "declares" and the other, with confident superiority, "maintains". One is an anonymous "specialist", the other is "M. Blanc". No, there is no need for a "Round Table conference" in front of the rhinoceros frieze: a conference which would have brought together not only Abbé Breuil, Professor Graziosi, ourselves and soon Professor Almagro, but how many European university specialists in prehistoric art on one side, and Bernard Pierret, a cave-explorer from Périgueux, on the other!

And why should there be such a friendly meeting? In order to enable M. Bernard Pierret, supported by M. de Faccio, to tell us: "This one is good, that one is bad." But we do not need them—far from it!—to uphold the authenticity of a mammoth or to recognise in passing the talents of M. Gérin, the little telegraph linesman. You know—the famous Gérin bison! But we shall speak of him later. He deserves it.

Entrance free—but only by Request

We refused no one during the official visits. Not even M. Segondat, a schoolmaster from the Dordogne, who passed himself off as a journalist to get into Rouffignac and as a "Prehistorian" [sic] to stay there.

It is true that when he came out, for he had to come out at last—we did not leave him to brood alone over the friezes—he gave us the advantage of his high opinion. "It's really very fine, very fine, but . . ." But what? Well, M. Segondat was not satisfied with a horse and with one horn of a rhinoceros. Never mind, dear friend, but you must tell us that. We will try to do better next time. How would you like your horn? Longer or more curving? More sharply pointed?—though you know, a pretty little blunted point has charm! No doubt we should not have refused entry to M. Bernard Pierret if he had asked for it. But he never did. Never! Our address, or rather our addresses, were well known enough, and even if letters wandered from the Alps to the Pyrenees and from Paris to the Dordogne, they always arrived in the end. How often, when we asked for a telephone call, did the operator cut us short, having already understood "ROUF——": Rouffignac! Yes, yes, the cave country! And we were put through at once.

There are about twenty years between us, and THAT ALONE was a sufficient reason why M. Bernard Pierret should make a written request. We do not speak of other reasons; there are too many, let us be merciful. Unless, of course, M. Charles Plassard had not allowed M. Bernard Pierret to enter his cave. As its owner, he had every right to refuse. Had he not the best of reasons for doing so? But we shall speak of that again. It, too, deserves it.

Now Breuil comes back . . .

On the evening of August 10, after the Italian professor's visit, we left the Dordogne, one of us for the Pyrenees, the other for the Alps. Fortunately France is quite small. In the evening of the

12th we had a new meeting with Abbé Breuil in Les Eyzies itself, at the Hôtel Cro-Magnon, which our master had made his headquarters. He wanted to see Rouffignac again, and he was accompanied by Sir Frederick Handley Page. The Abbé was in great form and led the visit from the start, refusing help. "With my stick and my lamp I don't need a guide."

We should willingly have given a mammoth as a prize—there were so many!—to Max Olivier-Lacamp to go with us. Was it not he who described the Abbé's visit of July 17 in these terms? "One can easily imagine the two discoverers afire with enthusiasm, communicating their excitement to the venerable Master of Prehistory and leading this old man, hardly out of the Paris train, into the depths of a cavern where the air is loaded with carbonic acid." No, my dear friend—for we called him, too, our friend—it was not like that. The Abbé was bound and gagged, and we took away his cigarettes, and we released him after twelve hours only when he consented to recognise the interest of the paintings and engravings we showed him. That was why the visit took twelve hours. What a magnificent proof of endurance!

Under the Great Ceiling the Abbé and Sir Frederick Handley Page exchanged a few words while Miss Mary Handley Page and the other members of the expedition went down to the lower galleries through the great crater of the Stream. And our ascent from the deep galleries, and our exit from the cave, were quicker than our descent. "Five more bison! Three more mammoths!"

Miraculous apparitions continued and Rouffignac appeared more and more in the guise of a "Pyrenean cave", quite improperly competing with its sister at Lourdes.

Despite his eighty years, Abbé Breuil wanted to go down at all costs. We had to use the greatest persuasion and ingenuity to prevent him from setting eyes on this new treasure, for the descent was dangerous and we had no rope.

Last Counter-Attack in Périgord

In the last days of August there was a lull in the mammoths' war of movement. Communiqués ceased, yielding place to long analytical articles relating the Homeric swayings of the battle. Everyone was taking stock, and we could feel a real desire for historical objectivity in presenting the problem and diagnosing and curing the trouble.

Max Soriano then surveyed the most up-to-date methods of the ancillary sciences of archaeology and arrived at this wise conclusion: "All these investigations clearly require that the great public of sightseers and journalists should not come and confuse, with their 'many-fingered hands', faint traces perceptible only to practised eyes. So much the worse for my curiosity and that of my readers, who would like to go to these places and see for themselves. It was quite right to build that wall and set up that armoured door."

Jean Guichard, for his part, also summed up the case. At least, if that were necessary, he destroyed the legend of the *Maquisards* artists of Rouffignac, and he wondered about the "plot" against the truth.

"What remains of all this great plot, then? Nothing."

Would our mammoths of Rouffignac, who could not help them-selves, poor things, subside into a torpor preceding a great silence? No, they were to be stirred up once more. "*Coup de théâtre!*" rattled the teleprinters round the world. "Counter-attack by the Périgueux Spéléo-Club!" flared the Press.

From now on the battle raged in the heart of Périgueux itself, in "a room of the Barrière château, itself a modern structure but built hard by a Roman rampart which at least is very ancient."

A "limited" Conference

There Bernard Pierret held a Press conference on the model of ours in Paris. Standing, "he read a typewritten statement for about three-quarters of an hour". He began by defining his own com-petence. "We do not uphold the point of view of an expert, a pre-historian or a man of science. We are only cave-explorers...." Wise and prudent words! But then why did he declare, an hour later:

"As for the flint 'kidneys' found at the end of the western branch, these do not come from stone-cutting workshops but are blocks which have fallen from the roof and slid down the chimneys to the Stream."

It's quite true, M. Bernard Pierret; you are not by any means an historian, not even an elementary apprentice beginner. After a quarter of an hour of their first lesson my pupils could recognise a splinter of flint cut by human hands and discern the striking plane, the split surface and the percussion bulb....

Those far-away workshops in the northern section of Rouffignac prove that you are not a prehistorian. They prove that M. Séverin Blanc never went as far as that, for he is, after all, a prehistorian, and he could not have set foot there without seeing them.... The lecturer then read what he called his "decisive arguments". "I am quite definite. We did not see the engravings. We passed them by without seeing them. Others were able to see what had escaped us."

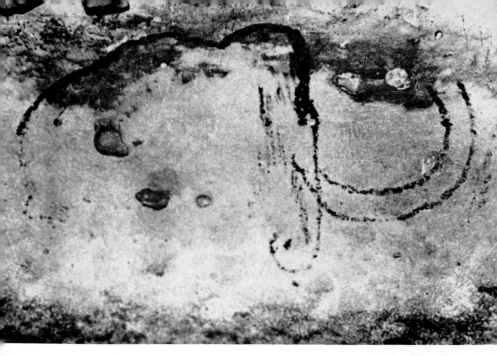

30. The Breuil Gallery: the last mammoth of the Great Frieze

31. The Breuil Gallery: two anthropomorphs engraved on the ceiling of
the extension to the gallery—left, Adam; right, Eve

32. The Breuil Gallery: the Mammoth Patriarch

33. The Sacred Way: the leader of the left-hand herd on the engraved panel of the Five Mammoths

That also is quite true, M. Bernard Pierret, but why add your Parthian shot: "This was the Corrèzian group"? M. Dubois dug up a half-bovid which was no other than a bison and immediately buried it in the Bulletin of the Second South-Western Regional Spelaeological Congress. You must admit that we had to be very sure of ourselves "to launch upon the world the mammoths of Rouffignac in a cave marked with a star in the Michelin guide". We must have been certain of our scientific diagnosis. But the lecturer continued:

"As for the paintings, we did our duty by reporting them to M. Blanc. He told us: 'They are fakes.' We had done our part."

Yes, indeed, your part was finished. What, then, was the use of this campaign? And why this pointless "Press conference"?

No doubt it enabled its author to give a model reading-lesson to a large audience, since from this point the conference degenerated into the studious reading of three letters.

Attractive Reading

The first was from M. François Bordes, a director of research at the National Scientific Research Centre and an excellent specialist on the loess of the Paris river basin, which he made the subject of his thesis. When I commented on this work on the loess to a mutual colleague, he said to me at once: "You speak well of him, but do you know he speaks very ill of you?" I answered calmly: "Oh, you know, we may both be wrong."

M. Bordes brought his guarantee to M. Bernard Pierret and to M. Blanc. Of course, he had never seen Rouffignac, but was that necessary to form an opinion? The detailed views of M. Blanc must be considered, he said, for he "has great experience of these questions". For the second time in the war of the mammoths, a doctor of science was content to see with the eyes of a school-teacher at Les Eyzies! Is that the attitude to science recommended by Claude Bernard or René Descartes? Are the sense of logic and the sense of humanity out of fashion in some of our scientific establishments? I refuse to believe it!

The second statement came from M. Jacques de Saintour, a geologist in Madagascar. He knew Rouffignac, for he had studied the flint strata there. He wrote: "When I last explored the cave, a few years ago, the drawings were not very numerous."

So there were *some* drawings? Decidedly, Rouffignac is a strange cave! Everyone flirts with it, more or less. Everyone snatches some treasure from it, but dare not go farther.

M

After all, it was a good thing we knew nothing of all this, of all these extravagances with the Pierrets, the De Faccios, the Dubois, the De Sainteurs and other imitators of François de Belleforest. We were even ignorant of our cave's gravest sin with Canon Tarde— yes, with a canon from a cathedral! To dare to enter and to get wedded to this cave of Rouffignac, must not one be a native of this countryside?

"*Little Lascaux*" [*sic*].

Finally, a third letter brought a revelation. Citizen Gérin, at last, the team-mate of Bernard Pierret in the glorious hours of 1945–1949, now living at Oran and as inquisitive as all distant correspondents, declared: "I made drawings on the roof at a place I called 'Little Lascaux'."

"Questions came thick and fast," noted Jean Guichard, the careful secretary of the conference. "Where, when and how were these drawings made? What drawings?" But Bernard Pierret knew nothing. The work of art was conceived when he himself was exploring the cave, but he saw nothing at all. We can understand why impartial observers were dissatisfied. And the Press conference fizzled out—or rather, it was about to begin. But the Gérin balloon was launched by Press and Radio. It was soon to collapse.

That same evening a letter left for Oran, addressed to a friend of mine. He was asked to find the man Gérin, but he arrived too late; Gabriel Gérin was out in the wilds, very usefully employed in setting up telegraph poles. Really, we were getting some distinguished scientific opponents! A weekly publication, *Benjamin-Actualité*, was quicker and luckier. It had a local correspondent at Oran, and he hurried to find Gabriel Gérin, the "forger" of Rouffignac. Let us see what Gérin had to say:

"When we founded our Club, our first expedition was to the cave of Miremont, *alias* Rouffignac. Two of our comrades knew it already, and they showed us some drawings. (Everyone seems to have seen them.) That was in the summer of 1948. I can't tell you whether those drawings were 20,000 years or only a few months old. We found about ten that day. There may have been many more already. The first we saw were 800 yards from the entrance to the cave."

These were evidently the black paintings on the Great Ceiling, at a halting-place before the descent to the Stream. As the interview goes on, we learn sensational facts:

"During one of our later expeditions I had to wait in a small chamber for my companions to come up.   We had pitched our tent in this chamber, above a deep well.   There were drawings on the walls of this low chamber.   While I waited, I had the idea of making drawings with lamp-smoke.   I imitated those I had seen at Lascaux."

The Gérin Bison

The reporter continues: "At my request, M. Gérin took a pencil and a sheet of paper and drew a bison like those he had drawn in the cave."   And *Benjamin-Actualité* published this "unique documentary evidence"!

Poor, poor youth of August 1956, who could admire this work of art in their magazine and believe quite seriously, for it was written, that they had a copy of Lascaux, painted at Rouffignac, before their eyes!   An enthusiastic and friendly group, sitting round a table, discussed the work of the "forger" of Rouffignac at length.   The word "FORGER" is printed in letters half an inch high in the text of the magazine.   True, it is carefully framed between inverted commas.   Was this a *Bison priscus* or a *Bos primigenius*, a *Bison bonasus* —why not, after all?   He had a kindly look—or the *Bison priscus*, ancestor of the *bonasus* and uncle of the *americanus*?

Some critics then thought they could distinguish various vegetable shapes.   I heard talk of "potatoes" and "beetroots".   Finally everyone agreed on wild salsify.   And indeed, Gérin's bison did look rather like a bulbous and distorted salsify.

And it was drawn in black smoke, too!   That was why fifty or a hundred persons, all the notables of Périgueux, were astir.   Oh, yes, all the notables of Périgueux, for among the honourable audience were the President of the Family Allowances Office, the Departmental Director of the Health Service (whose medical skill might have been useful) and the Senior Assistant to the Mayor, not to mention famous names in the world of science such as Professor Pittard of Geneva, and the Comtesse de Saint-Périer.   We pass over others. . . .

No doubt we should be offered a "confrontation" in the depths of Rouffignac, at which M. Gérin (Gabriel) would attend in person to show us where his drawings were, in case we did not know the difference between the Gérin salsify—pardon us, the Gérin bison— drawn in soot with an acetylene lamp, and a real bison of the real Rouffignac drawn in manganese!   Well, such a meeting is unnecessary.   One fine September day, when it was still quite dark in the maze of lower galleries leading to the Stream over a deep well, we examined some excellent and real bison.   And at last we discovered, a few yards farther along, on the left-hand wall, a perfect "Gérin salsify-bison" really drawn in black with the smoke of an acetylene lamp. But it would have been better to change the burner, for the lamp must have smoked abominably! However, this bison-like drawing is closely related to the hen and the duck drawn on the roofs of the eastern galleries, also with the smoke of an acetylene lamp.

So you see, everyone is right. There *are* "forgeries" in Rouffignac. Let us be reconciled! Let us embrace!

A serious Difference of Opinion

No, this was no occasion for embracing, except perhaps for the purpose of throttling, when Bernard Pierret had finished his lecture and the real Press conference began in the form of a few discreet little questions, recorded here by Jean Guichard (*Nouvelle République de Bordeaux*, 1.9.56, p. 3).

Question. The owner of the cave, M. Plassard, says he had a serious difference with you. What was that about?

Answer. In 1949 M. Plassard had the entrance to the cavern sealed. Until then he had allowed us to explore it freely. Now he told us we should find the key at a farmhouse. If you had not found the key [or the farmer?] WHAT WOULD YOU HAVE DONE IN MY PLACE?

I imagine that a well-regulated scenario would have made a long pause here. There should have been a moment of suspense, during which a few angels might brush the Périgordian notabilities present with their soft wings. What would the President of the Family Allowances Office, who was also the former owner of the Pradelie estate into which the cave opens, have done? He was not there, but the question concerned him. What would the Prefect of the Dordogne, who was Bernard Pierret's administrative chief, have done?

What exactly would the Resident Inspector of the Academy at Périgueux have done? He, too, was Bernard Pierret's administrative superior. Why, of course, they would all have done what you and I would have done as honest men who respect other people's property. WHAT WOULD YOU HAVE DONE IN MY PLACE? asked Bernard Pierret at Périgueux on August 31, 1956. WE BROKE OPEN THE GATE. That's all. WE BROKE IN. It wasn't difficult. And he added: "M. Plassard was very angry with us at the time, but it was all arranged afterwards."

Yes, it was all arranged because M. Plassard, who was a good fellow and a humane and fatherly man, forgave the culprits and withdrew his complaint to the police.

SCIENTIFIC PEACE RESTORED

Canon Tarde, "Inventor"

A few days later the debate was transferred to the Corrèze. M. de Chalup, President of the Brive Syndicat d'Initiatives, found in his château at Cosnac, near Brive, an old coloured map of Périgord accompanied by a text attributed to Canon Jean Tarde which mentioned Rouffignac and its "paintings in several places". The paper was written in 1606 and published in 1625. It therefore gave first priority to the Canon of La Roque-Gajac.

At the same time, the same map in colour, with his commentary, was on sale at Montignac-sur-Vézère, where it was bought and photographed to be presented at the meeting of the Historical and Archaeological Society of Périgord on September 6. And the official record of that meeting says: "Allowing for the time the map spent at the photographer's, Montignac may come before Brive, allowing for possible indiscretions."

How I dislike this doubt! Detective-historians, to your posts! Slice, cut and prune; Brive or Montignac? Montignac or Brive? O happy Périgord, where we can still be absorbed by such noble problems in 1956!

Finally the scene of operations moved north, and on September 7 Abbé Breuil presented the drawings and paintings of Rouffignac at the Académie des Inscriptions et Belles-Lettres.

The Shade of Saïtapharnès

It was an opening session, uneventful even for a communication on prehistory, as is right and proper on the Quai Conti. Abbé Breuil, in excellent form, gave a clear summary of the chief arguments in favour of authenticity, which are recorded in the paper deposited at the Academy. It annihilates the few opposing arguments: the paintings come off on one's fingers (which means nothing at all); they date from the last war; they are copies of those at Font-de-Gaume, Cabrerets or Niaux, made with an acetylene lamp! But one feels that all this is out of date and that these poor late reasonings were not and are no longer reasonable. Without false modesty,

Abbé Breuil declares that he is probably "the only person who could make imitations of quaternary art as successful as those in question".

He solemnly reaffirms "the absolutely certain authenticity of the paintings and engravings". Lantern-slides in colour of the chief animal paintings discovered up to then illustrated his words. "I am certain," he concludes, "that if M. Blanc had taken the trouble to visit the cave before making up his mind, he would have realised his mistake."

M. Séverin Blanc was cornered, but he still could escape. At that same time he received an invitation to visit Rouffignac on September 12, and this visit enabled him to make the report for which he had been asked by the Department of Architecture.

Abbé Breuil's audience applauded politely and adjourned the discussion to a later date, when "all the evidence and documents have been placed at the disposal of competent persons", seeing that the exploration of the cavern is far from complete.

It is true that an immediate discussion would have been a delicate business. The results of the analyses on which the laboratory at Florence had been working since Professor Graziosi obtained his first specimens on August 9 were not yet known. The range of highly specialised subjects before the Academy is immense, and it is always difficult to give a decision outside one's own speciality. The tattered shade of Saïtapharnès and painful memories of Glozel hovered over the Academy, inciting its members to prudent reserve and wise reflection. It would have been vain to expect the "last word" that day. The answer could be given only at Rouffignac, and thirty world specialists were invited to make a detailed inspection of the cave on September 12. Including M. Séverin Blanc!

Ariège Jubilee

From Paris we went to the Ariège, where we had to prepare for the ceremonies organised by the Ariège Prehistoric Society to celebrate the fiftieth anniversary of the discovery of the paintings in the cave at Niaux. We also had to arrange the preparatory meeting of the Pyrenean Institute of Prehistoric Art. Early correspondence led us to expect fifty or sixty members, of eight different nationalities, to attend. This was quite a frightening success for a beginning. At Niaux itself a bronze medallion bearing the effigy of Abbé Breuil was set in its place and draped in the red and gold colours of the Ariège. It would be unveiled on Sunday, September 16, but what a busy week there would be before this solemn tribute!

On the morning of the 10th two cars left for Toulouse to meet, at seven o'clock, Professor Martin Almagro, of the University of Madrid, and his wife.

Summer Holidays at Rouffignac

For the first time, our wives were in the secret and would visit the fabulous cave.   They will long remember the "Rouffignac summer holidays" as exceptional.   First, we planned to make an expedition to the South of Spain and photograph the Pileta, the most southerly painted cave in the country, in the Serrania de Bonda.   This noble pretext offered hopes of seeing Granada, Seville, Cadiz, Cordoba and the like.

The luggage was ready and loaded on the cars, the passports were generously stamped with visas; everything was ready except the drivers, who were paddling in the "Sea of Mud" at Rouffignac. By way of compensation, those husbands offered their wives the same pleasure: to go and wade through the mud and count mammoths by the score!   Those were wonderful holidays, those summer holidays of 1956, when we had meant to go to Seville. . . .

As for our eldest boy, Jacques (over 6 ft. 2 in.), he could look forward to a trip to the Dalmatian coast instead of torture by mud. But in October, when he came back to help us make an exact record of the Henri Breuil gallery, he found it just as attractive and even more slippery, for it was more frequented, and better for tobogganing.

At 7 a.m. (French time) we arrived at Toulouse to fetch our eminent Spanish colleague, Professor Almagro.   He was ready, for Spanish time is the same as ours, and that was a good omen.   As holder of the Chair of Prehistory in Madrid and Director of the Senior Council of Prehistoric Research in Spain and of the Archaeological Museum of Barcelona, Professor Almagro is certainly one of the great figures of prehistoric art.

When we were his guests at Ampurias, where we had gone to give a few lectures on Pyrenean Art, in the early days of September, he told us he would like to examine a series of pictures in colour of Rouffignac.   The audience of teachers and students at the international course on archaeology were greatly impressed.   As for the Professor himself, he wanted to form an opinion on the spot, based on actual specimens of the mammoths and rhinoceroses of Rouffignac.

On our way from Toulouse to the Dordogne, via Gourdon, we narrowly escaped three serious motor accidents in three hours. We concluded that the mammoths of Rouffignac were kind and

would harm no one but their detractors.   And early in the afternoon the whole caravan, on foot this time, entered the cave.

The Moment of Truth

We will borrow Jean Guichard's account in the *Nouvelle République* of September 11, 1956, of the results of this study, made by the
greatest Spanish specialist after his greatest Italian colleague.

"Professor Almagro behaved like a clinician.   'Pass me the lamp,'
he said to me as though he were asking for a stethoscope, and,
perched on a cornice where I supported him as he bent backwards,
he promptly began to examine some painting or engraving.

"'I am a man of science,' he said.   'At the request of the Italian
Government, I am organising prehistoric excavations in Liguria,
and I know nothing of the quarrel of which you speak.   I have an
open mind.   My first intellectual attitude is one of systematic
doubt.   I shall search everywhere for a doubt,' he insisted in his
sonorous French.

"He was then facing the first painting: a rhinoceros.   (The rhinoceros rejected by Séverin Blanc in 1949—if he got that far.)   Now
he was silent, and the hush of a thousand years, falling again on the
cave, was poignant.   What would be his diagnosis?   Only Professor
Nougier remained calm and smiling.   Suddenly, M. Almagro's face
was transfigured.   The cold eyes twinkled and the lip, rather scorn-
ful until then, relaxed.   The clinician's expression yielded to that
of the art-lover.

"'It's admirable,' he said.   'But give me the lamp!'

"Jumping down from the slippery cornice he took me by the arm
and led me forward to look at an engraved mammoth more closely.

"'We must find some reason for doubting . . .'   We breathed more
freely.

"'You have to know a lot to forge them . . .'   We began to hope.
'I don't understand why there has been such a scandal about these
drawings.'"

Then they were genuine!

At last the thrilling moment, the moment of truth, had arrived!

In the dim and flickering light of the lamps, M. Almagro saw the
long procession of the Great Frieze of mammoths.   He stood rooted
to the spot.   Then, stepping back, he signed to his guides to go
away.   "Let me look," he said.

I stayed alone with him.   He could hardly conceal his excitement.   He was talking to himself in Spanish.   Step by step, fas-
cinated, he went nearer.   Reversing the earlier process, at every

step the art-lover became the clinician. And once more, in this cave that saw the unrolling of great magic rites, those of science were coldly displayed.

"But give me the lamp!"

"I was unable," writes Jean Guichard, "to rouse Professor Almagro from his meditation before the Great Ceiling. "

But when we returned to the modern world, with passion stilled and the light of summer found again, Professor Almagro said to me:

"This cave holds one of the finest collections of cave-paintings in the world. I tried hard to criticise, but I could not find a single argument in favour of forgery. The detractors of the Cro de Granville have taken up an unreasonable personal position. The Great Ceiling is painted in a style so pure and so beautiful that the campaign against these masterpieces is incredible."

That same evening we were all at Les Eyzies, under the leafy boughs of "Les Glycines", where we found many eminent Spanish, Italian and Dutch colleagues. Night fell and the moths fluttered round the lamps.

One Second—Face to Face

Suddenly, a 4 h.p. Renault stops. A shadow alights and becomes clear after taking a few steps. It's M. Séverin Blanc. We are face to face. We are alone together, he and I, isolated by the darkness of the road and by a noisy group of Spanish colleagues. He is my senior, and I say "Good evening" to him. The shadow is swallowed up again, followed by the slam of a door and the sound of a hasty departure. . . .

I understood at that moment what would happen the next day. No, the example of the great Cartailhac would not be followed. At one time I had hoped, we had hoped it would be. We could not believe he would persist, when confronted with the mammoths of Rouffignac, in his earlier attitude. He had not seen them, or he had seen them badly. There were excuses for him. We were ready to emphasise those excuses and facilitate a sceptic's *mea culpa* that we all wished to hear. A *mea culpa* would have added to his stature; it would have arranged everything; all would have been forgiven and forgotten; it would even have cancelled that "Diary of Rouffignac". Cartailhac had fought against Altamira. At the Lisbon Congress of 1880, he had left the hall in protest, saying: "All this is childish."

The discovery at La Mouthe, near Les Eyzies, of engravings

covered by archaeological deposits did not convert him to quaternary art. At last the discovery of Combarelles on September 8 and of Font-de-Gaume on September 15, 1901, convinced him. He made honourable amends. "These discoveries," he said, "show us that our science, like others, is writing a history that will never end, but of which the interest grows unceasingly."

The International Visit

At 8.30 a.m. the Mayor of Rouffignac arrived, with his sash of office carefully folded in his pocket. "You never know," he had been told the day before, and it was easier to have the sash ironed than to go back to the village for it. He was excited and amiable. The last battle was about to be fought on his territory, in a cave he had known as a child. One by one, the cars began to drive up, controlled as soon as they reached the red road by a discreet police service, and to set down their notables or their journalists.

Groups gathered and dispersed in the courtyard of the estate. Some colleagues put on their overalls in the open; others retired to the near-by stables, to the astonishment of a row of brown cows, thrusting their horned heads through the oval openings of their mangers. More than one archaeologist, as he pulled on his dungarees, must have wondered how those animals could get their horns through the slits.

By 9 a.m. the yard was crowded and wore the air of a Périgordian wedding feast. We had decided to let our foreign colleagues, Professors Graziosi and Almagro, lead the procession, while the two representatives of the Franco-Cantabrian countries flanked the group from France. After Abbé Breuil, "the Pope of Prehistory", as the representative of the Minister simply and affectionately called him a few days later, when the Niaux medallion was unveiled, came the "Primate of Spain" and the "Primate of Italy", both of whom had come to certify the authenticity of Rouffignac. Around them were many prehistorians, mostly university men, from Barcelona or Oviedo, Verona or Liége, Erlangen or Stockholm, and the National Directors of excavations, like the Dutch delegate, who were accustomed to international congresses and were delighted to meet again. French was the common language, for you can hardly be a prehistorian without knowing both our language and our country. All rejoiced at the prospect of passing direct judgment on works of parietal art. The French delegation, which was numerous, varied and of the highest distinction, rejoiced no less. The *Institut* was represented by Professor P. P. Grassé; the Sorbonne by Professor

A. Leroi-Gourhan, the successor of Marcel Griaule; Algiers by
Professor L. Balout; Poitiers by Professor R. Facon; the French Pre-
historic Society by our collaborator Claude Barrière, Henri Delporte
and Jacques Blanchard; the archaeologists by the Comte de Chalup,
and the amateur prehistorians by Mlle de Saint-Mathurin and M. F.
Lacorre and his wife, who founded the society of the Friends of Les
Eyzies. Count Max Bégouen had come from the Ariège in spite of
pressing family cares, and his arrival was a great comfort to us
"Pyreneans", as was the affectionate and friendly presence of
Norbert Casteret, the Prince of cave-explorers. Still others came,
known or unknown colleagues and sometimes friends who had
spontaneously responded to our call for this visit of scientific veri-
fication. The sheer numbers of the visitors, increased by the journalists who were not the least keen and curious, made the excursion
long and difficult, for certain examinations required time and solitude. But they all understood that they were taking part in a
première which was intended much more to make them want to
come back and work at Rouffignac than to give a complete picture
of it one day.

The Guest

The scientific visit of Professor P. P. Grassé on October 10
originated in the international visit of September 12. At the hour
stated, the Director of the 7th District was there, and the journalists
crowded round him. From a distance I heard him say to the
reporters: "Not invited; ordered to come!" He waved the registered letter of invitation, with a receipt for his signature, which he
had received from us a few days before. We apologise for it, but
how else should we or could we have warned him and been quite
sure that he had been notified?

No, Monsieur Blanc, it was not a "summons" but a proper
invitation. More than that, it was a chance for you, a last chance.
But you did not understand. I regret it very sincerely. I regret it
for the sake of prehistory, which we all serve with the same
devouring passion. And quite simply, I regret it for your sake,
too.

Professors Graziosi and Almagro decided to begin the inspection
at the Great Ceiling. Everyone slopped through the soft clay and
slipped over huge blocks fallen from the roof, to find himself lying
on his back, examining those intertwined lines, searching them with
the beam of his electric torch or sometimes skimming them dangerously with the flame of an acetylene lamp. Professor Grassé cut

short an argument started by Séverin Blanc by remarking: "We are here to find out the truth, not to quarrel."

An optical Illusion

The most important observation, which occurred to several visitors unaccustomed to examining prehistoric paintings ("there are gate-crashers here," a journalist noted) reached the ears of Professor Grassé, who expressed it aloud: "Several people have the impression that the lines of a horse pictured above us were drawn over the inscriptions."

This is a well-known optical illusion. The palaeolithic line is deep black and thin. The line of the inscriptions is broad and thick, with a series of arches corresponding with the movements of the lamp. These inscriptions are much faded and turning greyish, while the old lines have kept their original blackness. To an unpractised eye, the darker line seems to pass over the lighter.

An examination with magnifying binoculars a month later clearly showed Professor Grassé that the inscriptions were SUPERIMPOSED on the old palaeolithic lines. But on September 12 there could be no question of a scientific examination of this kind. We were too many.

Anatomical details were analysed by the zoologists and biologists present. Professor Grassé says again: "I was very much struck by the accuracy of the representations, which showed a very advanced anatomical knowledge of the animals depicted, as for instance in the anal aperture of the mammoths and the reversed curve of the horns in the woolly rhinoceros."

M. Jacques Blanchard, who is a great hunter and a perfect connoisseur of fauna past and present, also noticed characteristic details. The atmosphere was most pleasant. Everyone gave his opinion and quietly discussed that of his neighbour. Many were delighted to find perfectly genuine evidence for themselves. Crawling as they talked, or rather talking as they crawled, the leaders of the scientific caravan reached the last mammoth, "with the Roguish Eye". He also represents a profound scientific truth, but let us not reveal the secrets of his "anatomical" gaze. In passing, we did not forget the many flint-cutting workshops *in situ*.

The return by the Sacred Way was quicker, but the congress "functioned" for a long time in the Breuil gallery. The frieze of mammoths and the frieze of rhinos were minutely examined and subjected to the most varied criticisms. All the schools represented climbed up to the rhinos in turn—as art-lovers, clinicians, geologists, cave-explorers or chemists—to look for some cause for doubt, which they never found. "As the visit to the cave proceeded, the scientists' belief in its authenticity was reinforced."

Limits of Present-day Science

Sometimes, however, the most modern science cannot solve the problems that are laid before it. Scientific possibilities must be accurately known before making demands. When we were under the Great Ceiling I was discreetly summoned. Bold assertions were being made:

"It's very simple! All you have to do is to analyse these lines with radioactive carbon, as was done at Lascaux."

"No, sir. These lines cannot be analysed with Carbon 14."

"But what about Lascaux?"

I had to explain, or what might we not have read (written in good faith) the next day?

Analysis with carbon 14 was used at Lascaux on hearth ashes, not on the lines of paintings. The age indicated, 15,516 years, with a possible error of 900 years, more or less, fits these ashes and the Périgordian assegais that lay among them. That date does not apply to the paintings. Or, if you prefer it, it is applicable only as the table in your drawing-room is dated by the wall. At Lascaux the rocky walls are eternal, historically and prehistorically, but the paintings may be older or more recent than the wood ashes of the hearth discovered at the bottom of the well.

The chronological estimate is interesting, none the less, but that is because the assegais belong to what is called the Périgordian civilisation, and the polychrome paintings of Lascaux belong to the same period. It is as though a magnificent Buhl writing-table were found in an 18th-century "folly". There are many hearths at Rouffignac, especially in the first few hundred yards, but they are recent hearths, with many fragments of pottery. They do not date the paintings.

"But if you scrape the paintings, isn't it possible to work out a date?"

That is not possible, either. First of all, of what are the paintings made? (On September 12 we still had not the result of the chemical analysis, which was made known to us a few days later. We know now that the lines were drawn in manganese.)

Carbon 14

If the colouring matter is manganese, it cannot be analysed with radioactive carbon 14. If the colouring matter is wood charcoal, which is possible without the paintings being faked on that account, we must scrape the paint very carefully, avoiding the slightest contact with organic matter, which would enrich the sample and distort all our calculations, making the date much more recent. How many grammes of charcoal could a mammoth of the Great Frieze or a rhinoceros supply?

"Bah! You have so many. You can easily sacrifice one for analysis," a journalist said to me.

"Well, no! To begin with, they don't belong to me any more than to you. From now on they are part of a common heritage, that of humanity and its distant origins. They are of inestimable value. No one now has any right to take these works of art for unnecessary experiments. To make an analysis with carbon 14, aiming at a date as far back as that of the Rouffignac mammoths, you would need about 400 grammes (6,000 grains) of charcoal. Perhaps more. That means that all the paintings, if they were scraped, would not yield the necessary quantity. And in front of rocky walls stripped bare, we should hardly gain much if we could say six months hence, when we had the results of an analysis made in Chicago: 'You see, on this rocky wall—yes, there, on that site —there *was* a frieze of mammoths dating from 12,000 years before our era.'"

Why has no analysis been made? That is why. Because analysis was impossible. All possible examinations have been or will be made. Rouffignac, the victim of slander, owes it to herself to be the most scientifically studied and analysed of caves. The lessons it will yield will enable us, no doubt, to avoid another "Rouffignac crisis" in the future.

In the 20th century it is easy to believe that Science is all-powerful, especially in chemistry and physics. But this does not mean unlimited power, just as in the case of cave-paintings millenary age does not mean eternity. There comes a time at last when Science reaches its limit and gives place to Man. Finally, Man is the master and the Head.

A radiograph of a Van Gogh has technical interest, no doubt, but it is the human eye that passes judgment. Modern methods of analysis and batteries of retorts can only be the servants of prehistorians, not their masters.

It was very late when our procession started its return journey, after having outlined many problems. Some journalists found the time too long.

A Journalist in a Hurry with a nice blue Suit

We shall long remember the special correspondent of a great Paris daily paper, Jacques Perrier. He was a big, tall fellow and he arrived at the cave-entrance wearing a beautiful navy blue suit and looking very smart. That suit certainly gave him a "complex", and he was most anxious to come out with it as immaculate as when he went in. He was equally anxious—I don't know why—to get out of the cave as soon as possible, though we were quite comfortable inside.

Near the engraved mammoths' panel he came and asked me if he could go. We had come in together and we had to go out together; I could not abandon our other guests to lead him back. I made some evasive reply. In front of the mammoths' frieze he asked me again. "We're going back soon," I said. But the prospect of escape into the open air was too remote for him and his blue suit, which no longer seemed blue at all to me. It is true that the light in the cave was dim.

In front of the horse painted on the flint "kidney" he came up once more. "I am very sorry," I said. "I haven't got the key. Someone has gone to fetch it."

Facing the great mammoth on the roof, the mammoth that was 10 ft. long, I found him again. This time I said I had lost the key. He went out with the rest of us and with his fine blue suit, which was blue no longer, even in broad daylight.

"You'll see my story!" he snarled as we separated.

"You've dropped a brick," a colleague assured me. "You'll see what he'll do to your mammoths!"

I must confess we laughed heartily over his story—the story of the Journalist in a Hurry with a Fine Blue Suit. "Surrounded by a detachment of spelaeologists and specialists in prehistory," he wrote, "I found myself yesterday morning at the entrance to the cave of Rouffignac.

"At first sight, this cave strangely resembles the basements of the Bank of France. The entrance is guarded by a strong-room door.

"At 9.30 a.m., by the light of acetylene lamps, our visit began. At first all went well. The ground was muddy but that was not serious. After 1,200 yds., however, we had to stoop more and more. We were ploughing through mud 20 in. deep." (Are you an exaggerating Southerner, M. Perrier?) "Personally, I tried at first to save my trousers, giving up hope for my shoes, which were sunk in miry clay. I carefully wiped one muddy patch with my handkerchief, then another, then a third.   After a few minutes I gave up the hand-kerchief: we had to crawl on all fours.   Our advance was punctu-ated by the sound of forty squelching pairs of feet.   A sharp blow on the top of my head and a painful bump soon made me grasp the truth about underground expeditions.   I knew then that cave-exploring was a pursuit unsuitable for rather stout men over six feet tall (and wearing good blue suits), as I unfortunately was.

"On one occasion I felt a sharp burning in a fleshy part of my person.   I turned round and found I had been in contact with the flame of an acetylene lamp.   Cursing and swearing in Italian, Spanish and German rang in my ears."   (Only the French remem-bered their manners, it seems, and that was odd!)

"At last, when threatened with a cruel cramp, I could raise my head.   The roof got higher.   Our torment seemed to be coming to an end.

The Climax

"Then we reached the climax: the mammoths.   Professor Graziosi, who was alongside me, gave vent to his joy.   '*Magnifico!*' he exclaimed.   And to his friends he called: '*Avanti!*' (Forward!).

"Just when I felt I was bearing the whole weight of the roof, a light tap from a stick on my right shoulder and a girlish voice made me jump.   It was the owner's daughter.

"'You'll rub out the frescoes with your hair!   Be kind!   Lie on your back!'

"As I lay on a bed of mud, I saw a strange sight.   A roughly-drawn mammoth and rhinoceros seemed to be laughing at me.   An Italian scientist bestrode me.   He lit up the mammoth and said simply: 'Formidable!   Marvellous!   Exceptional!   Magnificent! Superb!'

"But M. Blanc did not share this exuberance.   'That,' he scoffed, 'an early palaeolithic mammoth!   Are you joking?   It's the work of a forger.'

"At that moment M. Romain Robert invited him to come and see a drawing of an ibex, which, it seemed, was superb.   'Come, M. Blanc, let's bury the hatchet!   Come and see.'

"'Monsieur,' answered Blanc with the accent of Cyrano, whose château of Bergerac is not far away, 'I look at what I choose.   The Minister'—a pause—'the Minister of Fine Arts, yes, the Minister himself has sent me a registered letter with a receipt for my signature, asking for a report.   What I shall tell him will make him laugh!'

"'I don't care a damn about that,' Professor Grassé interrupted.

34.   The Sacred Way: a large mammoth engraved on the ceiling

35.   The Great Ceiling: a painted bison on the left; a bison partly painted
and partly incised on the right

36.   The Great Ceiling: a large painted horse, 7 ft. 6 in. long

37.   The Mammoth with the Roguish Eye.   This drawing in the extension of the Sacred Way is fifteen hundred yards from the entrance to the cave —the farthest in of all the drawings

'Personal questions must give way to science. Gentlemen, no deviationism, I beg of you!'

"The atmosphere of the Hall of the 91 Mammoths was then very like that of a stormy session in the National Assembly.

"'Look at the hairs on that horse's pastern. Could a forger have drawn that? If so, you can hang me!'

"'And this,' said another voice, 'isn't this pretty?' It was an inscription, scribbled on the wall. 'Here Hector swore eternal love to Françoise.'

"Meanwhile Professor Nougier, who seemed to have sunk into the earth, shone his lamp on the walls around us, repeating all the time: 'Come and see my mammoths! Come and see my rhinos!'

"After this we were invited to admire, in a more comfortable position, the Mammoth with the Roguish Eye and the sentimental ibex" [sic].

A Homeric Return

"At last, after wandering for more than four hours underground, we were told the visit was over. But now came the hardest part of our task: to find the exit! No one knew the way back! For more than an hour we wandered from gallery to gallery, from mud-bath to mud-bath, from mammoth to rhinoceros, before we saw the light of day. I began to envy my neighbour, whom I had mocked a little earlier. He carried a small basket from which protruded a bottle of wine, a sausage and a roll of bread.

"Afterwards, as we gazed at the sun with the ecstasy of ship-wrecked mariners when they set foot on *terra firma*, the men of science held their council."

Let us be patient for an hour before we seek the sun with ecstasy. Let us let Jacques Perrier out at last, that he may have time to repair the damage done by the mud of Rouffignac. The armoured door closed behind the journalists, and the specialists held their meeting. This long and detailed visit, which was quite free, since we left the field to Professors Almagro and Graziosi, intervening only to find the way back, was to be summed up in a signed declaration containing our views on the visit and on Rouffignac itself.

A very few of our colleagues abstained, more or less on principle, because they thought the declaration ill-timed. Among them were Mlle de Saint-Mathurin and Professor L. Balout, of the Algiers Faculty of Letters. At the same time Professor Balout agreed very amiably to write something in the cave's Visitors' Book, which Mme Plassard, Jr. offered him soon after we came out. He wrote:

N

"To deny the authenticity of the works of prehistoric art in the Cave of Rouffignac would be a miracle. We have no right to perform it."

The Scientists give their Verdict

Professors Almagro and Graziosi took the initiative in drawing up the first declaration, clear and precise, which was signed by the great majority of the visitors: "Apart, of course, from modern scribblings, the paintings and engravings in the Rouffignac cave are AUTHENTIC. They are among the most interesting known specimens of quaternary art."

In a second declaration Professors Grassé and Leroi-Gourhan noted their desire to wait for the results of scientific analyses. But they added immediately that during their visit they had seen no evidence that the paintings were NOT GENUINE.

Thus, some said Rouffignac was genuine, while others said it was not false. There was only a shade of difference between the two scientific statements; a shade that some newspaper headlines tried to turn into a non-existent opposition. "Thirty scientists face to face . . . The Prehistorians could not agree . . . The majority favour authenticity . . ."

There can be no majority over such a problem. There can be only unanimity, for or against. But positive unanimity does not imply the same reasoning for all. Every scientist is susceptible to this or that argument, according to his own speciality, his training and his character. The scientific range of our visitors was such that it was only natural that different scientific requirements should be expressed.

Generally speaking, the signatories of the first motion had a very wide knowledge of Franco-Cantabrian art. Most of them were specialists in cave paintings, and the criteria, for many of them, lay in aesthetic values, the superimposition of lines, the outlines of the painted features and an appreciation of the patina.

The signatories of the second motion, as eminent specialists in allied subjects such as zoology or ethnology, required different criteria, such as examination of the superimposition of lines by scientific optical methods, with magnifying binoculars for instance, and the "internal" examination of the line in order to discover its chemical composition, with an analysis of the patina. We should also add that the two promoters of the first statement knew the paintings and engravings of Rouffignac from earlier visits, made at leisure and with due consideration.

And the two promoters of the second statement wished to repeat the visit, which had been too crowded on the morning of September 12. Their subsequent visits delighted them. Professor Leroi-Gourhan returned to the cave in the afternoon of that day, and Professor Grassé on October 10.

Manganese, Manganese!

A few days later the first results of chemical analyses arrived. From Florence, Professor Graziosi announced that the colouring matter used by the palaeolithic painters of Rouffignac was MAN-GANESE. And a few days after this, Professor Grassé confirmed that statement in a valuable and masterly way by a series of many and varied scientific tests, for which we are infinitely grateful to him.

When the armoured door swung open at last, early in the afternoon of September 12, and President Jacques Blanchard, perched on the bank in front of the cave, read out the statements drawn up by the scientists, we could consider the "battle of Rouffignac" ended —and won. Only M. Séverin Blanc reserved his opinion for "his Minister". Sitting on the ground at the cave entrance, he was scraping the mud off his boots before taking the road back to the plateau. He was both methodical and melancholy, having lost some of his earlier fluency. He was alone, too, until one of my pupils took pity on him and went to talk to him and break an embarrassing silence.

In the afternoon of the 12th another visit was arranged, for all had not been able to take part in the morning's excursion. Professor Leroi-Gourhan and Norbert Casteret made a second tour of Rouffignac. We were even able to make a more thorough inspection of the gallery of flint-cutting workshops, which prolonged the Sacred Way, and especially of the eastern galleries. We were able to study the damage done to the concretions before the cave was first closed by a gate in 1949.

The Sack of Miremont

For several hundred yards, both to right and to left, the beautiful concretions which used to be so admired by their owners, the "anemones" and "starfish", had been systematically rifled. The marks of picks are still plainly visible, leaving milky, flat streaks in the shining bed of calcite crystals. On the ground, oddly enough, in the brown clay, there is not the smallest splinter or the tiniest remnant of crystal. Norbert Casteret could not believe his eyes, yet he knows hundreds of caves and has seen untold pillage.

"It's incredible! Incredible!" he said, scanning gallery after gallery. We found only two or three starfish. Someone had laid rugs or sacks under the concretions and picked and picked until everything was fallen and destroyed. We recalled certain local memories, certain evenings a few years ago, when heavily-laden cars climbed the hill from the cave in the twilight.

At that time all the talk was of the Cave of Miremont. The Cave of Miremont was systematically looted. Why? Where were the crystals of Miremont bound for? Let us hope that here, too, chemical and petrographical analysis will give us an answer one day soon. Miremont could be interesting only in its natural state, and that interest vanished with this pillage. Miremont was dead, quite dead. That was why, following the example of the herald of Saint-Denis when royal personages passed away, we gave the pre-historic Cave of Miremont the name of the commune in which it lay: Rouffignac.

"Miremont is dead: long live Rouffignac!"

Casteret speaks

That same evening Norbert Casteret gave his own personal com-muniqué to the Press. He said:

"I have been privileged to discover personally six caves with drawings, paintings and sculptures, and I am enthusiastic after my visit to Rouffignac. I came, I saw and I was not only convinced of the genuineness of the works discovered by MM. Nougier and Robert, but I should class them among the MOST SENSATIONAL and the MOST NUMEROUS WE KNOW."

This opinion of a highly qualified pioneer went straight to our hearts. The afternoon brought further valuable confirmation. We recall the statement made by M. Laurière, at the very beginning of the controversy, that he had seen the paintings in 1938. When invited to take part in this latest visit, he was able to remember what he had seen quite clearly in spite of the eighteen years' interval. He made the following statement to several reporters, among them François Denjean (*Dépêche du Midi*, September 23, 1956):

"I declare that in 1938 I saw the three rhinoceroses, as they are today, the frieze of mammoths and one horse. But there were then much fewer scribblings and names on the walls. I make this statement in the interest of science and not for or against anyone."

This renewed testimony made an end of certain Périgordian allegations. It will be easy to show, one day, how the inscriptions increased after 1938—inscriptions which, also, have painfully changed Rouffignac. Some specimens are flagrant, and I cannot forget the wave of indignation among a crowd of 1,500 persons at a Paris lecture on Thursday, November 22, when I described certain rhinoceroses. Is it possible that in 1950?—well, yes, that is possible. And it will be possible as long as prehistory is regarded as a "useless science", as it has been described by a great administrator. To respect a work you must first know it and appreciate it as such.

Policemen will not save our prehistoric heritage from damage, clandestine excavation and systematic pillage. University chairs may do so. But to ensure that our caves and our dolmens are treated with respect, we should begin our teaching of history before the Gauls and learn the meaning of prehistory and its rich lessons. To teach this to our children and our scholars, we should first teach it to our schoolmasters and professors.

I shall long remember the keen attention of *normaliens* (High School pupils) in the Aisne department, in the spring of 1956, when I described to them the main phases of prehistoric evolution from the great discoveries of Professor Arambourg at Ternifine-Palikao to the marvellous Vix vase, found in the chariot-sepulchre at Châtil-lon-sur-Seine by my friend René Jouffroy. That was only an experiment, though a fine one. In the Dordogne, which is the prehistoric Department *par excellence*, those who often appear in the operational bulletins of the "war of mammoths" seldom do so to their advantage. They think they are prehistorians just because they come from Périgord. . . .

At the end of that afternoon (September 12), Louis Plassard had to lead a third visit. On the return to the Pradelie the Minister Plenipotentiary, who had at last SEEN Rouffignac, sat in the yard, scraping his boots with a knife and sharing a foot-bath with a member of a neighbouring Departmental Council. The expedition had been hard and hot, and the Minister murmured: "I am so happy" (scrape, scrape), "I am so very happy." His complete and simple contentment was a joy to us, too.

A few days later, a letter from Florence brought us the results of the first chemical analysis of colouring matter. Professor Graziosi was the first to declare: "Manganese."

The Academy of Sciences at Rouffignac

On October 10 we met once more at the Pradelie to receive Professor P. P. Grassé, of the *Institut*, M. Charlot, professor at the School of Physics and Chemistry of the City of Paris, and several of their colleagues. This was a scientific visit, if ever there was one.

Heavy and powerful accumulators to supply light, magnifying binoculars and test-tubes were carried into the painted cave. Samples of clay, manganese and colouring matter were taken from a section of the Great Ceiling.

The final results will be announced by Professor Grassé in due course. We may say, however, that valuable and useful confirmation was obtained of lines drawn in manganese, the disfigurement of paintings by inscriptions (e.g. on the mammoths of the Great Frieze, by the name "Barry", and on an ibex on the Great Ceiling by inscriptions dating from 1902). Engraved lines with a heavy patina yielded strong manganese reactions, the "dirt" of centuries, apparently fine manganese dust, and a limestone exudation clogging the lines of the mammoths on the Red Ceiling, which were covered, besides, with many 18th-century scribblings.

In spite of very great difficulties, scientific evidence of complete authenticity was increased by this visit. Some walls, like that which bears the fine group of five incised mammoths on the Sacred Way, are of soft chalk. It would have been impossible to set up the heavy stands of the binoculars on them without defacing and spoiling the drawings. Men balancing on each other's shoulders had to make shift to hold the "bino" a few millimetres from the wall, without touching it, and to hold it steady. And then, at the psychological moment, a beastly mist would obscure the view so painfully obtained! After a short rest, the human pyramid would rise again. . . .

"I see! I see!" Professor Grassé would exclaim. "There are crystallised efflorescences of calcite," he noted, "in one of the lines of the leading mammoth in the Grand Frieze." The presence of this efflorescence in lines painted in manganese was further confirmation. At every step and in every gallery, Professor Grassé's *dossier* became richer and the scientific harvest grew and ripened.

At Rouffignac, now, we no longer thought of the "war of mammoths" and their authenticity. We thought of the many tasks that would spring from Rouffignac, in every possible direction. The most-described cave in history would soon be also the most scientifically studied and depicted cave. It deserved to be.

For the mammoths of Rouffignac, a new era was beginning. At last they were entering the calm refuge of true science. The war was over, and the binoculars became the instruments of ratification of a deep scientific peace.

THE FORGERS UNMASKED

(Conclusion)

There has been a lot of talk of "forgeries" in this dreadful War of the Mammoths. I don't know whether our publisher was being mischievous when he asked us to write this book to follow up that of Fritz Mendax, which was entitled *The World of Forgers*. For a moment I was a little anxious about this. The big Larousse dictionary quickly put me right. It says:

"Forger: one who commits a forgery."

Now let us see the definition of a forgery:

"Something contrary to truth or to fact."

There we have our Rouffignac forgers! They are our opponents, who declare *urbi et orbi* at Périgueux or Les Eyzies that the truth is false! They are all those who call false that which is true!

We dare not nail them to the pillory. We must leave them time to expiate their sin between the writing and the printing of these lines. The forgers of Rouffignac still have a last chance. They can still make a last confession!

Yet it was a one-sided fight—we may say that since it is won. The forgers of Rouffignac were not up to the mark. Their wholly destructive plan of operations lacked cohesion; it was too flexible. After acetylene-smoke they relied on charcoal. And after that, there was nothing left!

After the *Maquis* came De Faccio, who solemnly withdrew, for he could not have done the deed. Then came Gérin; then who else could have executed these masterpieces of painting or engraving? Every week they beat a retreat and at last, in the isolation of Périgord, the Rouffignac forgers, at the top of their voices, demanded confrontations, group visits and meetings on the spot.

All this did them no good at all. Throughout the War of the Mammoths, the forgers of Rouffignac, all those who claim as false what is true—will there be any left in the end?—were, after all, only amateur forgers! They were amateur cave-explorers, little amateurs in prehistory, and very little amateurs in controversy.

Of course, I am not speaking of real forgers. They would have to be peculiarly learned and extremely clever. No one has been clever enough for that in all this business. Not even ourselves!

On the Mammoth Front.
Suresnes, November 28, 1956.

IV
APPENDIX OF DOCUMENTS
ON ROUFFIGNAC

ANNEXED DOCUMENTS

Comparison with Altamira. (A communiqué to the French Press Agency (A.F.P.) for the Press Conference at the Musée de l'Homme.)

Communication by Abbé Henri Breuil, Member of the *Institut*, Professor at the Collège de France, made at the Press Conference at the Musée de l'Homme, Aug. 3, 1956.

Declaration made by Professor Paolo Graziosi at the time of his visit to Rouffignac, Aug. 9, 1956.

Letter of Invitation addressed to M. Séverin Blanc.

Communication by Abbé Breuil to the Academy of Inscriptions and Literature (Académie des Inscriptions et Belles-Lettres), Sept. 7, 1956.

Declaration made by Professor Martin Almagro at the time of his visit to Rouffignac, Sept. 10, 1956.

Declaration of Professors Almagro and Graziosi at the time of the International Visit to Rouffignac, Sept. 12, 1956.

Declaration by Professors Grassé and Leroi-Gourhan at the time of the International Visit of Sept. 12, 1956.

Declaration made by Norbert Casteret at the time of the International Visit of Sept. 12, 1956.

Report by Professor P. P. Grassé, Member of the *Institut* and Professor at the Sorbonne.

Report by Professor P. Graziosi to the Architectural Department of the Ministry of National Education.

COMPARISON WITH ALTAMIRA

Just as the Jesuits were accused of having painted the admirable frescoes in the cave of Altamira (Spain), so the authorship of the masterpieces in the cave of Rouffignac, in Périgord, has been attributed to members of the *Maquis* (French "underground" resistance movement during the war).

M. Séverin Blanc, Director of the Prehistoric District including the Dordogne, seems to be the local spokesman of all those who visited this cave (perhaps too well known) without noticing paintings or engravings there, or, if they did see anything, failed to understand its importance, owing to their ignorance, their incompetence or their sheer carelessness.

Professor Louis-René Nougier and Romain Robert are surprised at this campaign, aimed, no doubt, in the first place at themselves. They are indignant that it should also be aimed, over their heads, at their respected Master, Abbé Henri Breuil, of the *Institut*, the man who, by more than sixty years of work, research and constant discoveries in France and throughout the World, has won, without contest or denial, the first place among world specialists on Prehistoric Art.

In complete agreement with this great scientist, in their own names and in his, Professor L.-R. Nougier and M. Robert will present next week, in Paris, a second provisional estimate of these discoveries, more complete than the first, with all the essential evidence and a common statement which will be made to the entire Paris Press.

Communiqué to the French Press Agency (l'Agence Française de Presse), end of July, 1956.

DECLARATION

BY THE ABBÉ HENRI BREUIL

OF THE INSTITUT

With Professor Louis-René Nougier and Romain Robert, Founder-President of the Prehistoric Society of the Ariège, on July 17, 1956, I visited the cave of Rouffignac (Dordogne), where the prospectors had reported prehistoric paintings and engravings discovered on June 26, 1956.

This cave is immense. For twelve hours we concentrated our efforts on the left-hand branch, the only one where incised drawings and paintings had been reported. These drawings are made in black and usually in an excellent style, and I consider their AUTHENTICITY to be QUITE CERTAIN. I learned that M. Séverin Blanc had made a statement. I consider his statement to be WITHOUT THE SLIGHTEST SCIENTIFIC VALUE.

M. Blanc maintains that the works are forgeries dating from the last war, for he and M. de Joly had examined the cave thoroughly and had seen no drawings. I am not aware that M. de Joly has ever studied this subject, and though M. Blanc is fairly familiar with the caves at Les Eyzies (La Mouthe, Font-de-Gaume, Combarelles, etc.), I do not know of his having made discoveries of this kind or having any special qualifications except his willingness to show the caves to strangers. In any case, he is certainly making a misstatement when he says these drawings are copies of those in the Font-de-Gaume (for the rhinoceros), Cabreret (for the mammoths) and Niaux (for the bison and ibex), for the only similarity between the latter and those at Rouffignac lies in the fact that they represent animals of the same species. The truth is much simpler: M. Blanc did not know how to distinguish the drawings, which are far from obvious and need looking for, though they are easy to decipher once they are found.

Those on the roof, near the well at the left-hand end of the west gallery, are unfortunately overlaid with a great many inscriptions in smoke-black, which also cover drawings in other parts of the cave.

These inscriptions are quite legible and fairly often accompanied by dates, many of the 18th and the first half of the 19th century. Many of them may be traced in municipal and departmental records, and the dates verified. It takes *a long time* to make such drawings, which are usually large, in lamp-black, and they show that the drawings existed at a date when nothing was known of quaternary art.

There is only very slight and rare crystallisation on the engraved or painted figures, though this is very frequent in other caves or galleries where there has been little or no stalagmitic concretion. In the great gallery I visited there are no stalagmites or concretions in any shape or form. This appears to me to be due to the clayey, watertight nature of the soil (there are no cracks in the roof).

There are no infiltrations of water in this great corridor, except in the south-west corner of the cavern, where a heavy flow of extremely sticky clay comes from a blocked entrance or fissure through which a mass of tertiary kaolin clay has oozed in from the plateau above.

Elsewhere, except for a few massive slabs which have fallen from the roof, the floor is of very old, compact, clayey soil, very firm and almost everywhere perforated with large oval holes of some depth, very like the sleeping-hollows of the great bear in the Pyrenean caves where this animal used to hibernate. There are no concretions or bones, which proves that the surrounding clay contains no lime and is acid. The bears' claw-marks, of which there are many on the walls, contain no more concretions than the incised drawings. The latter, when they represent some object, are well preserved, either on low ceilings or on walls which are vertical or slightly set back, where the rock has remained light in colour.

Below the backward-sloping part of the wall, however, there are surfaces with a reversed slope, like desks, where innumerable hollows between ribs can be seen. All these grooves are completely choked with the black grime of centuries due to the slow precipitation of dust from air coming from outside, or to smoke made by earlier visitors which contained impalpable charcoal, or to dust left behind by bats, bears or men who reached these points.

This is the rule in every cave which is open to the outside air, and in Lascaux among others. On these "desks" or shelves I saw no true drawings, but I did not search much for them there, for they were limited to the roof-friezes and vertical or concave walls. This constitutes perfectly valid indirect evidence of great age.

Apart from this, the making of engravings, sometimes deeply incised, must have caused small grains of clayey white chalk, detached by the instrument used to cut into the rock, to fall to the ground.   I saw no such white particles on the black surface of the floor, the colour of which is due to the dust mentioned above.   The reason is that the centuries-old dust on the floor has covered the chalk.   This is another argument for the extreme age of the drawings.

Moreover, it is a commonplace for me to say that I am probably today the only person who could attempt to make imitations of quaternary Art as successful as those I am discussing, for they show, to the highest possible degree, the technique of the purest Magdalenian or pre-Magdalenian work.   In fact, if we wanted to find a model for the Rouffignac rhinoceros, we should have to seek it in the early Périgordian work of the Trilobite cave (in the Yonne) and the Colombière (in the Ain).   I am certain that if M. Blanc had taken the trouble to visit the cavern before giving an opinion, he would have realised his great mistake.

No doubt, he may be forgiven for having been unable to discover or understand the paintings, which are by no means conspicuous, but we cannot allow him in 1956 to drivel about *Albigeois*, *Camisards* or *Maquisards*, who were mere successors of the rebels against the First Empire, much discussed fifty years ago, in order to explain the other caves of Les Eyzies.

(Signed): Abbé Henri BREUIL,
de l'Institut.

SECOND LIST OF WORKS OF ART
IN THE CAVERN OF ROUFFIGNAC
IN PÉRIGORD

(July 30, 1956)

	Paintings	Incised Drawings	Total
Mammoths . . .	27	43	70
Ibex	11	—	11
Horses . . .	7	2	9
Rhinoceros . . .	6	—	6
Bison	8	4	12
Unidentified Animals? .	—	5	5
	59	54	113

To the 113 animals should be added a very large number of scrolls and finger-tracings.

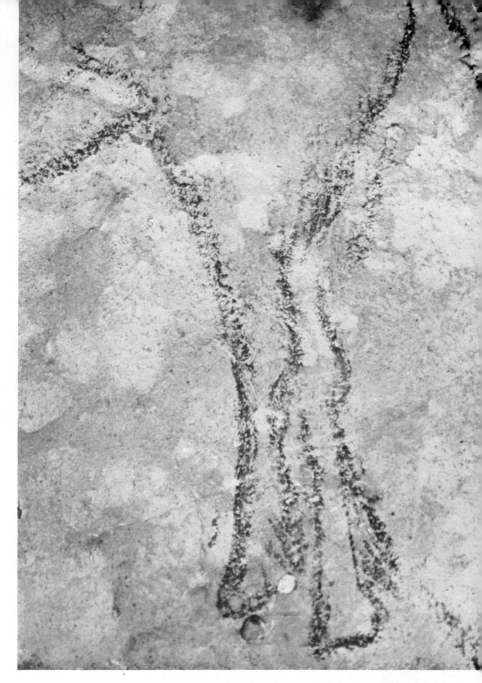

38. The Great Ceiling: detail of the hind legs of the large painted horse

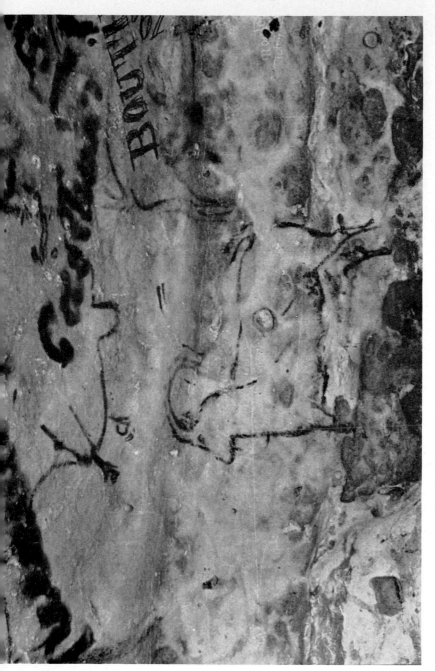

39. The Great Ceiling, right-hand cornice: the "Dalbavie" ibex

DECLARATION

BY PROFESSOR PAOLO GRAZIOSI,

OF THE UNIVERSITY OF FLORENCE

Rouffignac-en-Périgord, August 9, 1956

I attended the Prehistoric Congress at Poitiers and I heard the announcement made by the prospectors of the Cave of Rouffignac-en-Périgord, Professor Louis-René Nougier and M. Romain Robert. I had the pleasure of making a careful examination of the first photographic records of this fine discovery. I immediately realised its great value and importance, as did all the Congress members.

On my return to Italy I was surprised to hear rumours concerning the authenticity of these works of art. That is why I did not hesitate to leave Florence immediately in order to form a personal opinion on the specimens themselves, when the discoverers asked me to come and pronounce judgment.

After having examined the paintings and drawings discovered hitherto very attentively for many hours, I can affirm most categorically that these paintings and drawings are among the finest and most interesting that the whole series of palaeolithic rock paintings has yielded to us until the present time. I am absolutely astonished that anyone should have started a controversy over the authenticity of these specimens. It is enough to have normal experience of prehistoric art to realise at once, not only their genuineness, but their extraordinary interest.

Such a controversy, which I find inconceivable, can be explained only by the fact that it has been started by persons who have not seen the specimens of painting and drawing as a whole. The material is enormously rich.

I wish to emphasise the exceptional beauty and delicacy of the drawings on the "Great Ceiling", which are conspicuous in spite of the many modern inscriptions made over them in more than a century. I hope it will be possible, by appropriate means, to remove these inscriptions in order to bring out the splendour of the works.

o

In the names of all Italian scientists, I rejoice sincerely at the enrichment of the artistic heritage of France by this fine discovery at Rouffignac, which we owe to the keen intelligence of our learned French colleagues, Professor Louis-René Nougier and Romain Robert.

I wish to address a solemn tribute to that great Master of Pre-historic Art, Abbé Henri Breuil, Member of the *Institut*, who was the first to visit the dark depths of Rouffignac with the prospectors and who emphasised the importance of their discovery.

LETTER TO MONSIEUR SÉVERIN BLANC,

Regional Director of Antiquities of the Dordogne

Tarascon-sur-Ariège, September 1, 1956.

Monsieur le Directeur,

Professor Louis-René Nougier and Romain Robert, Founder and President of the Prehistoric Society of the Ariège, have the honour to invite you, in their own names and in that of Monsieur Charles Plassard, the owner of the cave of Rouffignac, to visit the cave and examine the paintings and engravings which it contains.

This visit will enable you to make the report for which you have been asked by the Administration of Fine Arts.

The meeting is fixed at the Domaine de la Pradelie, Rouffignac, Dordogne, for Wednesday, September 12, at 9 a.m. sharp.

Please accept, etc. . . .

(Signed) Prof. L.-R. Nougier,
Director of the Pyrenean Institute of Prehistoric Art.

Romain Robert,
Founder-President of the Prehistoric Society of the Ariège.

ABBÉ BREUIL'S REPORT

THE PAINTED CAVERN OF ROUFFIGNAC (CRO DE GRANVILLE), DORDOGNE

Discovered by Professor L.-R. Nougier and R. Robert

Report by Abbé Henri Breuil, Member of the *Institut* and Honorary Professor at the Collège de France.
(Communicated to the Académie des Inscriptions et Belles-Lettres, September 7, 1956.)

I.—THE DISCOVERY

On June 26, 1956, M. Louis-René Nougier, Professor of Prehistoric Archaeology at the Faculty of Letters of Toulouse and Director of the Pyrenean Institute of Prehistoric Art, and M. Romain Robert, Founder and President of the Prehistorical Society of the Ariège, discovered numerous and very fine paintings and engraved drawings in the cave of the Cro de Granville at Rouffignac (Dordogne), on the estate of La Pradelie.

This estate, on which is the entrance to the cavern extending under his considerable property, was acquired in 1929 by M. Charles Plassard, a distinguished industrialist, who wished to purchase for his son land including woods and arable fields in this picturesque district.

With his son Louis, M. Plassard set about developing the property. Being interested in natural science, he and his family wished to know the great cave that lay under their land. While exploring the westernmost branch they thought they saw drawings, though these were partly covered by more recent inscriptions: these were on a great ceiling, more than 800 yards from the entrance. As the Plassard family had been on friendly terms for about ten years with M. Louis-René Nougier, now Professor of Prehistoric Archaeology at the Faculty of Letters at Toulouse, they told him of their observations in conversation at Menton in 1955. M. Nougier wished to check this report, and he carried out his wish by visiting the cave in June 1956. He was accompanied by his friend, M. Romain Robert, Founder-President of the Prehistorical Society of the Ariège, with whom he has collaborated for many years, notably in excavations in the cave at Bédeilhac (Magdalenian and Neolithic) and the Grotte de la Vache (Magdalenian).

Both men had visited most of the painted caves in the Franco-Cantabrian mountain chain. M. Plassard and his son Louis kindly offered to guide them. The exploration began in the western branch: here they found, about 600 yards from the entrance, on the left-hand wall, the first drawings, which represented two mammoths fighting. After observing many other engraved drawings MM. Nougier and Robert arrived at the great low ceiling, about 800 yards from the mouth of the cave. Here they confirmed the truth of M. Plassard's story. They also found many other painted or incised drawings during their underground expedition. A few days later, young M. Plassard, in his turn, discovered a low chamber opening to the right of the gallery. Its red clay roof bore a series of incised drawings: five large mammoths.

In subsequent expeditions MM. Nougier and Robert found more paintings and drawings "in several places" different from the first, to quote a phrase used by Canon Tarde in 1606. There were also paintings in the "secondary gallery of the Two Mammoths" and in the deep gallery of the Stream.

We shall give later an analysis of the specimens found up to the present day. Thanks to the kindness of M. Plassard and his family, the prospectors will be able to continue their systematic exploration of the rest of the cave, which is hardly begun, in order to publish full details one day. The preparation of this report will take some time and require great exertions, both physical and graphological. MM. Nougier and Robert therefore intend to publish at the end of this year (1956) a monograph on one of the most important sections of the cave, a gallery opening to the right, some distance before the "Great Ceiling". They have named this chamber "the Henri Breuil Gallery" in memory of my visit of July 17, 1956. From the beginning, MM. Nougier and Robert took advantage of my long experience to ask me, before anyone else, to come and verify the authenticity and artistic character of the works they had discovered. I responded to their invitation three weeks after the discovery. I spent a whole day of about twelve hours in the cave, and I was able to examine all the drawings found up to that time and to form an exact idea of them.

I went there for a second time on August 13 with some English friends, guided by the Plassards and M. Robert, and I took advantage of this visit to follow up certain points of special interest, but I stayed only six hours.

It is my duty to associate as closely as I can with this communication the two prospectors of the cave, MM. Nougier and Robert, and also the Plassard family, who made this tiring visit easier for me. It is to all of them that we owe the many facts set forth in this report on the cave of Rouffignac. M. Robert has added many really remarkable colour-photographs which illustrate this report and are his work.

II.—HISTORY AND EARLIER VISITORS

On the Pradelie estate in the commune of Rouffignac (Dordogne), between two branches of a stream called the Manaurie, under a recess which is very largely filled up, a low opening, facing south-west, gives access to one of the most complex caverns in Périgord and, perhaps, in France. The cave has been known for several centuries and was much visited at one time, being mentioned in all the old guides to Périgord. This is proved by many inscriptions in various parts of the cave. In view of the great complexity of the galleries, this suggests that an experienced guide was always on the spot to conduct tourists.

In a description published in 1610 a Sarlade Canon, Jean Tarde, who was a disciple and friend of Galileo, declares that in the Cro du Cluzeau (as the cave was called then—later Cro de Granville and Grotte de Miremont) there were *Paintings in several places showing traces of all sorts of animals.* Older reports are now being searched for in the National Library.

Canon Jean Tarde is believed to have written his description of this "admirable underground cave" in 1606. Thus the Rouffignac cave was known at the beginning of the 17th century, and probably in the 16th century. From that time on, there are many mentions of "paintings", in 1670 and 1699, for example. The cave was visited more and more: in 1721, 1746 and 1759. This last "cave-exploring expedition" was made by about forty persons, including a corresponding member of the Academy, two barristers and six priests.

Gabriel Bouquier, of Terrasson, made an excellent plan of the cave in 1759. Gonthier, of Miremont, made another in 1765. Bouquier's plan has a picturesque and very detailed descriptive caption. On it the letter Y indicates "the gallery where M. de Barry lost his way for an hour". Now, on two painted mammoths in the Great Frieze we find the inscription "Barry" traced in smoke with an oil lamp or a candle. This inscription is much fainter than more recent specimens. It is also fainter than the firm, clear manganese painting of the mammoths over which it is made.

The cave was visited constantly during the 18th and 19th centuries. M. Martel took an interest in it. He had a plan made by MM. Rupin and Ph. and A. Lalande, of Brive, in 1893. The Périgord Spéléo-Club, with M. Bernard Pierret, worked there in 1948–1949 and made a plan which differed little from Martel's.'[1]

The discovery, more interesting from the tourist's point of view, of the prehistoric caves in the valley of the Vézère, which have incomparable rock formations, started a decline in visits to the old cavern. Moreover, Rouffignac is largely bare of stalagmitic concretions. These exist only in the East gallery, where they were wickedly looted in the 19th and 20th centuries. Sticky mud makes it difficult to walk at some points, but there is usually no danger except that of losing one's shoes, falling into the occasional shafts that communicate with the underground stream, or breaking one's leg in a hole.

A few people who are interested in parietal cave-paintings have been to see the place. I made a very short visit in 1915 to accompany the entomologist and distinguished African explorer M. Charles Alluaud, who is a specialist on carabides and wished to collect some specimens of a cave-dwelling *Trechus* long known to be peculiar to this cavern. Our visit lasted barely two hours and was confined to a gallery on the left where M. Alluaud was delighted to find the insect he sought. Owing to the nature of the walls, which are formed of very soft clayey limestone studded at various levels with large flint nodules, and to the enormous mass of sticky mud, I

---

[1] Since the war M. Bernard Pierret, a school-teacher at Périgord and President of the Périgord Spelaeological Society (see *Le Périgord Souterrain*, pp. 104–14), has made many expeditions to the cave. Dismissing the upper storey explored by Martel as well known, he and his friends concentrated on the lower level, where there is a network of underground streams. Their work was certainly excellent and very difficult and praiseworthy. In his little book, which deals solely with cave-exploring, M. Pierret devotes ten pages to the Miremont-Granville cave and quotes some of the early writers who explored it. Although Plate XVI, which shows his underground camp and his tent, includes in the background the three chief rhinoceroses of the east gallery, he makes no mention of them or of any other decorations in his text. These drawings, shown here in a purely spelaeological context, had escaped my attention. It seems that M. Pierret, like myself, only became aware of them later and then unfortunately reported them to M. Blanc, who was not well qualified and said not a word about the drawings to me or to the Minister.

hardly expected to find drawings. On the roof, however, I noticed some of those human finger-tracings we call "macaronis", and that made me think the cave might yield results if it were examined carefully, but I did not come back at the time, being taken up with travels abroad and other important work. I confided my very dubious opinion to Abbé Glory, who also made a brief and very incomplete exploration, as did M. Blanc, according to himself. M. de Joly, President of the Spelaeological Society of France, made a brief visit purely as a cave-explorer and M. Pierret acted as his guide.

Two persons let it be known that they had seen drawings in the cave. One was M. R. de Laurière, a native of the district, who owns the château of La Marzelle at Fleurac, a village near Rouffignac (1938). The other was M. Dubois, who reported an incised "bovid" in 1955 but did not make a sketch of it; he wrote his name on one of the fine rhinoceroses with yellow clay. He and his companions also saw figures drawn in black, but M. Plassard told them M. Blanc had said they were fakes, and they did not mention them.

III.—TOPOGRAPHY AND FILLING UP

Immediately inside the entrance a large, rather low gallery starts in an east-west direction and soon links with two other great lateral galleries on its right, running north. This is the first system of converging, branching corridors. At its western terminal point, in a place marked "pothole" on Martel's plan, this southern branch joins another branch, leading north, which is very large. Great masses of sticky mud have flowed from this pothole. It also marks the centre of masses of slabs fallen from the roof, and this has raised the floor of the gallery at a point under the breach in the vault, which is now blocked. The slabs fell down after the time when the cave was inhabited by bears, for they have partly buried their winter nests; moreover, on the near-by walls, the belt of claw-marks, which are usually just within reach of man, and were made by young bears standing upright, are here on a level with the fallen slabs or barely higher. On the other hand, the layer of sticky clay partly covers the slabs. For more than 500 yards farther the gallery continues to run north, but after 300 yards it divides into two large branches, which divide in their turn.

Here the floor is not very damp or sticky but consists of hard clay, slowly cracking as it dries and studded with numerous shallow pits. These oval pits seem to be nests scooped out by the bears, into which these animals and successive visitors have accidentally knocked many lumps of flint, making passage difficult.

The width of this western gallery is fairly constant (4 to 10 yds.), though it gradually narrows. The ceiling is usually smooth; at first it is as high as a man standing upright, but it gets steadily lower as you advance, and you are sometimes forced to go on all fours, but never to crawl. The only obstacles under foot are the bears' winter nests. I think this explanation of the pits is true, and I do not believe they were formed by suction from holes underneath, first, because the clay, which is drying and cracking, is very firm, and secondly, because the edges of the pits often overhang but their floors are flat and not at all funnel-shaped.

Often, in spite of the many slides left by recent visitors, you can see the marks of the claws that dug the pits. Large, angular lumps of flint have accumulated in the pits, and one of the reasons for their number is probably that when two or three lumps had fallen into his nest the bear found it uncomfortable to lie in and dug another.

Many large flint "kidneys" which have fallen from the walls are found, then, in these pits, mixed with clay fallen from their edges and occasional fragments of pottery of various bygone ages. (A spindle was also found there.) There are also a few pieces of charcoal and flint chips, often fairly well formed but unfinished and without patina or polish. Though some of these blocks have evidently yielded several chips, no trace of a regular nucleus has been found so far. I do not think these specimens of flint-cutting are earlier than the pottery, and this (or these) are not older than the Bronze or Iron Age. Supporting evidence is supplied by a sheep's jaw, of the same period and well preserved; the only bone we have found in the gallery. No doubt men came in to gather and roughly cut these flints, which are incidentally of very good quality, and then to make them, outside the cave, into spikes for fitting on the *tribulum*, as I have seen done at the present day with planting-boards in Spain. In 1915 I noticed similar fragments in the part of the cave immediately inside the entrance. Flints and potsherds are also to be found in the bank outside the opening.

To sum up, we have found until now no reliable relics of the Stone Age or remains of bears' bones, although many bears lived there for a long time. Why? Bones do not seem to have lasted in this gallery. The floor, which is composed of Tertiary kaolin clay, is apparently acid, and comes from granitic alluvia brought down in the Tertiary period from the Limousin.

At the same time, there is not the smallest sign of chalky infiltration in this gallery; no stalactite, no stalagmite, no draperies, no parietal flow or platform anywhere. This is due to the water-tight and uncracked nature of the chalky limestone ceiling. We shall return to this point when we consider the drawings.

The very old, hard clay floor is earlier than the bears in spite of the many claw-marks, scratchings and nests. But the bears must have left footprints, for I found magnificent prints of the Cave Bear on an exactly similar floor at Altamira, and I saw them there again, intact but forgotten, in 1954. I suppose some will be found some day at Rouffignac, along the foot of a wall or in some corner which has been spared by visitors' feet.

The walls are generally inlaid with two horizontal bands of large flints without any signs of an attempt to extract them, as there were enough on the floor for all purposes. The limestone is a very clayey chalk, fragile but fairly even in quality and not mixed with sand as at Lascaux or with quartz grains and coral as it is around Les Eyzies.

The rock strata appear to be horizontal. Two continuous layers of flint "kidneys" have formed belts of harder material which project continuously from the smooth walls. Between them lies a depressed intermediate belt in the form of a concave frieze. On this are many incised drawings and a few paintings. The others are on the fairly smooth roof surfaces, always within arm's length (except over the well near the fork mentioned before). All the drawings found up to now are in one of these two positions: on the walls, between the two red belts of flints, and here and there on the ceilings.

IV.—PALAEOLITHIC DECORATION OF THE CAVERN

The drawings of animals found by MM. Nougier and Robert with the eager help of M. Plassard and his son were observed, in the south gallery, only in a side chamber on the right, a little before the "pothole". This chamber had been filled up with soft secondary clay which had oozed down from the pothole and had reached the roof, staining it red, which is unusual. The colour has remained, while the other ceilings show no such staining. The five or six mammoths found nearest to the entrance up to now are there. They were discovered by young M. Plassard on the eve of my visit of July 17.

All the other drawings incised on the ceilings are scattered irregularly all along the gallery up to a point rather beyond the "well". Though they are often rather mixed, these drawings are all easy to decipher, and they are often fairly large—up to three and even six feet long. A small number are unfinished or rather carelessly done. There are other, but fewer drawings on the walls, in separate groups, and these are much less mixed. Where the walls get lower as you approach the end of the gallery, their decoration is more sparse. I am told that no drawing goes down into the "well".

Drawings painted in black lines are very seldom incised as well, but one bison is half painted (behind) and half incised (in front), unless the paint on the fore-quarters has simply disappeared.

The black-painted figures are fairly far apart, but they are distributed only over the walls of the first part of the gallery.[1] Besides the Rhinoceros Frieze, mammoths may often be seen following one another closely, and fairly often the leaders of two files walking in opposite directions meet, as they do in the incised drawings. Other animals have been very rarely depicted in this long, wide corridor.

But above and to the right of the "well" and in the first few yards of the next gallery, painting in black lines is completely dominant. Here is the "great black ceiling" on which several of the finest mammoths and rhinoceroses are found, as well as some bison and horses and all the ibex known until now in this cave.

During our visit of July 17 M. Nougier noted the number and species of the figures painted or incised in this part of the cave:

First count, July 17

61 mammoths	24 painted	37 incised
12 bison	9 ,,	3 ,,
8 ibex	8 ,,	0 ,,
6 horses	5 ,,	1 ,,
4 rhinoceros	4 ,,	0 ,,
	50 painted	41 incised

Total: 91 figures of five species.

[1] The Breuil gallery is noteworthy for the Great Frieze in black of three rhinoceroses and the immense frieze of eleven mammoths, seven in the right-hand and four in the left-hand group. The two leaders meet head-on.

Later discoveries increased the figures as follows:

	Painted	Incised	Totals
Mammoths	31	47	78
Bison	13	4	17
Ibex	11	0	11
Horses	7	2	9
Rhinoceros	6	4	10
Felines	0	2	2
Unidentified	0	1	1
	68	60	128
			of 6 species

This is only a provisional total.

More recently (at the end of September 1956) the total of mammoths reached 91. The total of animals is therefore over 140.

Still more recently, M. Louis Plassard discovered in another gallery a ceiling with an area of over 1,124 sq. ft., covered with finger-traceries and no doubt with incised drawings, including anthropomorphic figures. The Rouffignac cave is therefore far from having said its last word.

In the foregoing tables there is no mention of the very numerous markings or strokes incised vertically or criss-cross on the lower convex friezes under the animals walking in file. Could these strokes represent grassy vegetation? They are not always easy to distinguish from the bears' claw-marks in the same places.

On the incised ceilings of the gallery there are rather numerous longitudinal lines, sometimes tens of yards long and occasionally barbed, which end in circular designs. These may have been topographical direction-signs. As these ceilings are nearly always very low, the signs were and remained perfectly visible, even in a dim light. Their age is uncertain.

There are no real "macaroni" lines in the area I visited, but among the best incised drawings of animals are a good many three-line "serpents" or scrolls, carefully executed, of which we shall speak again, and well-defined spiral signs which may be reference points.

As regards the paintings, which are all in black lines or very lightly shaded with small strokes, they are as a rule very carefully done. The incised figures are often lightly cut but sometimes cut more deeply, though without being actually carved, which would have been easy in this soft rock. Some are very sketchy but most of them are carefully detailed and traced by a very firm, steady hand.

V.—PROOFS OF AUTHENTICITY OF THE FIGURES

In many caves where there are chalky infiltrations, more or less thick concretions have been formed on the drawings. This is the case in most of the ornamented caves in the district of Les Eyzies, and the fact carried general conviction in 1902. The coral limestone, though hard, is porous and a good deal cracked, so that it usually admits many infiltrations. This is not so at Lascaux, even less so at Rouffignac: there have been *no infiltrations* even through very soft clayey chalk and therefore *no concretions due to infiltration.* As a rule, also, there is *no hardening* of the decorated surfaces and the rock has not absorbed the colouring matter (as sandstone and granitic rocks do in the open air).

At sites so far away (at present) from the outside atmosphere and its variations of temperature there has been no condensation of water vapour coming in at a higher temperature and containing more moisture, and therefore there has been no damage due to the condensation of atmospheric vapour.

What is needed to form a test-layer or to change the walls in such a way as to glaze and modify the painted and incised surfaces, so that they can be distinguished from the work of possible forgers? Such questions can be put, *mutatis mutandis,* about other caves such as Lascaux, Altamira, Marsoulas, and the rest.

Let us see what signs I have observed which have the same indicative value as to the authenticity of Rouffignac.

On July 17 I noticed that the long cornices of the walls of the gallery I was visiting, where the painted or incised friezes of mammoths and rhinoceroses are situated, show three zones in which the figures differ.

There is an upper concave zone under the overhang where the colour is well preserved and the rock is clean and healthy. Then comes a middle zone corresponding with the greatest depth of the concavity, where the paint tends to fade away more and more as it goes lower and often disappears completely, except for a few patches left here and there. Finally, there is a lower zone, forming a shelf, if one may call it that, which is blackened or dirtied by dust coming through all the pores in the rock.

In many cases the white middle zone is soft to the touch and the rock there seems to be eaten away. In some cases observed on August 13 this white substance was dry and hard and had formed very small clots of calcite which had made the black colouring matter paler but had then fixed it. What is this process of white efflorescence (equally visible at Lascaux on a few drawings in the axial corridor and at the beginning of the right-hand gallery, on the lower parts of some very large figures whose upper parts have very largely faded away)? I am not sure. Does this efflorescence arise from a very slight sweating of the rock—so slight that it does not run? Or is it due to the condensation of water vapour from the air (in this case carrying carbonic and corrosive acid) which has been caused, in a drier atmosphere, to solidify into granules? I leave all whom it may concern to decide this point. In any case the process is extremely slow. Since the surface affected at Rouffignac is now dry, it has ceased there, but in any case the progressive disappearance of black lines as they go down and the very small concretions produced show the age of drawings partly effaced by this phenomenon.

But as the three rhinoceroses are placed above the white zone or hardly touch it, they have not suffered from the process as the neighbouring mammoths have. I count on Dr. Grassé to explain this phenomenon.

As for the third zone, where the "dust of centuries" lies, unfortunately it does not affect any drawing yet discovered, but it carries many criss-cross strokes, some made by bears' claws and others, perhaps, by artists to represent the pasture on which the mammoths and rhinoceroses were walking. All these incisions are completely clogged by the black dust of ages due to the slow precipitation of airborne dust from outside, to smoke made by former visitors which contained fine charcoal powder and to dirt left by bats, bears or people who reached that point. I need hardly say that this dust does not settle on the ceilings or the upper part of the concave walls, or on vertical walls.

I saw only one drawing, more rubbed than incised, which had disturbed this dust and might be attributed to a member of the *Maquis*. It was the kind of drawing that abounds in public lavatories.

Another detail may be mentioned. There are drawings on the ceilings, among them an enormous unfinished rhinoceros head and the body of another, smaller rhinoceros,[1] the lines of which gradually become fainter before they disappear. This is a process of slow

---

[1] Note in passing that the horns of the large head overlapping the body of the little rhinoceros running before it reminded me that the very long horn of the female white African rhinoceros is used to guide her young as they go. The same may be true of her near relation, the woolly rhinoceros, and this is an illustration of it.

disintegration, grain by grain, of overhanging surfaces under the influence of gravity, and it cannot be counterfeited.

On the other hand the execution of drawings which are sometimes deeply incised has necessarily been accompanied by the fall to the ground of particles of clayey chalk detached by the tool which cut into the rock. Yet I never detected such white particles on the surface blackness of the floor, which is due to the dust of ages already mentioned. That dust also lies along the walls, where visitors' feet do not tread, and on projections in the walls. The dust has overlaid the chalk particles and made them invisible. This is another argument for the great age of the drawings.

Their number, which grows every day, and the impeccable perfection of their splendid style, quite in conformity with that of a certain stage of development in palaeolithic art, are also "aesthetic" arguments of great weight, as are the absolute sureness of the executant's touch and his perfect knowledge of the anatomy and covering of the subjects he depicts. Even the far too many contacts between the palaeolithic paintings and incised drawings of Rouffignac and the innumerable modern scribblings go to confirm the earlier date of the drawings and their relative positions.

The wide, low ceiling with fine black paintings, near the "well" of which we have spoken, extends to the left over the wide, gaping mouth of the well, so that this part of it is inaccessible today. Visitors' names are therefore limited to the surface above the firm clay floor of the gallery, An examination of the lip of the well on the gallery side shows why. A great mass of clay has fallen into the well, and the scar left where it came away from the ceiling can be seen. The fall took place after the animals were drawn, but long before the arrival of visitors in the last two centuries, who have written their names on the bare surface.

Now, these inscriptions, which are very legible, are often accompanied by dates, many from the 18th and the first half of the 19th century. Many of them may be traced in municipal or departmental records, and the dates checked. To make such inscriptions, which are usually large, with lamp-smoke takes *a long time*, and they show that the animal drawings (on which they are always superimposed, whereas the drawings never overlap them) existed at a date when nothing was known of quaternary art.

It is well to point out that not a single animal drawing in Rouffignac was made with smoke from a flame, acetylene or other, as persons without real experience of the subject have alleged. Let us recall on this point that at the beginning of this century Professor Moissan, on being asked by Dr. Capitan why there were no traces of lamp or other smoke in untouched galleries with prehistoric drawings, replied that the very fine powdering of the carbon contained in smoke made it possible for the oxygen in the air to turn it very quickly, or fairly quickly, into carbonic acid, as I have observed many times during a long career as a cave-explorer. This explains, among other things, how it is that a name traced in this way *over* an old black line may be in process of re-absorption, which makes it look older than the under-drawing made with a more stable substance (in this case manganese, according to the first analysis made by Professor Graziosi).

Séverin Blanc (after Breton at Cabrerets) tried to test the permanence of the black lines of a Rouffignac rhinoceros with the tip of his finger, which turned black, and he concluded, like his predecessor and with no better reason, that the line was recent. That means absolutely nothing. It happens wherever concretion has not "fixed" the colouring matter, that is to say, in more than half of all cave paintings, including Cabrerets (*pace* Breton!), Cougnac, Marsoulas, Niaux, Trois-Frères, Altamira, etc. etc.

Monsieur Séverin Blanc also maintained (according to the Press) that these were fakes made by *Maquisards* during the last war. He (?) and others visited the cave before 1948 and did not, or could not, see any drawings, but other people had seen some in 1938! Although M. Blanc knows Les Eyzies caves (La Mouthe, Font-de-Gaume, Les Combarelles, etc.) fairly well, I do not know of his having made any discovery of this kind or having any particular qualification except his praiseworthy readiness to conduct strangers through the caves. In any case, he made another undeniable misstatement in declaring that these drawings are copies of those at Font-de-Gaume in the case of the rhinoceros, Cabrerets in that of the mammoths and Niaux in that of the ibex, for the only resemblance between those drawings and the ones at Rouffignac is in the fact that they represent the same species of animals. The truth is much simpler: M. Blanc and others could not distinguish or understand these drawings, which are far from conspicuous and need looking for, though they are easy to decipher once they are found.

The very legitimate doubts of M. Pierret and his fellow cave-explorers led them to concentrate their praiseworthy efforts on the lower "live" level of the cave, where streams flow, as he notes in his little book. If, as is likely, they caught a glimpse of black drawings on the Great Ceiling, they did not realise their importance.

Pierret accused M. de Faccio of being the artist, and got an emphatically negative reply. He now accuses a man who is at Oran but whose skill as an artist is hardly equal to the occasion, from all I hear.

VI.—The Place in the Evolution of Cave-Painting of the Artistic Collection at Rouffignac

One fact must be plain to every observer: up to now, all the figures found have been of the same date, whether incised or painted in black lines, and they suggest a single artist or a group of artists belonging to a single school. Of course, they can be compared artistically with some drawings in other caves, but not to the same degree, and this is not surprising. Within the general style which predominates in any classical period, every studio or master has his own manner, which his pupils imitate and specialists can identify today. The same thing happened in the Reindeer Age, when there could be no question of modern imitations. The most striking comparison is that with the panel of black drawings of mammoths and oxen at Cabrerets, which, moreover, is notably older.

A determining factor may be the very limited choice of animals for portrayal, in which the mammoth plays a disproportionate part and the rhinoceros is more prominent than he is anywhere else, while bison and horses, which are legion elsewhere, are barely represented. Primeval oxen are omitted altogether, though they abound in the black line-drawings of Lascaux and Cabrerets (where they are associated with mammoths). The stag and reindeer are completely absent, bison and horses are few, while there is an abundance of rhinoceros, very rare elsewhere. This cannot be explained as a simple climatic selection of local fauna. The animal data of Rouffignac can be justified only by reference to different selective considerations, especially those of tribal, sociological and perhaps totemic origin. It is difficult to understand why we should find no representation of *cervidés* at a time when stags and reindeer were certainly abundant. The relative frequency of ibex, here grouped together at a single point but usually rare in drawings in the caves of Périgord, is an interesting fact. There are more pictures of them in the Pyrenean caves. One can only say that the exceptional predominance of the mammoth, his association with numbers of woolly rhinoceros, and the simplicity of the technique of black-line drawing used by the painters, all tend to fix the brief moment with which Rouffignac must be identified rather far back in the series of phases of cave painting.

Yet the style of the Rouffignac drawings does not place them in the first cycle of cave painting. In spite of their extreme pictorial sobriety (a sort of reaction from the two-coloured and many-coloured scheme of Lascaux) we have to do with a quite distinct and more austere form of art, by no means to be connected with the style where distorted perspective is in evidence, as it is up to the end of the Lascaux period. At first sight this seems to indicate an improved Magdalenian style, probably developed at an early stage, having regard to the discreet monochrome of the paintings, all of which are linear.

So, to sum up: no sign of distorted perspective. No typical "macaroni" drawing apart from the scrolls. The latter, however, may be compared with the serpentine and supposedly magic lines found on the Late Gravettian stones of La Colombière, on those of the chronologically related Trilobite cave and in the oldest drawings of bison in the sanctuary of the Trois-Frères cave, which I believe also to be Gravettian.

The age of the Rouffignac drawings would seem, then, to belong to the beginning of the second cycle in quaternary art.

These artistic specimens, both paintings and incised drawings, may belong either to the last phase of the Gravettian period or, more likely, to a phase described as pre-Magdalenian, by Denis Peyrony, in the deposits of Laugerie-Haute. This phase is super-imposed on Périgordian and anterior to all Solutrean cycles. We recall the finest specimen Denis Peyrony found there, an admirable pierced *bâton* engraved with two fighting mammoths, like the many in the cave of Rouffignac.

Indeed, the incised drawings of La Colombière (Ain) were a prelude to the introduction into upper palaeolithic art of correct perspective and the avoidance, of which signs are seen at Lascaux in its most recent drawings, of the distorted perspective of the first cycle of this art. Confirmation of this relatively distant date of the art of Rouffignac, at the beginning of this last cycle, may be found in the abundance of mammoths and rhinoceroses.

We may still ask what led men at such a far-off time to venture into this underground maze, even supposing there were then easier entrances which are masked today. This was an exploit greatly exceeding the much easier entry into the great decorated caves we have known until now, the topography of all of which is relatively simple. What are the 1,500 yards of Niaux or the 750 yards of

P

Trois-Frères and the Tuc beside Rouffignac, with more than 10 kms. (6 miles) of galleries? Even more than those other great caves, Rouffignac called for a reliable source of light which could be quickly renewed.

Every decorated cave brings fort a crop of new facts and prospects concerning the art and habits of early men, and we must congratulate MM. Nougier, Robert and Plassard, the prospectors of the works of art of the Cro de Granville-Rouffignac, for their contribution.[1] It did not escape the controversies that the first discoveries set in motion but to which, it seems to me, we need pay no further attention.

Abbé H. BREUIL.

[1] We must be grateful for the interest and physico-chemical assistance of the distinguished Professor Grassé, of the Academy of Sciences, from whom I hope to get a great deal of light on the technique of the paintings, the phenomena of change in the drawings and the general physics of caves and their atmosphere.

DECLARATION

BY Professor Martin Almagro OF THE University OF Madrid

Rouffignac-en-Périgord, September 11, 1956

Having been invited to give my opinion on the authenticity of the paintings and incised drawings in the cave of Rouffignac in Périgord, I came to examine the whole body of art at Rouffignac in a completely critical spirit.

I systematically sought all possible evidence of non-authenticity.

I declare in the most unequivocal and categorical manner that I found none.

The paintings and drawings at Rouffignac are incontestably authentic and they form one of the finest collections of rock-drawings in the world.

The Great Ceiling is painted in a style so pure and so beautiful that the campaign waged against these masterpieces is incredible.

After the coloured paintings of Lascaux and Altamira, this is the most important cave in the world.

I rejoice at this wonderful discovery and at the priceless contribution made to the French and human heritage by Professor R.-L. Nougier, occupant of the chair of Prehistoric Archaeology at the University of Toulouse, and Romain Robert, Founder-President of the Prehistoric Society of the Ariège, whose remarkable work for science we have often been able to appreciate.

I join with Professor Paolo Graziosi, of the University of Florence, in hoping that it will be possible by suitable means to remove the inscriptions which deface the paintings in order to bring out the full splendour of these works.

I wish to address a solemn tribute to the great Master of prehistoric art, Abbé Henri Breuil, who was the first to confirm the authenticity of the works of art at Rouffignac and to emphasise their great value.

FIRST DECLARATION

MADE BY PROFESSORS ALMAGRO AND GRAZIOSI ON THEIR VISIT TO
ROUFFIGNAC, SEPTEMBER 12, 1956

Professor Paolo Graziosi, of the University of Florence, and
Professor Martin Almagro, of the University of Madrid, repeat that
apart, of course, from the modern inscriptions, *the paintings and
incised drawings in the Cave of Rouffignac in Périgord, reported by
Professor L.-R. Nougier and Romain Robert, are authentic.*
They are *among the finest known specimens* of quaternary art.

Professors Almagro and Graziosi thus confirm the first opinion
of Abbé Henri Breuil, and they wish to express their affectionate
regard for this eminent man of science.

The following persons, after having visited the Cave of Rouffignac
in Périgord under the guidance of Professors Graziosi and Almagro,
associate themselves entirely with this declaration:

Antonio Beltran *Catedratico* of the University of Saragossa.

E. Ripoll Perello, Conservator of the Barcelona Museum and
Professor at the University.

Dr. Jorda Cerda, Professor at the University of Oviedo.

Dr. R. Facon, of the University of Poitiers.

Comte Henri de Chalup-Cosnac.

F. Lacorre, founder of the "Friends of Les Eyzies."

J.-M. Thomas Casagiroux, Spelaeologist and Geologist.

J.-M. Corominas, of the Museum of Banolas.

Norbert Casteret.

Miguel Fuste, Professor at the University of Barcelona.

Dr. S. Villaseca Salvador, Commissioner for Excavation at
Tarragona.

Dr. Guinea, Professor at the University of Valladolid.

Dr. P. Glazema, Director of Archaeological Excavations in the
Netherlands.

Maria Trias, Conservator of the Barcelona Archaeological
Museum.

José-Manuel Tabanera, Professor at the University of Madrid.
Professor Lothar Zotz, of the University of Erlangen.
E. Quaduardo, Provincial Commissioner for Archaeological
Excavation in Guadalajara.
Madame Lacorre.
M. Max Bégoüen.
M. J. Blanchard, former President of the S.P.F.
Dr. Miguel Oliva Prat, Conservator of the Gerona Museum.
Altrian, Conservator of the Teruel Museum.

SECOND DECLARATION

PROFESSORS GRASSÉ AND LEROI-GOURHAN

(Visit of September 12, 1956)

The undersigned declare that, while suspending final judgment until the publication of the results of a strict scientific analysis, they found during their visit *no evidence of non-authenticity* of the paintings and drawings.

P. P. Grassé, of the French Academy of Sciences, Professor at the Sorbonne.

Professor Leroi-Gourhan, of the Sorbonne.

Professor Zorzi, Director of the Museum of Natural History of Verona.

Madame P. M. Grand-Chastel, of the French Prehistorical Society.

Hélène Danthine, Professor at the University of Liége.

Carl Axel Althin, Professor at the University of Lund.

Dr. Gisela Freund, Tutor at the University of Erlangen.

DECLARATION

BY M. NORBERT CASTERET

(September 12, 1956)

I have had the privilege of discovering personally six caves containing incised drawings, paintings and sculptures, and I am enthusiastic about my visit to Rouffignac.

I have come, I have seen and I have been convinced of the authenticity of the works of Art discovered by MM. Nougier and Robert, which I class among the MOST SENSATIONAL and the MOST NUMEROUS KNOWN.

(Signed) NORBERT CASTERET.

REPORT OF PROFESSOR P. P. GRASSÉ,

(Professor at the Sorbonne, Member of the *Institut*)

After his first visit, September 12, 1956

Having been kindly invited by MM. Nougier, Robert and Plassard to visit the Cave of Cro de Granville, situated half-way between Rouffignac and Les Eyzies, I was able to examine closely a considerable number of drawings and engravings. Such a visit, being necessarily hasty and superficial, does not enable me to give a final judgment on the authenticity of the wall-decorations in the cave. None the less, a certain number of facts which seem rather important were observed during this visit. Here they are:

1. All the drawings were made with the same material and the same technique. There are more or less broad strokes of blackish matter which forms crusts nearly one-third of a millimetre thick in places. This pigment has not absorbed the substratum; it remains on the surface, as though clinging to the roughness of the rock. It seems to be a pasty material, applied either by the finger-tip or with a rough paint-brush. Nothing can be said of its nature except that it is not smoke-black from a candle or an acetylene lamp.

The uniformity of the technique employed by the artist is such that one is tempted to attribute all the drawings in the cave to a single hand. The fact that the same material has been used in the execution of all the drawings puts us in the following dilemma: either all the drawings are genuine, or all are false.

2. The incised drawings seen on the side walls and also on the roof are cut in the chalk, which is extremely soft. A finger-nail can dig into it easily.

Marks which may be considered old, notably the bears' claw-marks, are hardly more glazed than the incised lines. Some of the latter have sharp edges and crumbs of chalk in their hollows, and this makes them look fresh. Others are flattened as though worn down.

3. I am not qualified to draw any useful lesson from a comparison of the technique used in the drawings and engravings of

Cro de Granville and that of the paintings at Lascaux, Altamira, Font-de-Gaume, etc. What I can certify is that the drawings and paintings are nearly always very accurate in their zoology. Thus, in the case of the mammoth, I note the curve of the tusks, the very characteristic domed shape of the skull, the downward slope of the spine and the form of the anal region. In the *Rhinoceros tichorhinus* I note the general outline, the shape of the head, the very peculiar and often opposite curves of the two horns, etc. The hair on the species depicted, which are nearly all in their winter pelts, is distributed with really remarkable accuracy. In the case of the mammoths the placing is just as it has been found to be on the fully fleshed specimens found in the ice of North Russia and Siberia.

An immediate and important conclusion may be drawn from this brief visit. The forger, if there is a forger, is neither a *Maquisard* nor a Boy Scout, as some have maintained. He is a man who knew prehistoric animals well and was able to depict their leading features. An artist relying on published works on palaeolithic art might possibly have committed such a forgery, and nothing is impossible in the way of fraud! However, some of the details shown, especially in the case of the mammoth, require in the executant a very exact knowledge of anatomy which, leaving the zoologist aside, can only be acquired by a hunter cutting up his prey.

Some visitors have pointed out that some of the prehistoric drawings appear to be drawn over relatively recent inscriptions made with the smoke of a candle or an acetylene lamp. After examining these superimpositions very closely, I have not been able to determine their order quite certainly. This order, which is of capital importance in establishing the age of the drawings, can be detected quite definitely only by means of magnifying binoculars and chemical analysis of the colouring matter.

In truth, as the signatories of the second resolution presented after the visit, of whom I am one, have declared, no fact could be found in the course of this first examination which demonstrated the non-authenticity of the drawings and engravings in the cave in question.

The mentions of drawings of animals on the walls of Cro de Granville which are to be found in the writings of old authors (of the 17th and 18th centuries) are very strong evidence in favour of authenticity. The number of the paintings and incised drawings and their position, which would make them very difficult to execute in the present state of the cave, reinforce this argument.

The very "palaeolithic" style of all the pictures seems to us a fact to be noted on the credit side of authenticity. Some of the

Cro de Granville mammoths immediately recall engravings on bones found in the rock cavity of La Madeleine.

But none of these arguments in itself removes all doubts. To escape from the jungle of controversy and put an end to personal quarrels (and Heaven knows they have been many in this deplorable affair!) we must turn to Science and all its technical equipment.

Here are a few suggestions among many others:

1. A very careful chemical analysis of the colouring matter used to make the drawings.

2. Examination with the microscope and by chemical analysis of the superimposed scribblings and paintings.

3. A comparative study of the incised lines in order to determine the nature of the tool used to trace them.

4. An exhaustive study of the micro-climate of the cave and the amount of CO^2 (carbon dioxide) and water vapour in the air.

5. A study of air currents in the cave.

6. A search for tools and fossils in the floor of the cave; determination of the pH in the soil, etc.

Research under headings 4 and 5 will explain the state of preservation of the paintings and the patina on the drawings.

As the recording of these paintings and drawings does not seem to be finished, it is possible that new questions for prehistorians will arise and that other researches besides those we have suggested may have to be undertaken.

(Signed) Professor Pierre Grassé

de'l Institut.

REPORT OF PROFESSOR PAOLO GRAZIOSI

TO THE DEPARTMENT OF ARCHITECTURE

Florence, September 21, 1956

Ministry of National Education,
7 rue de Valois,
Paris, 1.

I have the honour to submit to you my report on the results of my visits to the cave of Rouffignac-en-Périgord, which I made on August 11, 12 and 13 and September 12, 1956, in order to form an opinion on the authenticity of the paintings and incised drawings discovered by M. Louis-René Nougier, Professor of Prehistoric Archaeology at the Faculty of Letters of the University of Toulouse and Director of the Pyrenean Institute of Prehistoric Art, and M. Romain Robert, Founder-President of the Prehistoric Society of the Ariège, which paintings were also authenticated by the eminent Master, Professor Henri Breuil, a member of the *Institut*.

I was invited to give an opinion on the paintings at Rouffignac as a result of a controversy raised by members of the Spéléo-Club or Périgord, local men of science and reporters of the Paris Press regarding the authenticity of these same paintings.

As the Press has already made known, my conclusions from my previous visits to the cave were definitely favourable to their authenticity and to their palaeolithic origin.

The last visit, which was made, as is well known, on September 12 with many French and foreign men of science, including M. Séverin Blanc, who maintained the theory of non-authenticity, could only confirm me in my opinion.

First of all it must be noted that there are in the Rouffignac cave, as in several palaeolithic painted caves, innumerable modern scribblings which may date from the present time to several centuries before it, or even earlier. Many of these consist of writings made with carbide lamps or candles or engraved (with names, dates, etc.) and also of more or less clumsy figures such, for instance, as the representations of birds in one side gallery.

It goes without saying that there can be no question here of fixing the palaeolithic age of all the figures in the great Cave of Rouffignac. We can only determine whether, at Rouffignac, there has been a deliberate attempt to make partial or total forgeries to deceive the public, or whether this is really a great body of Franco-Cantabrian art without any sign of a forger's work.

My affirmation of the authenticity and palaeolithic origin of the drawings and paintings of pleistocene fauna at Rouffignac is based on the following data:

1. *Style of the paintings and drawings.*

The style is very clearly that of Franco-Cantabrian art, both in the general movement of the figures and in the carefully treated details. It is absurd to believe, as has been suggested, that members of the *Maquis* or youths belonging to the Périgord Spéléo-Club may have executed such drawings. In fact, their execution would require the genius of a gifted artist who was also a great specialist in palaeolithic art. There is no detail of these drawings that is clumsy or unskilful or drawn in any other manner than that which is typical of Franco-Cantabrian art. If these were forgeries—and in that case they would constitute a fraud on a great scale which would have required months and months of well-organised work—I think very few members of the very small circle of specialists in prehistoric art could have produced them; and here I am speaking of the drawing only, for apart from this the physical condition of the pictures, especially the incised drawings, admits of no fraud.

2. *Subjects.*

The animals display anatomical details so accurately drawn and so realistic that only persons with complete knowledge of the morphology and even the outward appearance of extinct fauna (such as the mammoth, for instance) could reproduce these animals.

3. *Physical condition*

(*a*) *Paintings.* The black outline of the paintings naturally varies in freshness according to the places where the paintings are made. We have shining black strokes (recalling, for example, those of the paintings in the cave of Niaux in the Ariège) wherever the greater humidity of the rock surface has caused better preservation of the paint itself, as may be observed in many decorated caves. Where the wall is drier or more exposed the paint tends to crumble into powder and disappear. In this way one may observe in certain parts of the Great Ceiling and elsewhere some figures which are fainter than others.

An example: in the frieze of mammoths in the Breuil gallery the upper part of the animals is well preserved, while in the lower part the paint has almost entirely vanished except for a few small traces. Now, it is interesting to note that the rock here is clearly divided into two distinct bands, the upper (where the paint has been preserved) being the more damp, while the lower band (where the paint has almost vanished) is drier. We cannot possibly suppose that a forger would have thought of carrying his fraud to such a degree of subtlety.

If one examines the black line of some painted figures carefully and at close range one sees that it has undergone a slight chromatic change tending towards brown. Such a change can occur only over a period of many years.

(b) *Incised drawings.* According to their position on the wall the drawings, as well as the surface of the rock itself, may show different kinds of patina. In some cases the patina is definitely different from that of the inside of the rock and must have taken a very long time to develop. Generally speaking, it is the same on the line and on the rocky surface. This does not mean that the patina on the line and that of the surface cannot be of the same colour as the internal patina. When both the surface and the line are dark, the difference between these and the tone of any modern signs cut on the same wall is very clearly seen. The latter stand out in a lighter tone.

4. During the visit of September 12 the person who believed most firmly that the paintings were not genuine thought he had found a proof of fraud in the fact that more than once, and especially on the Great Ceiling, the black lines of the palaeolithic figures seem to pass over the modern inscriptions (writings and dates) made with candle-smoke.

It is true that one may get this impression at first sight, and that it might lead one to think the pictures of animals were painted after inscriptions which are only a few tens of years old. But on this point we must put on record that this is a true optical illusion, which may be seen in other painted caves (for example, at Portel in the Ariège). The smoke of a candle or other lamp deposits on the painted surface volatile particles produced by combustion which are very unstable and tend to disappear in a short time. Indeed, in this same cave of Rouffignac, it may be seen that writings made with candle-smoke at times which are not very far apart show very different states of preservation. Often a few tens of years have sufficed to make these writings almost invisible.

Writings made over the palaeolithic figures have naturally suffered the same fate. Since the lines of the old drawing, when made, for example, with manganese, have in many cases remained quite fresh and clear, it is natural that they should seem to be superimposed on the scribblings, which, on the contrary, have faded to a very faint and almost totally effaced black tone.

Apart from all this, it is really absurd, after all, to suppose that forgers with profound knowledge of palaeolithic art and associated questions, who were ready to organise a work of forgery so long, so difficult and on such a scale, would have chosen for the execution of their largest groups of forgeries, such as the painted ceiling at Rouffignac, the one rock surface in the cave which is almost completely covered with modern writings.

In addition to these observations on the intrinsic character of the pictures, one might advance other arguments in favour of the authenticity of the paintings and incised drawings of Rouffignac. I will not linger on this point, because these arguments would not apply to the nature of the pictures in itself.

I may recall, however, that in the 17th and 18th centuries some writers referring to the cave of Miremont (that is, of Rouffignac) spoke of animal pictures inside the cave. In various places one sees paintings covered with names and dates some of which can be found in the writings of these authors, which date from a time when both palaeolithic wall-painting and also the morphology of certain extinct animals were unknown. The mammoth was then quite unknown.

Moreover, M. de Laurière, of Orleans, has assured us that during a visit to the Rouffignac cave in 1938 he saw the friezes of rhinoceroses and mammoths, which he definitely recognised on revisiting the same cave at the present time. This at least excludes the possibility of a recent forgery, which has also been suggested.

During the visit of September 12 some of the visitors suggested chemical analysis of the paintings to establish their authenticity. For my part I do not see how one could arrive at a definite conclusion on this point after such an analysis. I think all it could indicate is the nature of the substance used to make the paintings, but this would enable us to establish whether it was a colouring matter in use among palaeolithic artists.

Still in the matter of analysis and on the plane of theory, one could try to recover and to analyse the particles deposited by candle-smoke on the black lines in places where the scribblings have almost faded away, in order to offer the sceptics one more proof where it does not seem, at first sight, that the scribblings overlie the paintings. But to analyse the slight traces of products of combustion from a candle which may still be sticking to the surface of the paint is surely not an easy task or one that could give us final results, either because of the difficult conditions under which one must work in the cave with very small quantities of material, or because one would never dare to decide whether any carbonaceous substance which might be isolated in the laboratory from colouring matter removed from the painting had been on the surface of the painted sign or under it. However, one might attempt to make this analysis on the spot by working out an appropriate method, although in my opinion all this is not worth the trouble, in view of the fact that this "optical illusion" is repeated identically in other caves in connexion with paintings on the authenticity of which no doubt exists.

(Signed) PAOLO GRAZIOSI,
*Professor of Anthropology
and Palaeontology at the
University of Florence.*

REPORT OF PROFESSOR M. ALMAGRO, OF THE UNIVERSITY OF MADRID

Martin Almagro Basch, holder of the Chair of Prehistory of the University of Madrid and Director of the Prehistorical Section of the Upper Council for Scientific Research, has the honour to report to the Minister of National Education on the visit made to the cave of Rouffignac, in the Dordogne, for the purpose of expert examination.

After examining the paintings and incised drawings which can be seen in the cave and which have been criticised by some of his French colleagues, the Professor undersigned wishes to point out that the paintings and drawings at Rouffignac as a whole will require careful copying and analysis, for the cave has been visited for centuries and it shows traces of the passage of modern man through the galleries. This work will undoubtedly clear some of the fine creations of quaternary art of later drawings and paintings. There are various engraved signs, people's names and drawings made with smoke or charcoal which complicate the task of a careful observer.

But though all this exists, it is nothing new. In most other caves containing rock paintings which have become known until now there are similar adherences and additions, but owing to their technique and the way in which the drawings are conceived and the feeling which is expressed in their execution the creations of quaternary art cannot be confused with later additions.

The problem at Rouffignac was to establish whether this was a new discovery of creations of quaternary art or whether the cave, which is still partly in process of scientific exploration, contains only the modern and deliberate or spontaneous work of amateurs or mischievous forgers. It may be clearly stated that one of the most interesting bodies of quaternary art, unknown before Professor Nougier and M. R. Robert made their researches, exists at Rouffignac. The paintings and drawings at Rouffignac are fine paintings and drawings forming a new contribution which will enrich the artistic heritage of France. Some of these artistic creations are torn by the scratching of bears; others have been partly damaged by damp or by rocky concretions, but all belong in every detail to the undisputed line of creation of quaternary art. Such details, and many others, rule out any argument that these works are false, and even any doubt as to their authenticity.

The undersigned does not think it necessary to add to this report, which cannot be analytical in the absence of graphical records such as he does not possess in relation to every artistic specimen requiring analysis. Such analysis could be attempted only with the help of calculations and photographs which do not yet exist, but are being prepared by the discoverers. The undersigned Professor wishes to state that he does not think chemical analysis, which many may regard as a final test, will yield useful information, although it is possible to analyse the colouring matter adhering to rock which is soft but in many places friable and on the point of crumbling away. It would be a new thing for such analyses to shed fresh light on the question. It would be a new feature, perhaps peculiar to this cave. Any chemists who are allowed to intervene should do so with great circumspection. As a prehistorian I can state that until now, every time analyses of traces of rock-colouring have been undertaken, they have shed little special light on chronological questions, in spite of the attempts made on these lines at the suggestion of the undersigned and that of the late Professor Obermaïer at the Universities of Berlin, Madrid and Barcelona.

The opinion of the undersigned, which favours authenticity, will be set forth in greater detail, as it should be, in scientific publications. He does not intend to add any more to this report, which, with respect, aims only to sustain before the high authority of Your Excellency an opinion formed after long hours of study and a life partly dedicated to the better knowledge of quaternary art.